MAR 2006

the Seasoned Traveler

GEORGE BAUER

the Seasoned Traveler

A GUIDE FOR BABY BOOMERS AND BEYOND

INSIDERS' GUIDE®

GUILFORD, CONNECTICUT
AN IMPRINT OF THE GLOBE PEQUOT PRESS

To buy books in quantity for corporate use
or incentives, call **(800) 962–0973, ext. 4551,**
or e-mail **premiums@GlobePequot.com**.

INSIDERS' GUIDE®

Library of Congress Cataloging-in-Publication Data

Bauer, George, 1948–
    The seasoned traveler : a guide for baby boomers and beyond / George
  Bauer. — 1st ed.
        p. cm.
    Includes index.
    ISBN 0-7627-3858-8
    1. Travel. 2. Older people–Travel.   I. Title.
  G151.B38 2005
  910 ' .2 ' 02–dc22

2005015627

Design: Linda Loiewski
Photography: Kevan Ward

Manufactured in the United States of America
First Edition/First Printing

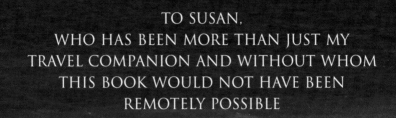
TO SUSAN,
WHO HAS BEEN MORE THAN JUST MY
TRAVEL COMPANION AND WITHOUT WHOM
THIS BOOK WOULD NOT HAVE BEEN
REMOTELY POSSIBLE

Seasoned travelers recognize cultural symbols in many forms: the proud display of national and state flags, the allure of holiday candles, or the ubiquitous canals and bicycles of Amsterdam.

Winter brings its own joys to travelers: Christmas markets brimming with handcrafts and sweet treats, cozy candlelight gatherings aboard a Rhine River cruise, and snowbound villages, such as Malbun, a ski resort in the mountains of Liechtenstein.

Meditative moments often produce our best travel memories—whether at a place of worship, in a quiet garden, or beholding the bounty of a local market or a meticulously groomed vineyard.

Friendly faces, full of warmth and welcome, enhance our visits around the world, whether they be to elegant European cities, colorful Caribbean waterfronts, or hallowed monuments of the past.

Nature offers her own distinctive delights to travelers, providing a beauty that is the envy of architects and engineers worldwide.

Ashdod, 12,981 k
8,063 mi.

Santo Tomas, 950
Guatemala 1,529 k

Kogoshima City 6,960 mi.
Japan 11,318 km.

Zakinthos, Greece
6,070 mi. 9,712 k

CONTENTS

PREFACE AND ACKNOWLEDGMENTS

I've been traveling on my own since I was fourteen. I vividly recall the first time I buckled myself into a seat aboard a commercial airplane as the prop jet rumbled down the runway at New York's LaGuardia Airport and vaulted into the air over Flushing Bay. I was airborne, streaking through the night sky toward Lexington, Kentucky, to meet a former classmate who had moved with her family from the Hudson Valley to Bluegrass Country. I remember that first airline meal—back then it really was a meal—and that, shockingly, it came with a three-pack of cigarettes. I declined the smokes but savored the experience of dining in the sky.

From then on I cannot remember a time when I was not traveling or dreaming about traveling. When I graduated from high school, the only gift I requested was a bus pass. At the time Greyhound was offering a special ticket—$99 for ninety-nine days anywhere the coach line traveled in the United States and Canada. I blocked out a trip and left the driving to them, heading from the East Coast across the northern plains to Seattle, down the West Coast, and back east. It was my first of many visits to the Grand Canyon. I was speechless at its grandeur and couldn't wait to wake up before dawn to watch the sun paint brilliant images on the mighty rocks, as it has done for millions of years. My journey continued through the South and up the eastern seaboard. I had used all but nine of the ninety-nine days and visited forty states.

Trips overseas followed during my college and postcollegiate days. I became a journalist and volunteered for every assignment that required a plane ticket. Each year I took three or four vacations in the United States or beyond our borders. I lived in London for a year, traveled extensively, and met the woman who became my wife. Her love of travel equaled mine. We settled in the States and traveled every chance we could.

A few years ago I had what I thought was a great idea. Over the years I had met a lot of "older" people who traveled extensively—I called them seasoned travelers—but, sadly, I'd met even more people who, now heading into their sunset years, had not traveled widely. Many had discretionary income and time at their disposal. In my view these folks were missing out on one of life's most rewarding experiences. True, they went to the beach every summer or drove to the mountains, and perhaps they'd flown to London once or taken a cruise across the Caribbean, but I couldn't help thinking that all they needed was a gentle push to get them off their duffs and out into that big world I enjoyed so much. *The Seasoned Traveler* television show was born from that meditation—it would target new places and new experiences especially chosen for the mature traveler.

Once the TV series was sponsored and a debut date selected, the crew and I hit the road. We traveled across the United States, Canada, and Mexico, as well as the Caribbean and Bermuda. We visited destinations in South America, Europe, Africa, Asia, Australia, even Antarctica. But that was just part of my plan. I wanted the audience to discover the joys of hiking in America's breathtaking Four Corners region, biking through the Benelux countries of Western Europe, riding sleek trains in Mexico and Canada, sailing down beautiful rivers across the globe, tracing the heritage of ancient peoples, and even purchasing their own recreational vehicle or boat.

That's when it occurred to me that I should create a companion book for the show. After all, doesn't every show on public television have a

companion book? Don't local stations try to get viewers to buy it during pledge periods? And wouldn't a companion book for my program actually be a valuable resource, too? Good grief, I said, I'd better find a publisher and start writing.

So what follows is *The Seasoned Traveler* on paper, as a resource book for the mature traveler, not just those who love to travel and do so extensively, but for those who'd like to travel more but need a nudge to get started.

In the months I've been traveling for the series, people have concluded that I know a lot about travel, and they've asked questions about where they should go, when they should go, and how they should get there. Just recently an American woman in Mexico asked me to recommend the best "volunteer vacation." She's a widow with time on her hands and wants to help others. I told her to buy my book. After we both laughed, I hauled out my research on the best volunteer vacation companies and gave her a few leads. (Turn to chapter 11, Volunteer Vacations, if you want to learn more about these ventures.)

My goal here is to provide you with the tools you need to become a seasoned traveler. Whether you are a veteran or a newcomer, I offer insights on navigating the World Wide Web, discovering discounts, and the best places to visit on your next outing. I give you the facts and some personal opinion; then you can decide what's best for you. If you want to take a cruise, I provide some tips on whether to sail the seven seas or ride the great rivers of the world. Want to exercise your brain, instead of your brawn? I introduce you to the best brain-teaser holidays. I also suggest some great places to shop in both the United States and some wonderful cities abroad. And, in honor of my ninety-nine Greyhound days and the many more that have followed, I provide information on some charming towns, enchanting cities, and wonderful natural sites you might want to visit in each of the fifty states. Finally, at the end of the book, I share my trips and tips from *The Seasoned Traveler* TV series.

Baby boomers and beyond are leading the travel charge in this country. If you are missing the boat, the bus, the plane, or the RV, this book can help you get up and get moving. It's a dynamic and wonderful world out there. Why wait?

I thank Mary Norris, executive editor at The Globe Pequot Press, for recognizing that this new television series merited a companion book. She has been a calming and encouraging guide throughout the entire process. And even as I rush to the finish line, she is envisioning a series of books from *The Seasoned Traveler.*

Thanks also to Gillian Belnap, my book editor and savior. As I hurried from destination to destination, typing the manuscript on different computers and even handwriting it on paper napkins, she was the one who stepped back and grounded my efforts. She has helped me see the forest through the trees and has provided considerable expertise in molding this manuscript into a coherent final product. I am also grateful to the talented staff of The Globe Pequot Press, who produced and marketed this work, which I now hope will be the first of many books from *The Seasoned Traveler.*

I extend my gratitude to photographer Kevan Ward, whose still pictures grace many pages of this book and whose video has made the television show so appealing visually. I also thank Grand Circle Travel and Orbitz.com for underwriting my adventures, which will be seen on U.S. public television stations.

Above all, special thanks to my wife, Susan, who has endured not only my protracted absences while preparing the TV programs but also my many nights hunched over a computer to complete this book. Love always.

INTRODUCTION: BOOMERS AND BEYOND

There are more and more of us, we're more mobile than ever, and we have one important thing in common: We love to get away to new and exciting destinations. Over the past several months, I have met scores of mature travelers, from forty-seven to ninety-two. They are not content to sit home and watch the world go by. They want to be a part of that world as it goes by. If I were king, we would all be grabbing every opportunity to travel—at home and abroad.

THE GRAYING OF THE TOURIST INDUSTRY

We baby boomers are dashing past the fifty-year mark with breathtaking speed and in record numbers. Those who've already crossed that threshold are still around, living longer and living better. We're called everything from aging hippies, to geezers, the Greatest Generation, and even old farts. But we old farts want to learn more, see more, and have more fun.

For many of us that means traveling. It can be day trips within our own state, vacation outings in the U.S. of A., a train ride across Canada, or a special jaunt over an ocean to some far-off land of enchantment. We make these trips whether we live on a tight budget, get by on Social Security, or have lots of money in the bank. And we do it because we know travel is an important part of living. I met two sixtyish sisters near my home in Georgia a few years back. They told me, with some degree of pride, that neither had ever ventured outside the Peach State in her entire life. More power to them, I thought, but not for me and probably not for you. You are likely to be one of those mature Americans who takes two or three excursions every year, at least one of them outside the boundaries of the United States. Boomers and above are setting the pace for travel.

We're citizens of a nation where someone turns fifty every eight seconds. More than seventy-six million Americans are five decades old, or more. That's roughly one in four folks right here, right now. And by 2010 one of every three Americans will be eligible for that coveted AARP membership card. Sociologists tell us the aging rush will continue unabated until the middle of the twenty-first century.

There are forty million seniors sixty-five or beyond and, remarkably, this group now outnumbers American teenagers for the first time in our country's history. Five thousand Americans turn sixty-five each day. Three million people are at least eighty-five years young, and I'm meeting them on my travels. By 2030 that number will jump to eight million, and to twenty-eight million by 2050. And if you can believe it, there are thousands and thousands of folks who have passed the century mark. Their numbers will increase, too. Modern medicine, preventive health care, better diets, exercise, and quitting smoking have helped us reach ever-higher age plateaus.

Still, for a long time older folks have been the forgotten generations. Advertisers wooed the desirable hip and young crowd of eighteen- to forty-nine-year-olds. I decided we were important. That's why I created *The Seasoned Traveler* television program, aimed at viewers fifty and beyond, and why I wrote this book. We are just as important as some thirty-year-old.

THE GRAYING OF THE WORLD

Corporate America has perked up its collective ears, too, and is coming our way. Gap is going after the Gray. This retailer, which has been targeting clothes for infants, children, and casual-Friday workers, is seeking a new audience. As I write these words, Gap is planning on opening as many as a dozen new stores that focus on selling duds to baby-boomer women. The nation's largest specialty-apparel retailer is admitting there's a special consumer base well over the age of eighteen. As the *Wall Street Journal* has reported, "Boomers consider themselves younger, hipper, more willing to experiment. They may not want to dress 'young' anymore but they certainly don't want to dress old." Consultant Philip Kowalczyk told the paper that boomers "don't view themselves as approaching retirement. Fashion is still important and they have taken better care of their bodies." And Gap is not alone. Other clothiers, like Ann Taylor Stores and Talbots, have already blazed a business trail to our doors and bank accounts. Turn on the news any night, as mature folks do, and you'll see a preponderance of commercials for medicines, health aids, and beauty products.

Gap estimates the boomer fashion market as a $41 billion business. That should come as no surprise. After all, we old farts hold much of the nation's individual wealth, including discretionary income. The American Association of Retired Persons reports that the median net worth of the beyond-fifty set increased 36 percent between 1983 and 1998, to $134,000 a year, adjusting for inflation. Either we're near the top of our pay scales, if we work, or we've retired and have money for a rainy day. Some folks have enough money for a raging storm. In many cases the children have grown and gone, paying their own bills for a change, freeing Mom and Dad from that burden. Our homes are either paid off or well on the way. Most of us have what we need, our bills are under control, and we have more time to do more things—things that are awe inspiring, educational, or just plain fun.

The recreation vehicle industry has come calling and with great success. The people who bring you those great behemoths of the superhighways are awash in profits. RV sales went up by double digits in 2004, even with escalating costs for gasoline. The Recreation Vehicle Industry

Association reports that seven million American households own one of those sleek monsters, one of every twelve vehicle-owning homes. And you can bet your 401(k) there aren't many eighteen-year-olds driving an RV along the interstate.

Companies are now courting baby boomers and beyonders, knowing we are smart—indeed, smarter than our parents and grandparents—and we are healthier, too. If thousands of us are living to be one hundred, we must be doing something right. Today's jobs are less taxing physically than our fathers' jobs, and modern conveniences make out-of-work hours less stressful. That gives people more time for more adventure.

SO WHO ARE WE SEASONED TRAVELERS?

Several studies show that older Americans have traded in the rocker on the front porch for a ride on the wild side. AARP reports that over the last five years, there's been a 23 percent increase in travel across the United States by car, train, bus, and plane, and much of that is due to people like us. The Travel Industry Association of America says folks fifty-five and older increased their travel by 40 percent, twice the national average. Baby boomers generated the highest travel volume in the United States in 2003, taking 269 million trips, more than any other age group. We spend $500 million each and every year on travel. Mature Americans take the most day trips and some of the longest vacations, averaging at least seven nights.

Early retirees, those from fifty to sixty, are planning investment and retirement strategies as they send their children out on their own. Studies suggest that this group is doing so well financially, it has time for other pursuits—getting involved in community organizations and politics or traveling. So-called *young elders* (sixty to seventy) are slowing with age, but many are still healthy and are pursing hobbies and traveling. Many remain active and maintain high levels of disposable income. And many enjoy doting on grandchildren with gifts, while others take those grandchildren on trips across the country or to Europe.

Active elders are those from seventy to eighty. These folks are filling cruise ships, traveling abroad, and taking an active part in programs like Elderhostel in this country and Interhostel overseas. Finally, there are the *sunset elders,* who are between eighty and ninety-five or better. Although

many face declining health and activity levels, there are substantial numbers who decide to leave home on some type of trip. I've met them: single women over eighty traveling alone, even one man who is still traveling at ninety-two. It's remarkable to see them on the go.

That's who we are. This book will provide you, the post-fifty crowd, with practical information and resources to help you travel well and travel safely, which is my motto. Let's begin this journey together.

SEASONED TRAVELERS

CHAPTER 1

So here's the dilemma: We're all in this over-fifty lark together, but we're not all the same. When we pass a certain stage, those who are younger think of us as "old"—just plain "old." But as we now know, demographers see gradations of "old." As far as seasoned travelers are concerned, the younger end of the aging spectrum has different travel goals and desires than older folks. Take cruise travel, for a start. A couple in their fifties might find an ocean voyage too monotonous or mind numbing. A couple in their sixties, however, might like a cruise because it's part relaxation and part activity. But a pair of seventy-year-olds are likely quite happy to take a three-week cruise to several sites in South America, perhaps leaving the ship just a few times. They have time on their side, and they don't want to rush around from place to place. A cruise is an ideal chance to have the sea at their doorstep and to sample new and different cultures with ease.

Addressing the varying needs and desires among mature travelers is at the heart of both this book and *The Seasoned Traveler* television series. Surprisingly, it amounts to a forty-year spread, from fifty to ninety.

MORE ON THE STAGES OF "OLD"

The Wisconsin Department of Tourism has put out a special brochure on how to deal with the different stages of age. It differentiates between *baby boomers* and the more "mature" *seniors*. It notes that the latter, those sixty-five and up, prefer to take day trips that include visiting museums, historical places, or shopping malls. Boomers, on the other hand, prefer more active travel. They'd rather be on a bicycle than in a shopping mall. Seniors travel year-round, with summer and autumn forays the most popular. They are likely to stay with friends or relatives, while boomers prefer lodging in hotels or bed-and-breakfasts. Younger travelers are also more apt to book hotels through the Internet than older folks. The Wisconsin brochure also reports baby boomers often travel without extensive preparation, while older travelers plan things thoroughly.

Baby boomers consider travel a necessity, not a luxury. They need to get away from the rat race, and they want to do it on a regular basis. A weekend getaway in the next state may happen regularly, with a longer trip at least once a year. Given the exploding number of boomers, this should be comforting news to travel providers: Clearly, people who think travel is as necessary to life as watching a movie will provide plenty of business.

Post-retirees, on the other hand, may be less active and less interested in travel, especially now that airport security has escalated into an athletic event of its own. Or these folks may be on tighter budgets so that, while they have a lot of time, they may not have a great deal of money for touring. Still, I've met lots of people in this age group who use all their discretionary money for travel, at least one trip every year. Travel is too important to them.

Boomers are traveling more than their parents and grandparents. Perhaps their parents visited the "Old Country" after they retired, but boomers have been traveling since they were young, and many crossed the Continent on a Eurail pass as high school or college students. Having done Europe, these wanderers are looking for new horizons at age fifty-five. They go farther and farther afield, trudging across Alaskan wilderness, sailing a rubber pontoon as part of a cruise to Antarctica, or traveling the length of Vietnam just decades after the United States fought a costly war there.

One official of a group that serves older Americans said of five-decaders, "You're not likely to see them on bus tours of the U.S. because they already did that on their bikes or with backpacks." This group is interested in physically challenging trips or out-of-the-way destinations. They may also be interested in travel that's intellectually stimulating, as long as it's not downright boring. Senior travelers, on the other hand, may only embark on one major trip each year or every other year. Driving to Florida from their northern homes may be more important to this group than driving across the desert of Kuwait.

When I put together the concept for *The Seasoned Traveler* TV show, I knew that most of the existing travel series on public television tend to visit places in Europe. Research convinced me to find alternate destinations and to highlight different kinds of travel experiences. A week of marveling at the majestic caverns of America's Four Corners region, for example, would be more appealing to younger oldsters than a return visit to Paris.

Many of the early boomers are still too young to accept the concept of early-bird dinner specials or discounted airfares that peg them as seniors. They may not come around to that way of thinking for another decade or two. Boomers claim they don't want stuffy or stodgy. Art and history museums are less likely destinations than casinos or coral reefs. The just-past-fifty group says it wants vacations to be about fun. Interest in religious pilgrimages or heritage tours is still some way off for them. Many boomers think they still fit in with the thirty-year-olds at resorts like Sandals and Hedonism. Older travelers would no more be caught at a Sandals resort than they would paraglide across the Grand Canyon. The more seasoned set is often quite happy on quieter trips—birding, heritage tours, Elderhostel educational trips, volunteer vacations. This is also the crowd that enjoys package tours.

Boomers want instant gratification while on holiday. They know their parents had to scrimp and save for vacations, but they're different. This bunch will make a quick decision to fly to Barbados, stay in a luxury hotel, eat and drink well, and put the entire escapade on a credit card. Boomers turn to Web sites that offer last-minute travel deals for the weekend or for a fortnight. These habits have spawned a group of

SIX COUNTRIES IN SIXTEEN DAYS

A few summers ago my wife and I took our college-graduating daughter on a package trip to Europe. It was typical, six countries in sixteen days. The tour provider pointed out in the brochures that our trip was eighteen days but, of course, day one was the overnight flight to London and day eighteen was flying home from Frankfurt. We chose this coach excursion because, while our daughter had been to England several times, we wanted her to get a taste of the Continent.

At the time my wife and I had just passed the fateful fifty mark. But we thought the organized tour would be the best way to see all the sights we wanted in the time allotted. Like other boomers, we were time-deprived, we wanted the best comfort and care we could get, and we weren't necessarily interested in joining the rest of our forced "family" for an entire fortnight.

When we assembled in our London hotel on the first evening, we met an extraordinarily diverse group. There was a sixtyish couple from Kansas, a retired couple from Massachusetts and their two grown daughters, a younger husband and wife from California with her mother and their daughter, a retired woman from Arizona with her teenaged grandson, a retired woman from Alabama with two girls, a pre-retiree couple from Iowa with their high school grandson, a woman from Arizona with her grown daughter, a middle-aged woman from California and her adult daughter, four young women who had just graduated from Princeton University, two middle-aged women traveling together, and the three of us.

This trip was in the summer after September 11, when many Americans were still skittish about flying. Our loquacious, personable travel guide explained that forty people was typical on this trip. Our group was smaller, so we had more room to stretch out on the bus. After two days in England, we were whisked off to Paris on the Eurostar express train, where we boarded the coach that was to be our wheels for fourteen days, over 4,000 miles.

It took some time to break down the barriers, as each group opted to stick close together at first. Eventually the walls came down, and people from all across America started exchanging pleasantries and then life stories. It was a typical, maddening package tour, always on the move, never enough time to stop and savor something of interest. After all, we had to check into the next hotel, and dinner was served at 7:00 P.M. sharp.

But because each family had a reason to be there, the trip made sense, and by the end of the eighteen days, which were actually sixteen, we had become comfortable with the routine and our companions. To be sure, there was some grousing about others and some quiet criticism. Yet most of the travelers got what they expected and wanted. Those who had never been to Europe saw the highlights: London, Paris, Nice, Lucerne, Pisa, Rome, Sorrento, Naples, Florence, Venice, Salzburg, and the Rhine. They could plan longer trips to the places they liked most if they wanted to return. Those who knew they'd visit only once saw the highlights of Western Europe and probably went home satisfied and laden with photographs they will treasure for the rest of their lives. The oldest members of our tour were the most delighted with the journey, because everything was done for them and they could just sit back and enjoy. Travel is what you want as well as what you need. For my wife and me, the experience confirmed that such whirlwind trips are not for us. Our daughter, Lisa, loved it. She had seen some of the highlights of Europe, and the trip whetted her appetite for travel even more.

In the end roughly thirty Americans had a specific travel demand for those eighteen days in June 2002, and—for the most part—those demands were satisfied.

Internet services that deal in last-minute seats on planes and last-minute cabins on cruise ships. The older crowd usually takes plenty of time to plan its trips. These folks will do the reading, talk to others who've been to the destinations they're considering. Then they'll visit a travel agent for brochures and work with that agent, or with someone on the other end of a telephone line at a cruise or package-tour company. They're less likely to do it all themselves and less likely to want nonstop entertainment and excitement.

Boomers are less likely to take package tours. They want more interactivity when traveling. They don't want to hear lectures about hikes; they want to take hikes. However, this group will go on "active" tours; for example, they'll happily sign up for a bicycle circuit of Europe because while they pedal through the Belgian countryside, the tour provides meals and lodging while carrying their suitcases from place to place. Such tours also offer a chance to meet the locals and share stories with them, as well as their traveling companions.

Many mature wanderers are often looking for discounts and bargains. They'll settle for second class for at least part of the trip. They're generally content with what they get and can be model passengers. Younger mature travelers are time-deprived because many still work (they haven't quite made that first million yet). Their jobs are often demanding and stressful, so they seek high-class relaxation at a spa resort or on a small luxury cruise with just a few other passengers on board. Others want to play as hard as they work, so they'll opt for endless scuba dives, skiing the toughest Himalayan peaks, or marching miles through untouched rain forests. Boomers want to get the most out of the short time they have to enjoy their expedition.

Boomers tend not to be joiners. They're uncomfortable on a cruise liner crammed with 2,400 people. They shun organized activities. Still, having said that, the fifties folks often like to associate with people like themselves. While they're less willing to go on trips with people much older, they are generally tolerant of those similar in age, nationality, or occupation.

Contrast that with those sixty and above. They rarely have trouble getting along with their new travel companions, and many make new life-long friends while touring together. I have noticed on recent trips that the older travelers seemed eager to make friends with strangers. I have seen this time and again during trips for the TV series.

Mature travelers prefer prepared tours with expert local guides who can show off the sights of their communities and countries. Still, while they want to be taken to tourist spots, they also want plenty of free time to explore each travel site. Thirty minutes may not be enough for a first-time visitor to Vienna or Sydney. Some places are just too important to rush. They have said so, and many travel providers have responded by offering more free time, less rush, and longer stopovers. The sixty-fivers want good value, a worry-free holiday, and the chance to meet and social-ize with fellow travelers.

"BEEN THERE, DONE THAT"

One of the things I wrestled with in preparing our television series and this book was where to go. I learned very quickly that today's mature trav-elers have seen and done much more than their elders. They've explored much of the United States, visited Canada, had some connection with Mexico, and made several jaunts overseas. It seems some people are never home.

When I talked to the people at Grand Circle Travel in Boston, which is the major underwriter for *The Seasoned Traveler* series, I learned that boomers and seniors have been on the road, and often. The company says senior travelers are taking more trips, and they are seeking new destinations or experiences. Grand Circle found that two-thirds of travelers are looking for something new, different, and exciting. Just one-third of respondents to a company survey said they prefer familiar destinations. On a recent river cruise in Europe, I met a couple from Colorado in their sixties. They have taken that same river trip four times. They just love it, and each time they go, they say they look for something new, something they missed on a previous cruise. Grand Circle notes that the median age for those on bicycling vacations is fifty, jumping to sixty-five for its Overseas Adventure tours (which are smaller and more active in nature); the average age of those on its cruises is seventy-two years old.

Seasoned travelers have probably reached the "usual destinations" already. They've landed in London, passed through Paris, roamed Rome, feasted on Florence, visited Vienna, and marveled at Madrid. They have schussed down Alpine slopes, imbibed great wines in the French countryside, sailed the fjords of Norway, and hiked the Yorkshire Dales. Now this reliable group of adventurers is looking for the next hill to climb. Grand Circle bookings suggest a brave new world of travel. The number one destination is Egypt. Cairo; the pyramids; the port city of Alexandria; cruises down the Nile, the world's longest river; and a hop to the resort area near Sharm el-Sheikh offer fresh allure to older folks, even given the continuing tension and violence in the region. Southern Africa is the second most popular destination for Grand Circle customers. A safari to a game preserve strikes many folks as living on the edge. It is far from their neighborhoods, more rural than their backyards, and home to wildlife not seen in suburban America. Remarkably enough, the third destination of choice is Morocco in northwestern Africa, again in the face of ongoing terrorism. The fact that Morocco is so close to Europe, yet so different, seems to attract Westerners. Turkey is also a magnet for American tourists, and it, too, has been rocked by series of deadly terrorist attacks. But Turkey's history and fascinating culture are attracting more and more mature explorers.

The oldest among us have witnessed war and hatred up close, from World War II to Korea. Baby boomers grew up during the pain of Vietnam and the scourge of Watergate. The terrorist attacks of September 11, 2001, inflicted new pain on a new generation. But many of us feel we have to keep a perspective on such attacks, which is why a fifty-something woman from New England told the *Boston Globe* that she and her husband have every intention of continuing their long tradition of travel, especially overseas. There is so much to see, she noted, and by exercising good sense there is no justifiable reason for them to be afraid.

There is absolutely no end to the places we old farts want to visit, and there's no end to the adventures we can take. If you are in your fifties or sixties, the world is yours to savor. If you're seventy to eighty-five, there are still plenty of places to see and things to do, but you may want to take it a bit more slowly. It's a great time to be mature, even if we don't act it, and it's a great time to be traveling.

THE NEW FACE OF TRAVEL

CHAPTER 2

Terrorism is nothing new to Americans. We had been fortunate over the years as acts of hatred played out in other parts of the world, but, of course, recent history has shown that no place is immune from terrorist acts. The 1993 attack on the World Trade Center in New York City and the 1995 bombing of the Alfred P. Murrah Federal Building in Oklahoma City proved that such acts were not limited to the Middle East.

Then there was 9/11, which devastated the nation and taught us all a costly lesson. September 11, 2001, affected so much of our lives and our way of living, including the travel industry and all who travel. Airlines stumbled or fell into bankruptcy; some carriers may never emerge from that scourge. Tour companies lost millions of dollars, and for some the burden was so great, they closed down. Cities, states, and countries dependent on tourism revenue suffered and were slow to recover.

The airline hijackings forced changes in the way we travel. A new government agency, the Transportation Security Administration, became the guardian of the skies. Uncle Sam took other steps to make rail and ship travel more secure. All of it was necessary because every year 500 million people, 130 million cars and trucks, 2.5 million railcars, and 5.7 million cargo ships traverse our roads, rails, rivers, and shorelines. More than 600 million passengers embark on 89,000 domestic and international flights.

Driving became an alternative method of travel for millions. After 9/11 it just seemed safer and easier. But driving across borders took on new meaning. Entry into Mexico or Canada at some crossings required just a few minutes, while in other areas lengthy queues caused a prolonged wait. Returning to the United States from south or north of the border became a laborious and frustrating exercise. I'm reminded of a recent trip to Vancouver and then on to Vancouver Island in British Columbia. Upon arriving at the ferry terminal in Victoria for the trip to Washington State, my vehicle and I were inspected twice by American officials, once in Canada and once in the United States.

THE SILVER LINING

Still, there's something of a silver lining from the horror of September 11. The travel industry has changed, and many would say it's much better. The change has come about quickly, but the impact will remain for many years to come.

As the industry was trying to reformulate itself, it had help from seasoned travelers who led the way back onto airliners and cruise ships. While many Americans refused to fly or sail and opted for the safety of their own vehicles, it was mature adventurers who decided to be brave. They rebooked package tours, made airline reservations, jumped aboard ocean and river ships, and checked into hotels.

Even today, with sporadic acts of terrorism continuing across the globe, many middle-aged and older travelers seem undeterred. I mentioned earlier the terrorist threats in Egypt, Morocco, and Turkey, and yet I have come across senior travelers recently who say they have made plans to visit each of those countries and many more. A man from Iowa said he can't be worried about the possibility of a terrorist attack. If one comes, he told me, he's prepared for the consequences, but he's not going to change his plans out of fear.

Ailing airlines have been forced to restructure themselves and slim down. Streamlined flight schedules have resulted, along with simplified fare schemes and lower ticket prices. Rising world oil prices and their impact on airline fuel have dented the low-fare trend, however, and fuel surcharges may be an unfortunate component of the new reality in air travel.

Upstart air carriers continue to perform well, outpacing the old-school airlines. Southwest, AirTran, Midwest, and other low-fare, no-frills airlines not only survived 9/11 but thrived afterward. Their practices impacted the established carriers (American, Continental, Delta, Northwest, United, and USAirways), forced some carriers like America West to adapt and improve, and spawned even more alternative airlines. Delta developed Song, United unleashed Ted, and JetBlue came from nowhere to make a name for itself. Many of these low-price lines are limited in scope and coverage, but travelers are turning to them increasingly when they're going where these carriers fly.

As the airlines changed, so did the airline ticketing game. Paper tickets virtually disappeared. Even the Big Six have converted to electronic ticketing. The World Wide Web is bulging with new, and even newer, sites to purchase air tickets. All-purpose sites can plan your entire trip:

air tickets, auto rentals, hotels, admissions to attractions. Other Web addresses can allow travelers to shop around for the best bargains. In some cases the late bird gets the best worm, as some sites cater to last-minute bookings.

Trains and buses benefited, too. The fear of flying made rail travel seem a safer, more secure alternative. Traffic on Amtrak, the struggling U.S. passenger rail service, rose after 9/11, as did ridership on bus lines. Package tours on coaches were snapped up by older folks who couldn't be bothered to drive and didn't want the hassle of airport security. Specialized train services, like those in Alaska and across Canada, posted passenger increases.

Recreation vehicle purchases soared. Industrywide, RV sales increased by 13 percent in 2004, but I've talked to local dealers who have experienced even more explosive growth. An RV outlet in Atlanta posted a 32 percent gain in sales; in Albuquerque one dealer said the increase was 20 percent. Americans who did not want to endure the new realities of air travel flocked to campers like moths to a bright bulb. RV factories worked nonstop to build new motorized buses, travel trailers, and pop-up units. One dealer said it can take eight months for some RV orders to be fulfilled. Rising fuel prices seemed to have little effect on sales. One reason may be that while it takes a boatload of gasoline to fill up these monsters, some RVers park them for weeks, even months at a time, using no gas whatsoever. I've met recreation vehicle enthusiasts who say they've driven to all forty-nine states on the mainland—and they'd drive to Hawaii if they could.

Travel companies rose to the new challenge. Some package-tour firms made themselves leaner and greener. They reduced prices on some trips, added new and desirable destinations, and made a stronger advertising pitch for their products. Sales peaked again, with older travelers once more setting the pace and others following their example. In the next several chapters, I'll tell you how to benefit from the new world order in travel today, whether you are a travel pro or a newcomer to the experience.

We must never forget what happened in Lower Manhattan; North Arlington, Virginia; or southwestern Pennsylvania that bright and clear September day. But we must not let it prevent us from traveling the world around us. Many seasoned travelers have shown the way. It's time for everyone else to follow their lead.

DISCOVERING DISCOUNTS

CHAPTER 3

In the good old days, when people aged they were rewarded in many ways: discount shopping days at the supermarket and the mall, lower admission prices to movie theaters and most attractions, cheaper dinners if you got to certain restaurants early. Oh, yes, and travelers could save money when traveling, with price breaks from airlines and other travel providers.

While you may still get early-bird specials at the diner and reduced rates at grocery stores, the days of lower travel prices for seniors are fading fast. In this chapter I'll direct you to the best resources available if you plan to fly, take the train, or catch a bus.

AIR TRAVEL

Since airlines are so much a part of the travel experience, let's start there. Many U.S. carriers do still recognize mature fliers. Don't be afraid to ask.

TICKETS TO RIDE—FOR LESS

Alaska Airlines, (800) 426–0333; www.alaskaair.com. Senior Published Fares provides 10 percent discounts to passengers sixty-two-plus and to a companion of any age. Special promotional fares are often available to those sixty-five and above. These do not apply to companions, and these tickets are nonrefundable.

America West, (800) 235–9292; www.americawest.com. If you are sixty-two or older, you get a 10 percent discount off the cheapest fare, as does a companion, for certain destinations. The carrier also has a Senior Saver Pack of four coupon books for passengers sixty-two and over. Each coupon can be used for a one-way flight to any of the one hundred America West or America West Express cities.

American Airlines, (800) 237–7981 (Promotions Department); www.aa.com. The nation's biggest carrier offers 10 percent reductions to passengers sixty-five and above. Certain restrictions apply.

TransAir (ATA), (800) 435–9282; www.ata.com. American's budget carrier, serving more than forty cities in the U.S. mainland, Hawaii, and the Caribbean. ATA offers special fares for travelers sixty-two and older at all times.

Continental Airlines, (800) 525–0280; www.continental.com. Fliers at least sixty-five get 10 percent off tickets to domestic destinations with a fourteen-day advance purchase.

Delta Air Lines, (800) 221–1212; www.delta.com. Delta's low-cost offshoot, Song, flies from Florida cities to Boston, New York, and Las Vegas. The carrier also connects Atlanta to New York's John F. Kennedy Airport. Fares may be lower than Delta's senior discounts. Contact (800) 359–7664 or www.flysong.com.

Frontier Airlines, (800) 432–1359; www.frontierairlines.com. A 10 percent discount to passengers sixty-two-plus, and a companion of any age flies for the same rate.

Great Plains Airlines, (866) 929–8646; www.gpair.com. This regional airline serves half a dozen cities in the Midwest, New Mexico, and Washington,

DC. It offers single-class service on thirty-two-seat jets, and travelers sixty-two or better get a 10 percent fare break.

Hawaiian Air, (800) 367–5320; www.hawaiianair.com. You only have to be sixty to get a break here. Discounts vary on trips from the U.S. mainland to Hawaii, if seats are available.

Horizon Air, (800) 547–9708; www.horizonair.com. This carrier serves more than forty markets in the western United States and Canada, from the state of Arizona in the south to the province of Alberta in the north. If you're sixty-two or more, you and a companion qualify for a discount of 10 percent.

JetBlue Airways, (800) 538–2583; www.jetblue.com. JetBlue does not offer discounts to mature travelers.

Midwest Airlines, (800) 452–2022; www.midwestairlines.com. Midwest offers benefits to fliers fifty-five and older, the usual 10 percent.

Northwest Airlines, (800) 225–2525; www.nwa.com. This carrier's senior discounts are few and vary according to destination. It's worth inquiring when you make a reservation but don't expect a lot.

Southwest Airlines, (800) 435–9792; www.southwest.com. If you are sixty-five-plus, the carrier offers discounts that vary from city to city.

Spirit Airlines, (800) 772–7117; www.spiritair.com. Low-fare carrier serving as many as two dozen cities in Florida, as well as Chicago, Detroit, New York, Atlantic City, Los Angeles, Denver, Myrtle Beach, South Carolina, and San Juan, Puerto Rico.

United Air Lines, (800) 241–6522; www.united.com. Reduced fares for passengers sixty-five-plus. Also inquire about United's Silver Wings Plus Travel Club for folks fifty-five and above: (800) 720–1765 or www.silverwingsplus.com.

USA 3000 Airlines, (877) USA–3000; www.usa3000airlines.com. This low-cost carrier connects some Florida cities with towns up north like Chicago, Cleveland, and Baltimore; it does not offer senior discounts.

USAirways, (800) 428–4322 (AARP reservation line, 866–886–2277); www.usairways.com. Inquire about the AARP Savers discount program. A merger between USAirways and American West is anticipated before the end of 2005.

USAirways Shuttle, (800) 428–4322; www.usairways.com. The shuttle flies between Boston, New York, and Washington, DC, and provides some price reductions to AARP members.

Carriers can offer 10 percent discounts on the standard fares for customers sixty to sixty-five or older; at some of these airlines, seasoned-traveler 10 percent discounts also apply to a traveling companion of any age. Some carriers offer coupon books for multiple trips, a bonus for more frequent fliers. The booklets most often contain four coupons that can be redeemed for domestic or international destinations. You've heard or read about those department store gift cards that lose their value over time, right? Well, the same is true for airline coupons: They are valid for only a specific amount of time. If you buy in bulk, then, know the exact shelf life of the coupons. If you don't plan to travel much, steer clear of them.

Every so often air carriers will publish special promotional deals for seasoned travelers. Keep your good eye out for them. And when the airlines engage in a fare war, look for discounts. Even though fare cuts may apply to all travelers, there may be special bonuses for older fliers. All this is good news, although I have to admit you may actually do better shopping for lower prices online or through a travel agent than dealing exclusively with the carriers. And keep this in mind: Given the financial fluidity of the transportation industry, discounts could change or evaporate at any time. The smart consumer catches the bargains and runs with them to the nearest airport.

Many foreign airlines provide fare reductions to older adventurers. Aside from the American carriers, a dozen airlines serve Canada, four fly in Mexico, fifty-three operate in Europe, twenty-two in Asia, seven in Central America, and six in Africa; thirteen serve the Middle East, nine fly in South America, eleven travel to Australia and Oceania, and one carrier provides service to Antarctica.

Once again, it's a good idea to consult the carriers when you plan to fly, ask for a "goodie," or hop on the Internet and seek your fortune in flying.

DISCOUNTS ONLINE

In addition to travel providers, there are other ways to save a few dollars by using online travel agencies. The Big Three command the largest share of the market:

Expedia: **www.expedia.com**
Orbitz: **www.orbitz.com**
Travelocity: **www.travelocity.com**

One of the first Web sites to help folks find travel bargains was Priceline,

which encountered financial difficulties but has come back (www.price line.com).

I don't know about you, but when I consult these services, I sometimes get a few choices, a few airlines, or a couple of auto rental companies. Newer sites have thus burst onto the scene with claims they can do a better job of finding consumers the best deal out there.

America Online entered the fray in late 2004. AOL invested in Kayak Software Corporation, one of a group of firms whose software lets travelers scour hundreds of airline, hotel, and auto rental Web sites. Oddly, Kayak Software was developed by the founders of Orbitz, Expedia, and Travelocity, but now it's a competitor. One computer analyst said Kayak will become the main competitor for Travelocity. You can check it out at www.kayak.com.

There are other search engines, or aggregators, challenging the more established online travel agencies. These, too, claim they can scan up to 150 other sites, including the airlines themselves, to get you the absolute rock-bottom fare. Now, this could get very interesting, because if each promises the lowest rate, it could set off a bidding war among the various companies. This is the main competition for the Kayak system noted above.

MAJOR FOREIGN CARRIERS

Aer Lingus (Ireland):
www.aerlingus.com

Aeromexico: www.aeromexico.com

Air Canada: www.aircanada.ca

Air France: www.airfrance.com

Air Jamaica: www.airjamaica.com

Air New Zealand:
www.airnewzealand.com

Alitalia Airlines (Italy):
www.alitalia.com

Austrian Airlines: www.aua.com

British Airways:
www.britishairways.com

Cathay Pacific (China):
www.cathaypacific.com

EasyJet (Europe): www.easyjet.com

El Al (Israel): www.elal.co.il

Finnair: www.finnair.com

Hapag-Lloyd Express (Europe):
www.hlx.com

Iberia (Spain): www.iberia.com

Iceland Air: www.icelandair.com

Japan Air: www.jal.com

Kenya Airways:
www.kenya-airways.com

KLM (Netherlands): www.klm.com

Korean Air: www.koreanair.com

Kuwait Airlines:
www.kuwait-airways.com

Lan-Chile: www.lan.com

Lufthansa (Germany):
www.lufthansa.com

Mexicana Airlines:
www.mexicana.com

Olympic Airlines (Greece):
www.olympicair.com

Qantas (Australia):
www.qantas.com

Qatar (Persian Gulf):
www.qatarairways.com

Royal Jordanian Airlines:
www.rja.com

**Ryan International Airlines
(Europe):** www.flyryan.com

Sabena (Belgium): www.sabena.com

SAS (Scandinavia):
www.sas.com

Singapore Airlines:
www.singaporeair.com

South African Airways:
www.flysaa.com

Swiss International Airlines:
www.swiss.com

TAP (Portugal): www.tap.pt

Thai Airways: www.thaiair.com

Turkish Airlines: www.thy.com

Varig (Brazil): www.varig.com

Virgin Atlantic (Britain):
www.virgin.com

So how does this really work? After a seasoned traveler like yourself finds a flight, car rental, or hotel room you want, you are redirected to a supplier's site; there the transaction is completed and you get loyalty points if such programs exist. This helps you in two ways. You don't have to pay suppliers a fee to book on their Web sites, which can save you around $5.00 per ticket. And you get access to more providers.

Here's another advantage. Budget airlines like Southwest and JetBlue don't sell tickets through third-party sites, but they do work with aggregators like the ones below. They do this to keep distribution costs down and thus ticket prices low. So you win again.

But there is a downside to almost everything, and the downside here is that unlike Expedia, which provides one-stop shopping, you'll have to make a few stops along the way. It's your wallet and your choice.

Online Aggregators

www.farechaser.com
www.itasoftware.com
www.mobissimo
www.qixo.com ($20 fee)
www.sidestep.com

Other Discount Travel Sites

www.about.com: Information on budget travel, goods, and services.
www.bestfare.com
www.cheaptickets.com
www.etn.com: A worldwide discount airfare system, listing the best consolidator and discount fares; the site also lists reductions on cruises, vehicle rentals, and hotels.
www.farechase.com
www.hotwire.com
www.lastminutetravel.com
www.onetravel.com: International travel and adventure destinations
www.opondo.com: The European equivalent to Orbitz; Opondo, by the way, is an acronym for "Opportunity to Do"
www.simplyquick.com
www.travelbyus.com

www.traveldiscounts.com: Considered a great place to find bargain-
basement airfares

www.travelzoo.com

AUTO TRAVEL

As a seasoned traveler, you may want to save money on other forms of transportation, not just airlines. The American Automobile Association (AAA), the Canadian Automobile Assocation (CAA), and ARC Europe offer discounts on hotels, motels, and popular tourist attractions. Of course, their primary function is to assist motorists with maps, travel directions, and emergency roadside service. You can also get travel insurance and traveler's checks for your trip. Note, however, that you must be a dues-paying member of these organizations to take advantage of the reduced rates and other benefits.

Most major automobile rental companies offer senior travelers a 5 to 10 percent discount. Minimum age requirements vary from firm to firm; some require AARP membership, which is good because you only have to be fifty to get an AARP card. You may want to play one discount against another. See whether an AAA discount is better than AARP, for instance, or ask about other incentives. If your goal is to shave dollars off the price of your rental vehicle, you'll want to exercise every option you can. Still, I generally find that AAA and AARP have the same discount.

You can also try Breeze Net (www.bnm.com) for an overview of vehicle rentals at both domestic and overseas locations.

TRAIN TRAVEL

For those who love riding the rails, Amtrak, the nation's passenger railroad service, continues offering travelers sixty-two and above a 15 percent break on all fares, even on sale prices and All Aboard fares, which allow many stops. The discount is not permitted on the Auto Train from Virginia to Florida or for first-class accommodations on any train. For information, call (800) USA–RAIL or visit www.amtrak.com. Alaska Railroad offers some discounts to older folks; contact (800) 544–0552 or www.alaskarailroad.com.

For travel north of the continental U.S., the Canadian Rail system, VIA (www.viarail.ca/), offers the sixty-plus crowd a 10 percent fare decrease.

TRAVELER'S CHECKS

Just as an aside, traveler's checks are not what they used to be. During a recent trip to Mexico, I discovered most merchants don't like to deal with them, Mexican banks don't always cash them, and most travelers have decided it's easier to go to an automated teller machine and take out small amounts of cash when needed. You certainly don't want to pay for traveler's checks when their value has been diminished.

VIA Rail may ask you for proof of age. By the way, this 10 percent discount comes on top of other fare breaks that VIA may be providing.

Rail Europe offers lower-cost passes throughout Europe to all those who are sixty and beyond. Some of these provide worthwhile savings. BritRail offers a variety of senior travel passes in Great Britain. You can access the company in the United States by visiting www.raileurope.com or www.britrail.net.

There are similarly discounted passes offered by French Railpass (www.raileurope.com), Holland Senior Railpass (www.railpass.com/eurail/passes/holland), Norway Rail Pass (www.railpass.com/eurail/passes/norway), and Scanrail Pass in Scandinavia (www.scanrail.com), as well as on the Balkan Flexipass (some deductions apply; www.railpass.com/new/passes/pass/balkan).

Eurailpass, by the way—which offers unlimited travel across seventeen nations in Europe—does not offer any senior discounts, making individual country passes a better deal. And Eurostar, the train through the English Channel tunnel (Chunnel) from London to Paris, Brussels, and Amsterdam, gives seniors a 25 to 30 percent fare discount, as long as you order tickets ahead. If you are going to London and on to any of the other three cities on the Continent, this is an excellent deal in many ways. The senior discount is higher than you'd get on other forms of conveyance, and the Eurostar is an absolutely brilliant way to make the channel crossing. The train zips along at about 100 miles per hour, races smoothly through the Chunnel in twenty minutes, and avoids the waves that make the ferry or hovercraft crossings so unpleasant. No seasickness here, so you can eat safely on the train without worrying that your breakfast may come back to haunt you. For information, contact www.raileurope.com.

BUS TRAVEL

Finally, there's the bus. Greyhound does not have a senior discount program per se, but discounts are usually available to the over-fifty-five crowd. If you want to "leave the driving to us," contact the carrier at www.greyhound.com.

Happy trails!

TRAVEL AGENTS, TRAVEL PROVIDERS, AND THE WORLD WIDE WEB

Let's face it: We are all turning to the World Wide Web these days for world news, local weather, and research material, as well as travel information and fares. Most of us are wired and often take the time and effort to find what we need. But as we age, we may be less willing to expend the time and energy required to surf the Web to save a few dollars on a flight, a car rental, or a train ride. Fortunately, travelers have some options.

TRAVEL AGENTS

The travel agent was once a lofty individual, almost godlike in stature, the Oracle of Delphi for travel conundrums. She, or less likely he, had access to the vital information prospective tourists needed and the lowdown on fares for such trips. Of course, back then few people other than travel agents had the ability to book tickets themselves. Even fewer could access the computers of airlines and other travel providers, so the public beat a path to the travel professional's door. Today, with the Internet, anyone has the potential to be a travel agent.

Agents still offer a world of excursion information. A good travel specialist is well versed on many locations and has traveled extensively to far-flung regions of the world. Any agent worth her or his salt can navigate countless travel sites to get the best rates and deals for customers. These folks know how to use the World Wide Web, just as you or I do, but they have access to wholesale consolidator data that we may not be able to find.

In the good old days, travel agents did their work and did not charge patrons a dime. Airlines, tour companies, and hotels paid them a commission. After all, the agent took a great deal of work off the hands of providers. The airlines or other entities were happy to reimburse travel agents for their time and effort bringing in business. That stopped when the airlines encountered financial turbulence at the start of the twenty-first century. The ailing carriers, and even the not-so-ailing carriers, terminated their commissions to travel agents, who in turn passed along the costs to the traveling public in the form of a service fee. Some travel specialists have also contemplated, or actually resorted to, requiring a trip-planning deposit from customers. The fee is applied to the cost of a trip that may eventually be booked but is forfeited if the client doesn't use the agent's services.

As we often say, timing is everything, and the timing for imposing fees on clients could not have come more inauspiciously. The Web was ablaze with information for travelers, including ways to secure rooms, rent vans, and buy plane tickets. New sites multiplied, promising better deals and lower fares. The travel agent's ability to compete was compromised. On top of that, most travel companies created their own sites. Air carriers, hotels and motels, vehicle rental agencies, travel vendors, and tour companies are all after your business.

These are tough times for the Oracles of Delphi. On my wanderings for *The Seasoned Traveler* television program, I have met many travel agents who decry the current state of affairs. Some have reduced their hours, working only part time or arranging trips for neighborhood or church groups in their communities. Those agents who are still putting up the good fight say it has become very difficult to make a living, because they cannot compete effectively with hundreds of Web sites or even the telephone reservationists for air carriers. AirTran, for instance, opened a new call center in Carrollton, Georgia, with college students from the University of West Georgia and others taking reservations on the phone. These staffers make little money and work just a few hours each week, but they do help maximize reservations for the low-fare carrier. A travel agent is competing not only with the airline in this instance but also with a potential customer. You or I can call AirTran directly, thus saving ourselves the travel agent's fee for booking the exact same tickets.

As a result, there are some interesting changes in the travel business. Research firm PhoCusWright reports that the overall industry is growing about 5 percent a year, although travel agency bookings are about the same from year to year. So how is the industry growing? Simple. Online travel planning has mushroomed at a rate of 20 percent per year. PhoCusWright says one in three travelers in 2004 booked trips or flights online. Expedia is getting 39 percent of the online business, Travelocity commands 20 percent of the market, and Orbitz has 18 percent.

A study from Virginia Tech quantified the different benefits of using a travel agency, electronic travel services, and travel providers. Agents can make arrangements face-to-face or over the telephone and arrange all aspects of a trip for customers. They also assist with difficult situations, provide tips for better discounts, and offer timely refunds on cancellations. Key drawbacks: Access to travel specialists may be limited to the actual hours of operation, especially if agents are closed on Sunday or holidays, and agents must charge for their work.

Compare that with electronic travel services, through which you can make multiple types of reservations twenty-four hours a day, after comparison-shopping among many travel sites and services. On some Web sites you may be able to find a bargain price via auction, with far more success than you'd obtain using an individual travel agent. But the downside is that you must check all itineraries yourself—which can be very time consuming. You may not be able to locate all the discounts offered and not be able to reach someone who can help you find them.

TRAVEL PROVIDERS

When it comes to travel providers themselves, the Virginia Tech study gives them points for being able to check multiple itineraries day or night and make emergency arrangements quickly. A friend of mine still marvels at how Delta Air Lines helped her get a ticket from Atlanta to Honolulu quickly and inexpensively when her father suffered a stroke. Providers can also offer customers special benefits, with frequent-traveler programs, coupons, or other incentives.

On the negative side, travel providers cannot offer multiple reservations for autos and hotels, because they often have special arrangements with a particular rental agency or hotel chain. The car or hotel prices these services quote are often not the cheapest you can get. You may have discovered this; I confront the issue all the time. It's easy enough to book an airline ticket directly or claim frequent-flier miles, but the carrier always wants to connect you to the car rental firm with which it has a special arrangement. In every case I have found cheaper auto rentals or hotels on my own. And you may have noticed another inconvenience: Some of these providers require credit card payment from the moment you book a flight or rental. If you change your mind, you have to go through the process of getting a refund or credit.

So what's best for you? The answer is simple: the method that serves your needs and causes the fewest headaches. If you are busy and don't have time to cruise scores of Web sites for deals on plane tickets, hotel suites, and Hummer rentals, you should contact a travel specialist in your hometown, pay her or his fee, and let the agent do the work. If you are computer-illiterate or computer-uncomfortable, turn to a travel agency.

If you're busy and have a frequent-flier account with, say, Continental Airlines, the easiest solution is to connect to the Web site and book a flight. Or you could call the carrier's reservations number and, if you can endure the wait for an agent, get everything sorted out with one phone call. You should remember, though, that an airline's online ticket prices are often lower than those quoted by a customer service representative on the telephone.

THE WEB

Now, if you're computer-literate, and tired of reality shows on television, you might want to spend time on your computer and book up a storm.

You may contact a dozen or so Web sites and find the best price on every aspect of your upcoming adventure. If you're savvy, you'll check for surcharges, fuel add-ons, or special fees for overseas travel (such as a departure tax at airports).

Since nearly all of us can play the computer game, here are some resources for you to try. There are a few Web sites that are worth visiting when planning a trip: Fodors (www.fodors.com) will help with information about hotels and on-the-ground choices. Condé Nast Traveler (www.concierge.com) has options for airline travel, cars, and hotels as well as travel ideas and links to other travel services. Other sites, including www.smarterliving.com, www.away.com, and www.usatoday.com, provide a wealth of information about a variety of travel-related matters.

In addition to these sites, www.ustoa.com is an excellent Web site provided by the U.S. Tour Operators' Association. It has copious amounts of information to help you plan your excursion, no matter which method you employ to book it. The site has a section on consumer tips, including ways to budget for your tour and to avoid travel scams. The Tourism Offices Worldwide Directory, at www.towd.com, has addresses and telephone numbers for tourism offices globally.

If your tour plans involve a cruise, there's plenty of help available. The Centers for Disease Control and Prevention in Atlanta provides a "Green Sheet," which has inspection reports and updates on ship sanitation tests. After the spate of onboard illnesses, it might be valuable information. Go to www.cdc.gov/nceh/vsp/htm. The International Council of Cruise Lines, at www.iccl.com, publishes standards for cruise vessels' medical facilities. If you want helpful information about cruising, visit http://cruising.org or cruisecritic.com, especially if you are about to make your maiden voyage. (More tips in chapter 8, Adventures Afloat.)

And just to show you there's a site for almost any requirement, you might consider a visit to www.seatguru.com. This one will give you complete information on the airline seat that you've reserved online or that an agent may have reserved for you. Just tell Seatguru your flight number and seat assignment. The Web site will advise you about the location of the seat, legroom, the closest lavatories, and more. Of course, if you book a nonrefundable ticket, you won't be able to change your seat without some financial or other penalty, even if you don't like what you see.

CHOICES, CHOICES: WHAT'S THE BEST WAY TO BOOK?

Let's say you're planning a package tour, a cruise, or some similar excursion. You can visit the World Wide Web to learn more about such tours. Or you could call the tour provider directly. But some companies are notoriously bad about telephone response, and you may be on hold for lengthy periods. As a third option, you might call a travel agent in your town to help you decide which tour is best for you.

In the first instance, after scouring the Web, you may have to call each travel provider directly to discuss the fine points of your prospective trip—online communications often won't get all your questions answered. If you opt for the second method, you will hear from just one tour purveyor, when you might prefer to shop around for the best package, at the most convenient time, and the most reasonable price.

Or you might deal with an agent, presumably neutral, who can advise you on various options. She or he can provide tour books and travel guides and a synopsis of the various tour companies and their products. Agencies may have an advantage here because some tour companies market only through local travel agencies. Travel specialists can also

MORE TRAVEL-RELATED WEB SITES

www.airdeals.com provides information on consolidator airfares and other discounts.

www.airtech.com offers standby fares around the world, tells you about budget hotels in Europe, and can also give you information on bus and rail passes.

www.artoftravel.com tells you how to get cheap air flights.

www.bananatravel.com has a fare finder to get the lowest ticket price, but you must register for this service.

www.lowestfare.com is another place to find good quotes on airline tickets.

www.site59.com can help with last-minute travel deals.

www.travelhub.com provides discounts on air, car, hotel, and cruise costs.

www.travelsecret.com gives you the inside scoop on consolidator tickets and a wealth of budget travel information.

www.weekends.com can provide last-minute weekend deals, in both the United States and the United Kingdom.

www.windjammer.com is the site for Windjammer Barefoot Cruises, the largest operator of tall ships in the world, which can save you as much as 50 percent on a last-minute voyage. Offers are posted every Friday for departures ten days later.

---

assist you with passports, visas, and required immunizations. Here's another important advantage: Travel agents can be helpful if tours are canceled. They can probably get your money back more easily than you can on your own. When you book a journey, you rarely contemplate the necessity of canceling, but some emergency may intervene without warning. Too, trips are sometimes terminated for reasons beyond your control. Let's say you book a Christmas Markets tour to Germany, but not enough people sign up and the tour provider decides to cancel the trip. In most cases the firm will provide a refund expeditiously. But still, a travel agent, who has dealt with this same situation many times, may make the process less painful. And your agent may be able to reserve you a spot on an alternative trip if you still want to see a Christkindlmarkt or two.

I'm meeting seasoned travelers all the time, and many say they'd be lost without the Web in learning about travel and even making reservations. The smart ones are using some or all of the Internet addresses given here.

I could go on and on. You could visit all these sites and more and make your own plans, or you could decide to let someone else do it. Research conducted for the Walt Disney Company concluded that nine of ten leisure travelers value the advice of their very own travel agent in their very own community and assume that this person will be around when help is needed. The survey noted that travel specialists work for their clients, not a travel supplier.

And keep this in mind the next time you plan to call your favorite airline to book a reservation: In August 2004 Northwest Airlines began imposing a $5.00-per-ticket fee when booking through a customer service representative by telephone. The carrier charged $10 to make a flight reservation with an agent at an airport. American, USAirways, United, Continental, and Delta followed suit, as have many other smaller carriers. The fees generally apply to domestic and overseas tickets and even to frequent-flier awards. Flights booked at airport kiosks carry no fees at this point. Some airlines justify the fee by noting that customers will pay roughly $25 when using the services of a travel agent. Normally, the $5.00 fee is less than 2 percent of an average airline ticket's cost. The major carriers are always looking for ways to reduce costs—and services—to the traveling public.

On the other hand, Southwest Airlines, a leader in the no-frills, low-cost movement, does not at this time charge to speak to an airline service representative. JetBlue offers a $6.00 discount for customers making a round-trip reservation on the Web, while Independence Air offers a $10.00 reduction. The goal in each case is to drive consumers to these airlines' Web sites—and it seems to be working. JetBlue books 75 percent of its tickets online. Northwest, which led the way in those telephone surcharges, reserves only 16 percent of its tickets through its Web site.

So the choice is yours: travel agents, travel providers, or the wide world of the Web. You may use all three in the end, depending on your travel plans. Simple airplane tickets or car rentals can be completed eas-

BEST MATURE TRAVELER WEB SITES

www.adventuresabroad.com offers information about international study, work, and travel-related issues for people of all ages. Trips range from a fortnight in Florence learning the art of Italian cooking to a semester at a Spanish university learning the language and customs.

www.50plusexpeditions.com provides information on adventure travel for folks over fifty. It highlights active travel off the well-worn path for small groups across the globe.

www.frommers.com offers tips for special trips worldwide.

www.gct.com is Grand Circle Travel, a Boston-based tour company geared to seasoned travelers. It's the oldest and largest company of its kind.

www.smarterliving.com/senior: Smarter Living's Senior Travel Web site urges aging travelers to go creatively in the United States and overseas. It can offer tempting travel deals, some discounted heavily, along with travel tips and articles.

www.third.age.com/travel features a wide range of stories and travel information for fifty-and-above travelers.

www.travel.state.gov/older americans.html: The U.S. government is also involved in advising seniors about tourism. The State Department offers valuable tips for those about to travel abroad for the first time.

www.vantagetravel.com is the site of Vantage Deluxe World Travel, another Boston-based company dedicated to well-seasoned travelers.

www.wiredseniors.com: Look here for special senior-friendly itineraries.

ily online. Frequent-flier redemptions may mean a visit to the airline call center or Web site. An eighteen-day tour of South America may require calls to tour companies. And an involved trip to Europe to discover family roots may need assistance from a competent travel specialist.

No matter which method you choose, it's incumbent on you to do your own research. Know exactly where you want to travel, what you want to see, where you intend to stay, and how you want to get from place to place.

Travel is meant to be fun and rewarding, not misery and drudgery. Don't allow travel planning to ruin your holiday.

Here's the bottom line. There's a big, bold world out there for you to explore, conquer, and enjoy. Get out there and see it, the sooner the better. How you go and how you plan your trip are choices you can make depending on your lifestyle and desires. What is most important is that you get going and see as much as you can, as often as you can. So make your plans, do your research, and become a seasoned traveler.

ON-YOUR-OWN TRAVEL

CHAPTER 5

I'm sure you can remember because I certainly do. We were young, and our families lived less expansively than families do today. Life was simpler, but there were some important events. One was the Sunday drive, when our fathers would pile us into the family sedan and take us for a day out. Wasn't it sweet? Often we went just a few miles on undivided highways. We might take a picnic or stop at a local restaurant. Sometimes we didn't stop, but we went to see places unknown to us.

Those journeys may have been short, but they were wonderful because we got away from the house and transported to some magical new place. Once each year—I recall vividly—came the family vacation, always by car, but off to some new and exotic place. From our home in the mid–Hudson Valley of New York State, we would motor to the Berkshires of Massachusetts, the Adirondacks of New York, the distant coast of Maine, the hills of Pennsylvania, or the New Jersey shore.

Even today the thrill of the open road lures many travelers. A road trip connotes romance, adventure, exploration. The fact of the matter is that most of us take our vacations in our own cars, sport utility vehicles, or RVs rather than on a Boeing 767. Three-quarters of Americans prefer to travel on asphalt. Travel by personal vehicle increases with age, according to the Travel Industry Association of America. Travelers fifty-five and beyond spent more time on the road than any other age group. Older folks took 179 million such trips and spent nearly five nights per trip. Many people actually planned their travel route, booked a hotel or motel for the night, or counted on lodging from a friend or relative at the destination.

Others took the more adventurous approach. They got in the car and gunned the engine, without a great deal of planning. I recall meeting several older drivers at motels along interstate highways. They'd get up early each morning and get out on the road. They would drive a few hours and have lunch, then continue until they were tired, without ever making a motel reservation. At 4:00 P.M. they would leave the superhighway and head for a motel with a VACANCY sign. I always admired their carefree attitude, in the face of my prebooked hotel reservations.

More and more mature travelers are learning the value of going it alone. Couples are booking their own vacations, at home and abroad. Still, when it comes to travel overseas, some folks get positively nervous, while others are real pros. I've met them on my travels for the television series. Some are retired; some still work. They decide where they will go, read up on those locations, and divide the planning duties. One couple I met in Germany said they picked a location, decided what each of them wanted to see and do, then he booked the flights and planned the auto rental while she reserved hotel rooms and found the best restaurants to visit during their stay. They employed this tactic for travel within the United States, Canada, and Mexico as well as overseas. Whether you are fifty, sixty, seventy, or older, you can do this, too. And if you are tired of the travel regimen imposed by package tours, you can enter the brave new world of on-your-own travel.

READY, SET, GO!

So let's assume you have made the big decision. You will enjoy a two-week trip to Egypt and a sail down the Nile River. You are prepared to endure a long flight from the United States to Cairo, even willing to change planes in London or Paris. You are leaving your home, your children, and your grandchildren behind. You'll work with a travel agent on tickets, hotels, and connections to the river cruise ship. How do you make the necessary preparations for your journey?

The following guidelines apply whether you plot your own course, work with a travel agent, or book a package tour on the Internet. First of all, draw up an itinerary and photocopy the details. Give copies to those who need to know where you are and when. Make sure you add the names and telephone numbers of the places you'll be staying. Tell relatives and friends how to reach you.

Since you are going to Egypt, the U.S. State Department recommends you provide your contacts with your passport number and the numbers of other important documents, like your state driver's license. You should also give your friends the numbers of the credit cards and traveler's checks you will take on the trip. People back home may be able to notify officials of lost or stolen materials much faster than you can if you're helpless in Cairo.

Pack your medications properly. Make sure you have enough pills before you leave. A drug you are taking in this country may have a different name in other nations, or it may not be available at all. Take the telephone numbers and e-mail addresses of your physicians and pharmacists. If something out of the ordinary happens, you may be able to get replacement medications quickly. And here's an important point to consider: If you have a chronic medical condition, take a note from your health-care provider explaining your situation and describing the medications you are taking. A doctor in Egypt may then be able to prescribe pills similar to what you take at home.

Travel with prepaid telephone cards. Experts say these are the easiest, cheapest, and most convenient ways to make calls from overseas. If you have a cellular phone, you will most likely need to buy overseas service for Egypt. The provider will likely charge you a monthly fee, and calls may cost as much as $2.00 per minute, not to mention roaming charges. Hotels charge exorbitant rates to make local and overseas calls, too. You can avoid all of this by using phone cards. One estimate says one in three Americans on vacation use prepaid cards.

Prepare yourself physically and mentally for your trip. Get in shape. Make sure you have the proper vaccinations and inoculations. If you are going overseas, the State Department or the Centers for Disease Control and Prevention can advise you on the shots you'll need based on your destination. The last thing you need to spoil your trip is a bout of illness. Carry over-the-counter medications for headaches, fever, constipation, or diarrhea. Take precautions to safeguard your film and videotape against overexposure when coming through airport security. If in doubt, ask airport employees whether you should hand them the film before it goes through the security screening machinery.

Finally, travel wisely and safely when you reach your destination. Drive carefully if you rent a vehicle; driving in Cairo can be scary and dangerous. Remain alert at train stations, be careful where you walk, especially at night, and travel with companions when in doubt.

My wife, Susan, and I take these precautions whenever we travel, here at home or in other countries. In addition, if we plan to drive in other nations, we screen our routes thoroughly so we'll know exactly which roads to take, where to turn, and how to get there safely. This is especially helpful when you travel in non-English-speaking countries. It's hard enough driving in unfamiliar locations; it can be downright impossible to navigate when the road signs are in French, Greek, Russian, Chinese, or Arabic.

Don't overplan. Experts advise *not* scheduling every minute of your trip with something that must be seen or done. Be selective and budget time for rest and relaxation. It may be the once-in-a-lifetime experience you've anticipated, but you don't want to ruin the experience by overdoing it.

And don't overpack. Take what you need and no more. Take sturdy shoes, wash-and-wear clothing, and extra clothes for an emergency. Don't pack things you cannot afford to lose. You may want to take older clothes that you can discard before you return home. Don't take jewelry that, when worn, is an invitation to thieves. Travel light and smart.

ON-YOUR-OWN SAVINGS

If you've planned well, you've taken advantage of cost savings on your airline ticket, but be mindful that while a nonrefundable ticket booked six months in advance of your departure may sound like a tremendous deal, it will be a tremendously bad deal if you have to cancel your trip and you get no money back.

MONEY FOR THE ROAD

There's a great deal of debate about carrying money when you travel. Many travel gurus suggest you take a combination of cash, traveler's checks, and at least two major credit cards. If your destination is beyond American shores, take cards that will be accepted in those nations. Visa and MasterCard are welcomed in most countries. American Express is frowned upon by overseas merchants, who cite the high fee the company charges them. Some credit card companies will offer discounts on travel; others will cover some insurance on rental vehicles or replace lost or stolen airline tickets if purchased with that credit card. If you are far from home, you will want to be sure you have the most appropriate plastic money.

It's fine to convert dollars into foreign currency before you leave, as long as you don't have to pay an arm and a leg for it. Traveler's check fees are generally small; don't settle for hefty surcharges to change U.S. dollars into Egyptian pounds. These forms of payment are accepted by fewer merchants and banks than they once were. Many smart travelers now exchange money at an automated teller machine when they arrive at their destination. Here's what you do: Use your bank debit card and withdraw some of the money you'll need for your trip. There may be a withdrawal limit at some overseas banks. Your hometown bank will charge you a fee, as will the bank abroad. In return, you'll get the most favorable exchange rate, and you won't have to pay interest on a cash withdrawal against a credit card. Now, with that cash in your hands, make sure you put it into a protective wallet inside your clothes so pickpockets don't have a chance to lighten your financial load. If you stay with friends, relatives, or at a large hotel, you may want to use a hotel safe or secure place in the home you're visiting.

That's another reason to withdraw only small amounts of cash from the ATM: You won't have to worry about a huge chunk of change being lost or stolen. If you use traveler's checks, make sure the serial numbers are separate from the money. If the checks are lost or stolen, you can take the numbers to the bank and get the checks replaced.

If you go it alone on the reservations, watch for scams or other bad deals online. The adage has never been so relevant: If it looks too good to be true, it probably is. Some unscrupulous companies may try to sell you some variation on the "Buy Now, Travel Later" plan. Seniors are told to purchase certificates for travel now and redeem them later. By procuring these certificates, you may be stuck with something you can't use. Don't be suckered by this salesmanship. Say no now to the travel-later scam. *No* is such a short, simple word—yet often so difficult to utter.

You may have heard or read about travel discount clubs, which might seem like a fantastic opportunity. Members pay a certain (often steep) membership fee with the promise of extraordinary travel opportunities. To benefit from these fully, however, you might need to use the club several weeks each year—and many of us aren't in a position to do that. Don't be tempted by clubs that say your membership can be bequeathed to family members. Make sure your travel program states this clearly and unequivocally. Be careful, too, of travel clubs that take memberships up front and promise travel at a future date. There is no guarantee any such opportunities will be available when you want them.

If you travel alone and book your hotel room, don't ask for luxury hotel rooms at check-in, when you pay rock-bottom prices. Hotels may not be able or willing to guarantee upgrades. I have asked for them on several occasions myself, but—even when they were promised by telephone reservationists or online—those perks disappeared when I arrived at the hotel. Airlines are a bit more forthcoming. Reservationists will generally tell you they can't upgrade you on the telephone (but do always ask the gate personnel if such a move is possible).

If saving money is important to you, shop around for the best bargains, but be certain you are dealing with legitimate ticket sellers. As you book, use a credit card for advance purchases. Should you change your plans, cancel your vacation, or be subjected to some scam, your credit card firm will handle the matter. And if you are worried about any misdeeds or potential cancellations, buy trip insurance—but understand that this insurance will not come into force in the case of fraud or bankruptcy by the travel seller. It all goes back to where we started: Do your research, and don't let anyone take advantage of you.

LOGISTICS AND LEGALITIES

Once you have cleared all those hurdles, you may have a new one to vault. If you've never traveled overseas—and millions of Americans haven't— you'll need to apply for a U.S. passport. Apply early, as it can take four-to-eight weeks for the government to issue the document. You can apply two

TRAVEL TIP: HOW TO GET BUMPED UP

The best way to get moved up to business or first class is to look the part. On some of the airlines I travel, if I wear a jacket and tie, I'll go to the head of the cabin. If I wear blue jeans and an old shirt, I stay where I am. Wearing sneakers can also condemn you to coach. So the next time you fly, dress up and ask if there's a chance for an upgrade. You might be pleasantly surprised.

ways: in person or by mail. There are Passport Agency offices in Boston, Chicago, Honolulu, Houston, Los Angeles, Miami, New Orleans, New York, Philadelphia, San Francisco, Seattle, Stamford, Connecticut, and Washington, DC. For locations and telephone numbers, you can contact www.firstgov.gov and go to the State Department Web page.

Depending on your specific circumstances (for example, whether you are applying for a passport for the first time or renewing an existing passport), application is made either in person or by mail. You can inquire about procedures at most post offices, but my best advice is to go online at www.firstgov.gov and click on "Get or Renew a Passport," which takes you to the State Department page. Here you will find all the details of how, when, and where to apply, and also what documents are required for your specific application. Note that some applications require a *certified* birth certificate.

As you await the passport, learn about the countries you plan to visit. There are volumes of printed material and reams of files on the Internet. You should also go to the State Department's information sheet for the latest updates on your intended destination. The government will tell you about current political and health conditions, crime, currency, and entry regulations. The State Department also issues travel warnings, recommending that Americans avoid travel to some nations if conditions warrant.

Make sure the country you plan to visit does not require an entry visa. Most don't, but some still do. By all means, take a driver's license or other form of identification as a backup to your passport. If you are

WHAT *NOT* TO BUY

On your trip, do not purchase products or souvenirs made from endangered species. This ban includes:

- All products made from sea turtles
- All ivory (from Asia and Africa)
- Furs from spotted cats as well as furs from marine mammals
- Feathers and feather products from wild birds
- Live or stuffed birds from Australia, the Caribbean, and several nations in Latin America
- Most crocodile or cayman leather
- Most coral

visiting a nation requiring a travel visa, give yourself and the host country plenty of time to issue a visa and send it to you.

Be certain your health insurance is current and that your insurer will cover you in case of illness or accident far from home. You should be able to purchase special short-term policies for travel abroad. Keep in mind that the Medicare program does not provide for payment of hospital or medical services received outside the United States. Some Medicare supplement plans offer foreign medical coverage at no extra cost for Medicare-eligible travelers. These are reimbursement plans, which means you pay for the bills up front, get receipts, and submit them for payment. Scrutinize the policy closely to see whether it contains a payment ceiling.

Again, you might consider trip insurance to prevent against losses should you have to cancel the holiday for any reason. The airlines generally give you a refund if you have a legitimate medical excuse, but some travel companies may not be so nice. I see no need to purchase airline accident insurance. You probably have a life insurance policy by now, so there's no need to pay for another policy.

Even if you take precautions, you may still become ill overseas. If that happens, contact the consular officer or the U.S. embassy in the country you're visiting for assistance, or have someone make the connection for you.

When you reach your foreign destination, you may decide to drive in that country. Know whether your auto insurance covers you outside your home territory. Some credit card companies, as noted above, will cover the collision damage waiver if you rent a vehicle using their card. If you feel the slightest bit uncomfortable about motoring in other nations, purchase insurance even if you have to pay for it. Unfamiliarity breeds nerves, which may lead to an accident. At least you'll be covered, and it's a small enough price to pay for peace of mind.

If you travel into troubled regions and plan to stay longer than a fortnight, the government recommends you register with the nearest American embassy or consulate. This will assist officials in locating you in case of civil unrest or natural disaster.

If you shop, remember you may have to pay U.S. customs duty on certain items or if you exceed the limit allowed for overseas purchases.

DESTINATIONS: A CARIBBEAN HOLIDAY

Earlier I talked about the popularity of going to Egypt. A Caribbean holiday is similarly attractive to many mature American tourists. After all, it's close to home, easy to get to, and brimming with a wide diversity of experiences. The Caribbean is influenced by Britain, France, the Netherlands, and the United States, all of which have island colonies. Six million Americans visit the Caribbean each and every year. The islands extend nearly 1,800 miles, from the Caymans and Cuba in the west to Barbados on the eastern edge. The high season is from mid-December through mid-April, when northerners seek to escape bitter cold and mounting snow. Spring and summer bring lower rates, but travel to the Caribbean from June until November can be dicey, especially in an active Atlantic hurricane season.

There are some special precautions you should follow when going to the Caribbean. For information on health conditions, contact the Centers for Disease Control and Prevention's twenty-four-hour hotline. The telephone number in Atlanta is (404) 332–4559. Officials can advise you on current health conditions, required immunizations, and preventive health measures. For example, typhoid immunization is recommended if you fly to Jamaica or Haiti, where polio is also a risk, even today, just as it is in the Dominican Republic. Malaria is prevalent in Haiti and in some rural areas of the Dominican Republic that border Haiti and on the island of Hispaniola. In recent years hurricanes not only did extensive damage to many Caribbean islands, but also led to serious health problems across the region. Inquire about the purity of drinking water when you arrive in an island-nation. Bottled water may be necessary in some places.

Every island has entry requirements, but they are generally quite lenient. Most countries allow you to visit for anywhere from two weeks to three months if you show proof of U.S. citizenship and a return ticket home. Just to be absolutely safe, it is best to bring your passport. Some countries charge a departure tax of up to $25. According to the U.S. State Department, none of the islands requires a visa.

Some folks may opt to bring their own boats or planes to the region. In that case you should consult the embassy, consulate, or tourism office to learn what is required before you can bring your craft into and out of the island-nations.

If you rent a car or motor scooter in the Greater Caribbean region, remember that many of the islands require driving on the left. Be sure you understand the rules of the road in each country before you set out. Crime has also become a persistent nuisance in the Caribbean. Most of the misdeeds, including thievery, pickpocketing, and purse snatching, are considered petty crimes. But more violent crimes, like rape and assaults on visitors, are also rising. Worst of all, some murders are reported against tourists in the region. Those planning to visit Jamaica must be especially careful if they are planning to visit Kingston, the capital. Years of gang-, drug-, and extortion-related violence have led to thousands of deaths and fear among residents and tourists alike. If you must visit Jamaica, go to the other end of the island for your holiday, near Montego Bay. Better yet, go to some other island.

Most Caribbean lands have a very strict policy against drug use, possession, or sale. In some places, if you're arrested for carrying even small amounts of marijuana, you can be charged as a drug trafficker. Some islands could sentence you to twenty years in prison and mete out a hefty fine. I have read about the penalties given to those charged with narcotics offenses—they can be harsh indeed.

If your travel plans include swimming in the Atlantic Ocean or the Caribbean Sea, remember that the surf can be rough, and rip currents

are potentially deadly. The government reports that drowning is one of the leading causes of death for Americans in the Caribbean. Be careful when diving into water that may contain hidden rocks, and be on your guard for stings by jellyfish or other sea creatures.

While most of the Caribbean islands are warm and welcoming, remember that Cuba is still off-limits to Americans, even though more and more Yankees show up there every year. There are strict rules relating to travel and business transactions that you should understand before you embark on such a mission. If you are determined to see the sun set near Havana, there is a way around the diplomatic roadblock. Many Americans fly from Canada to Cuba or travel to Mexico and then change planes to Havana. There are direct flights from Mexico City and Cancún each day.

MORE DESTINATIONS: SOUTH OF THE BORDER

Speaking of Mexico, up to fifteen million citizens of the United States travel south of the border each year, and nearly half a million Americans live there year-round. Mexico has much to recommend it. (See chapter

TRAVELING SOLO

There is, of course, another meaning to *on-your-own travel:* traveling solo. Increasing numbers of men and women are traveling alone. They're widows or widowers, divorced, or single. Many mature solo travelers, especially women, opt for package tours, which provide safety, security, and few travel headaches. Unfortunately, there is an evil known as the "single supplement," a nefarious rule whereby solo travelers must pay more to use a single room. It applies whether you tour with a group or blaze your own trail. It is patently unfair and discourages some singles from embarking on a trip. A few travel companies waive this charge, while others double up single men or women to defray costs.

I think the travel and hospitality industry should wise up and eliminate these supplemental charges. If a woman has the courage to go on a trip by herself, only to be told she will have to pay $500 more for the same travel experience as a couple, she might feel justified in telling the travel company she will take her travel dollars elsewhere. Here's a tip on this matter: Some tour firms will eliminate the single supplement for people who book cruises or tours very early. The companies know it's one fewer room they'll have to sell, so they make a deal with the early booker. Inquire about this option when you reserve your next boat ride or holiday trip.

I've been on tours on which several single women, and to a lesser degree men, were traveling solo. These people found other singles quickly and formed companionships or developed long-term friendships. We should applaud those solo travelers who have the desire and the gumption to get out and get moving. There's no point in penalizing them.

13, *The Seasoned Traveler* on TV, for a synopsis of my two trips to Mexico for the premiere season.) Still, visitors to our southern neighbor can experience problems.

Before you set off, read up on the places you intend to visit. A bookstore, library, travel agent, Web search, or call to the embassy can provide valuable information. In addition, check with the State Department on new information or travel warnings that may apply to parts of the country. Consular Information Sheets and possible travel warnings can be obtained by calling State at (202) 647–5225 or sending a fax request to (202) 647–3000.

Mexico has long had an unfortunate reputation for health problems, which sometimes affect those who visit. Most of us grow up hearing the phrase "Don't drink the water" connected to trips there. It's still true. Hotels provide purified water, as do restaurants. Ice cubes are made from purified water. Use tap water only for bathing or cleaning teeth. Vegetables should be peeled, washed thoroughly, or cooked before consumption. Be careful about raw veggies, like lettuce or tomatoes.

For information on health concerns, call the CDC international traveler's hotline at (404) 332–4559. Remember, too, that some parts of rural Mexico have inferior medical facilities, and that such places may not accept traditional medical insurance coverage. Consult officials about purchasing special short-term insurance to cover yourself should you suffer serious illness or become involved in an accident. Tourists from the United States are not required to present immunization certification, but wise travelers will make certain they are vaccinated against diphtheria, tetanus, polio, typhoid, and hepatitis.

Malaria and yellow fever may be found in some sections of the country. Know where you plan to go, know what the risks are, and take the necessary precautions. That includes dealing with air pollution. Mexico City has some of the foulest air on earth. It can be downright dangerous from December to May. The capital's huge population and excessive reliance on automobiles and trucks, along with its high altitude, make dirty air a major concern to the elderly and people who have high blood pressure or respiratory or cardiac problems. Several people who live in Mexico City have told me that it's best to avoid visiting the city if there's the slightest possibility of health problems. I suggest that if you have any concerns at all, you visit others parts of the nation.

Enjoy your stay in Mexico, and follow the precautions that you would employ in any other foreign destination. At the hotel, leave your valuables in a safe or other secure place. Be vigilant when you're out on the street or on public transportation. Be wary of pickpockets.

If you drive, you need to understand the laws regarding border crossing. You must carry appropriate immigration forms, vehicle registration, and proof of ownership or a rental leasing contract. In addition, have your driver's license and a valid credit card in the name of the person leasing the vehicle. The next step is to present the documents to the Vehicular Control Module, located in customs. This agency will process an importation permit. It's valid for six months, and you'll need to carry this paper at all times. Once you have completed this bureaucratic exercise, you can drive back and forth across the border without worry. Other persons can drive the vehicle, as long as the owner is along for the ride. This is, of course, much more difficult and cumbersome than driving into Canada, but then Mexico is an entirely different world.

No matter where in the world you drive, remember that safety is your highest priority. The State Department says more than one million deaths occur each year across the globe in road accidents, 70 percent of which occur in so-called developing countries. More than 200 Americans are killed each year in highway mishaps abroad. I can't stress enough that you have to act responsibly when you drive. Your life and your enjoyment depend on it.

Good planning and good sense are the keys to a safe trip, whether it's across the States, to Mexico, the Caribbean, Canada, or beyond. I'm a big proponent of travel on your own. If you know what you want to see, you can plan how to explore it on your own. That's especially true in the areas mentioned above. It can also be true for Latin America, Europe, Africa, Asia, and Australia. Do your homework, plan your route, book your hotels, organize the sites you want to see, and get going.

Some last bits of advice: When you are far from home, never show it. Look as though you belong, and don't carry a tourist map where crooks can see it. And in our post-9/11 world, travelers must now be cognizant of the risk of terrorist attacks. Be vigilant, be safe, but be happy.

THE OPEN ROAD

CHAPTER 6

As you get more comfortable traveling on your own, you'll probably spend lots of time on American highways. And at the end of your travel day, you'll need a place to stop for the night, or for longer periods on vacations. Many folks choose hotels, motels, resorts, or bed-and-breakfasts. Others rent homes, cottages, or cabins for their time in the mountains or on the beach. Our superhighways are saturated with big buses, camper vans, and travel trailers. But a growing number of adventurers are turning to the recreation vehicle, and lots of seniors spend many weeks or months in these metal mini palaces, loving every minute of it. I call this crowd the "RV superseasoned travelers." Nearly eight million Americans have their own lodging solution right there in the driveway.

KINDS OF RVS

For the uninformed, and I counted myself among them until recently, there are all kinds of RVs. Although drivers pull some of them, most people think of a recreation vehicle as a motorized vehicle. These giants seem larger than cabin cruisers, and they can cost as much as a suburban house in an upper-crust neighborhood.

There are, in fact, two kinds of RVs—motorized and nonmotorized. Motorized RVs come in three sizes: Class A, the giants of the industry, large coaches that extend 40 feet or longer; Class B, the smallest, actually vans with a kitchen, bath, and bedroom; and Class C, the midlevel single units that average from 20 to 30 feet long and have a sleeping compartment over the cab. The nonmotorized are trailers, including tag-along pop-up tents, travel trailers, and fifth-wheels. The latter are gooseneck travel trailers attached to mega pickup trucks. They can be every bit as luxurious as a Class A vehicle. The good thing about them is, once you remove the trailer from the truck, you can use the pickup to drive around in; you don't have to tow a car.

THE RV LIFE

RVs have become a culture, not just a pastime. They are vacation vehicles for families, part- or full-time homes for retirees, and a heavyweight magic carpet to take families to exciting destinations across the United States and into Canada and Mexico. On my last trip to Mexico, I learned how many RVers get their vehicles south of the border with a minimum of effort. They drive to cities like El Paso, Texas, or Tucson, Arizona, and load their RVs onto flatbed trains. The trains carry scores of vehicles through northern Mexico to places like Copper Canyon or resort communities farther south. Drivers ride along on the trains and save themselves the trauma driving many of Mexico's horrible highways and crossing the hundreds of speed bumps near towns and cities. It seems the industry is thinking of everything.

I recently met a senior RV fanatic. She regaled me with stories of years of RVing with her now deceased husband. She'd been everywhere in the big van, except one spot: "If we could have driven to Hawaii," she said, "we'd have been to all fifty states." What is most remarkable about all this is that despite escalating prices for gasoline, folks are purchasing recreational gizmos at a remarkable rate. Ownership has increased 50 percent among people fifty-five and above since 1980 and shows no signs of slowing. Half of the RVs on the road today are owned and operated by mature travelers—and as the nation continues to gray, that growth will continue. A study by the University of Michigan shows that RV ownership rates rise with age, the highest levels being among those fifty-five to seventy-four. The industry now has a marketing campaign aimed at the next generation, those thirty-five to fifty-five who may be contemplating a big purchase of a big vehicle.

Recreation vehicles have become popular for many reasons. They provide freedom of movement to millions of vacationers. For those who cannot or who will not camp or backpack, a trailer or RV is an excellent way to enjoy the wide, wide world outdoors without much struggle—assuming, of course, that you can find an RV campsite. The vehicles are as roomy as some motel rooms or hotel suites, and most have living, dining, and bathroom facilities right on board. You can come and go as you please, explore nature up close at national parks and forests, and eat onboard, thus avoiding the need to dine at costly restaurants or fast-food outlets.

The RV life fosters a sense of community and fellowship. Camping facilities are often crammed with travelers who have stories to swap. Lifelong friendships are forged, and many RVers form clubs or groups that meet every year to renew acquaintances. Everyone I have talked with says the same thing: RV owners have a common bond as well as their individual stories. They have similar interests, and they help each other in many ways. I have listened to scores of the committed who insist RVers are the finest people on the face of the earth.

The industry that sells these behemoths of the open road likes to point out that older Americans remain the fastest-growing population group, and that this group will continue to lead RV ownership. It notes that mature travelers have combined incomes of more than $800 billion from jobs, pensions, retirement funds, investments, and Social Security, about 51 percent of the nation's discretionary income.

Have you ever noticed who's driving these road rigs? It's often men who look old enough to be my father, or even my grandfather. Yet these folks seem quite at home and quite capable at maneuvering these vehicles, which are five or ten times larger than my humble sport utility vehicle. Many men and women claim they feel much safer in an RV because it's bigger, higher, and stronger than most cars and small trucks.

I have sometimes wondered why people, especially those who reach a certain age, seem so drawn to the metal monsters. Here's what they say:

The big boats are comfortable, mobile, and more accommodating than a sterile hotel room. There's a queen-size bed in a good-size bedroom. The bed is fitted with your own sheets and pillowcases; your own towels are in the bathroom. There is plenty of heat or air-conditioning when the weather heads to extremes. You carry your clothes from the house to the RV, leaving everything there for the entire trip. Your kitchen comes complete with a stove, oven, and microwave, and some new units even have dishwashers. You can eat what you want, when you want, how you want. Some units can sleep up to six or eight, so the children or grandchildren can come along. It's cheaper to plug in at an RV campground than it is to stay in a motel for a night.

RVers hold annual conventions, regional rallies, campouts, and tailgate parties. They join groups like the Good Sam Club, Family Campers and RVers, the Family Motor Coach Association, and the Escapees RV Club. Recreation vehicles can take northerners to warmer climates for the winter and southerners to New England for autumn leaves. Some people spend weeks or months at desirable locations. I've heard from folks who've passed months in the desert of southern Arizona, at a beach in Florida, or on the Alaskan peninsula. Some seniors live in their vehicles and claim the mortgage interest on their income taxes as a first or second home. (Of course, there are guidelines for how long you must live in the unit to claim the credit.)

And some RVers enjoy the fact they can take part-time jobs as national and state park employees, at amusement parks, or in other fields. They make money that supplements their retirement and Social Security income, gives them some meaningful work, and offers a break from the routine. I met a man from Maryland who was spending several months at an RV park along the Florida Gulf Coast. He works for the park's owner, collecting trash and doing repairs. He admits he can't stand the thought of spending months sitting on the beach or just watching the sun set. So he spends a few hours each day working, in return for a reduction in his RV campsite rental.

READY TO BUY?

Some of the smaller recreation vehicles, like travel trailers, can be purchased for under $10,000, but top-of-the-line motor homes can cost $200,000 or more. I saw one Class A so loaded with options that it cost

$420,000. That's more than some older folks ever paid for a house. That's why on *The Seasoned Traveler* television series, I advise those considering an RV to rent one for a week or two to determine whether RV life is the life for them. I have rented a motorized travel vehicle on several occasions. A weekly rental can exceed $2,000 when you factor in costs for insurance and gasoline. But that's still a small price to pay compared with the quarter of a million dollars you can shell out to purchase your own vehicle, especially if you decide after one summer that you can't stand it.

Some things to keep in mind: Most dealers want to finance these vehicles for ten to fifteen years, which can make payments quite high. Recreation vehicles depreciate rapidly—some dealers admit that the RV will drop 20 percent in value when you drive it off the lot. People keep their vehicles for a few years, then most folks buy up. Because so many people are aging and interested, the resale market is fairly healthy. I visited a couple from Maine spending the winter down south. They were fairly new to the RV culture. They had purchased a used Class A that was ten years old. They got a good price on it and had come to enjoy the life. They told me they would be looking for a newer and larger motor home within the next year or two.

Given the initial cost and depreciation, many owners feel obligated to use their RVs every weekend or for much of the year. Once you hit the road, you may find it hard to get a space in an RV park, mostly on summer weekends or holidays. Repairs and maintenance can be a huge headache. Many repair shops don't have space to work on a 40-foot steel giant. Some repairs can take days to accomplish. It's impossible to change a flat tire on a multi-ton vehicle, so you have to wait for emergency roadside help. If you buy an RV, be sure you have such an emergency package.

If you leave home for many months, you need to tow a car or van so you can get around once you park your bus. And did I mention that the motor homes get 8 to 10 miles per gallon on the highway, and the price of gas isn't likely to fall anytime soon?

If you plan to buy, there are scores of options that dealers would love to sell you, many more than you can get on a car or truck. Know what options you want and negotiate them with the salesperson. Don't let anyone sell you options you don't really want. Getting data on the value of a used RV is also much more difficult than for other vehicles. You can't go to the normal *Kelley Blue Book* or Edmunds guide to get a feel for used RV prices. The only sources are the *NADA Consumer Recreational Vehicle Appraisal Guide* or the special *Kelley Blue Book Motor Home Guide,* the *Kelley Travel Trailer Guide,* and/or the same company's *Manufactured Housing Guide.*

A recreation vehicle can be one of the most important purchases of your life, especially if you have your heart set on a 40-footer with a million amenities. Don't rush into this. Read all you can. Talk to RVers. Visit as many showrooms as you can, don't buy the first vehicle you see, and don't let anyone take advantage of you.

The industry says financing an RV is relatively easy and straightforward. My view is that nothing is easy and straightforward anymore. On top of the purchase, remember that you must insure these mammoths, and the premiums can be much higher than for your two family cars or SUVs.

CAMPING IN YOUR RV

So what do you do with that big baby after you buy it? There are some great books and informative Web sites that can tell you. The National

HELP FOR THE RV BUYER

There are many terrific resources available if you're considering the big step. You can go to your local library to read up on the RV life, culture, and reality. Woodall's publishes a series of excellent books on RVing, camping, and campground sites. They're considered the bibles of the business. They are very informational and quite inexpensive. For those of you who are Internet junkies, www.rvbookstore.com can provide up-to-date information about RV travel, new models, accessories, campsites, and much more. Other valuable sites for you to peruse include www.gorving.com, www.rvtravel.com, www.freedomroads.com, or www.rvia.org.

Association of RV Parks and Campgrounds represents more than 3,700 RV parks and campsites across the nation. ARVC also provides data on cabins and lodges, membership campgrounds and resorts, industry suppliers, and park developers. Its Web site is www.arvc.org, or you can telephone the group at (703) 241–8801. Some other potentially useful sites relevant to camping are www.rvpark.com and www.campusa.com.

One of the best-known camp services is KOA, with more than 500 campgrounds in the United States, Canada, Mexico, and Japan. KOA says it is the largest system of campsites in the world. It provides RV spaces and hookups, tent sites, showers and laundry facilities, stores, swimming pools, and Internet access. For those without a trailer, there are what the company calls Kamping Kabins and Kamping Kottages. You can reach KOA at www.koakampgrounds.com or by calling the corporate office in Billings, Montana, at (406) 248–7444.

Of course, national parks and forests, as well as many state, regional, county, and local parks, have campsites for tents and recreation vehicles. There are also private campgrounds and groups of campsite owners offering their services to hikers, backpackers, tenters, and those who drive motor homes. In the Northeast, for example, there's the New Hampshire Campground Owners Association, which represents 141 sites across the

Granite State. An online search engine allows you to find the right location for your needs, whether it's in the northern notches, the White Mountains, the state's big lakes, ski country, or the New Hampshire seacoast. The association says it enforces strict guidelines on camp owners and that all facilities are inspected annually to make sure they comply. You must understand that the organization is basically policing itself, so you have to trust that the association is serious about protecting the public's right to fine facilities. If you're planning a trip to New Hampshire for autumn leaf-peeping or winter cross-country schussing, you might want to start here in your search for an appropriate place to "tie up." To get a feel for the organization and its members, you can contact it online, at www.ucampnh.com.

If you plan to visit one of America's major national parks—let's say Yosemite in California—I don't have to tell you that camping berths come at a premium at this magnificent and desirable destination. Sites are reserved months in advance; if you are not among the "booked," you'll need to consult your RV parks book or go on the Internet to find public and private campgrounds nearby. Turn your browser to "Yosemite campsites." Or suppose you wish to visit Mexico, and you live in the desert region of New Mexico. The seaside town of Puerto Peñasco may be just your place. Once again, if you access the World Wide Web, you can learn a great deal about Puerto Peñasco, including the number of recreation vehicle resting sites. You can overlook the egregious spelling errors and get plenty of valuable information about the nine RV parks in the area and one in neighboring Lukeville, Arizona. The best way to unlock this wealth of information is to start with www.puerto-penasco.com and negotiate your way to the RV parks area. You'll find such information for almost any region. Hit the computer and ask your Internet search engine to locate campsites. "RV parks Alaska" or "RV parks Quebec" should yield results quickly and completely.

Given the increasing popularity of motorized and nonmotorized RVs, more and more holiday makers will be searching for the most desirable campgrounds. Some folks despair of finding parking spots, especially in peak travel seasons. They turn to campground membership groups to ensure availability of spaces at a price that isn't overly exorbitant. These are brokerage services for RV enthusiasts seeking reliable parking sites. It's the mobile version of those condominium time-share arrangements

so many people have latched on to. What you do in this case is buy a membership to join what's known as a "home resort." This can cost several thousand dollars, but it guarantees you a spot at the home resort. Each year, you are required to pay an annual fee to maintain your prerogative. You don't have to wait until you retire to join these clubs, and you can hand back your membership when you no longer wish to maintain it. The best way to discover more about these is to go online, search the keywords "camping membership," and comparison-shop.

Here's something to think about on the subject of RV campsites. On an RV trip to the Gulf Coast, I stayed at four parks. Two of them were closing down. They were near the beach, and developers had offered the park owners huge sums of money to sell their properties. In one case, thirty homes were to be built; in the other, a high-rise condominium would replace the forty-space RV resort. A Michigan man who owns a KOA resort told me that this is the way of the RV world. Some parks will close and newer, larger hyperparks will be created, with spaces for 500 or even 1,000 motor homes and trailers. That may be something to think about as you contemplate the RV life.

CASE STUDY: LET'S GO TO TENNESSEE

Let's say your travel plans are about to take you to Tennessee, in the Mid-South. Perhaps it's a trip to the mountains, to a university reunion, Dollywood amusement park, or the Grand Ole Opry near Nashville. You'd want to contact the Tennessee Association of RV Parks and Campgrounds, a group similar to the one in New Hampshire. This group lists its forty-plus sites, at least three of which are also marinas, should you be towing a boat as well. The campgrounds, RV parks, travel parks, log cabins, and marinas are listed by city with individual telephone numbers, Web sites, or e-mail addresses. To get started, go to www.kiz.com/campnet/mtml/cluborgs/tnarvc/tnarvc.htm.

Finally, I recall the wisdom of a Wisconsin woman. She and her husband had sold their house and furnishings and bought a 40-foot Class A. It was their home, moving from north to south depending on the weather. She professed to love her new home but said she sometimes wonders whether she wants to spend the rest of her life in a small space "with him," pointing to her husband. They both smiled. RVs can be really cramped, especially if you're stuck inside during several days of inclement weather.

Think long and hard about this decision. Make the right one for you. Oh, and bon voyage.

THE GREAT OUTDOORS

CHAPTER 7

Morning. You open the door of the RV to a beautiful new day and decide that after your "home"-cooked breakfast, you'll be out there exploring. Whether you are in the Rocky Mountains of Colorado, the Andes Mountains of Chile, or the Alps of Austria, the world is full of many-splendored outdoor places to experience.

NATIONAL AND STATE PARKS

Here at home your tax dollars are at work each year when the National Park Service offers its Golden Age Passport to seasoned travelers. Millions of folks take an opportunity to view the natural assets of America each year by scheduling stops at national parks from Acadia in Maine to Kilauea in Hawaii. There are, in fact, more than 390 national parks, national monuments, historic sites and parks, battlefields, recreation areas, and wildlife refuges across the fifty states. They offer up-close views of some of our most spectacular scenery and our most important history.

American citizens and permanent residents aged sixty-two and over can visit these treasures absolutely free with a Golden Age Passport. It's a lifetime entrance pass for the cardholder and passengers in the cardholder's vehicle for parks with a vehicle entrance fee. In parks that charge a per-person admission fee, the Golden Age Passport admits the cardholder, spouse, and children without charge. Beyond that, the passport offers a 50 percent discount on use fees for camping, swimming, parking, boat launching, and tours. To get one of these babies, you pay $10. You can procure one at a federal area where an entrance fee is charged. You must be able to prove you have reached your sixty-second birthday. No proof, no passport. Once you cross that special threshold, it makes a wonderful addition to your travel accessories. The government also issues a Golden Access Passport, which is a bit more generous than the Golden Age Passport. In NPS facilities that charge entrance fees, this card admits the passholder, spouse, children, parents, and even care assistants to disabled card members.

Our neighbor to the north also has a wide array of wild and wonderful places. Canadian national parks and national historic sites charge admission fees to most attractions, but there is a reduction in price for mature visitors. Provincial parks have a similar policy, so be sure to ask about price breaks and bring proof of age whenever your travel.

Each of the fifty states has an extensive network of parklands and accommodations. Millions flock to these green and open spaces for day visits, weekend escapes, or summer vacations. Parks in most states are appreciated by residents and out-of-staters as well.

As an illustration, let me share with you information provided by the state of Arkansas. If you inquire, as I did, the Natural State will send out a sixty-two-page *Arkansas State Parks Guide* with current information and dazzling color photos, including one on page fifty-two for the DeGray Lake Resort that was so enticing, I inquired about a visit for my wife and me last spring. Talk about effective marketing.

For those of you who might consider Arkansas dull and bland—and that presumably would not include former president Bill Clinton—you'll get an entirely new perspective on the state. The little guide describes the fifty-one state parks of Arkansas, in six regions. The Ozark Mountains are in the north and northwest, the Mississippi Delta encompasses the entire eastern frontier, the Crowley's Ridge area slices through the north-eastern part of the state, the Gulf Coastal Plain forms the southern and southwestern border, the Ouachita Mountains are in west-central Arkansas, and the Arkansas River Valley is just north of the Ouachitas. The fifty-one parks exude natural beauty, include historical sites and museums, and offer an array of recreational activities. I have to confess I was unaware of all Arkansas has to offer—and you may be, too. That's why guides like this are so valuable, especially to frequent travelers, in RVs or other vehicles.

In Arkansas, as in other states, you can visit a park during the day and also stay overnight. There are campsites, cabins, lodges, rent-a-camp, rent-a-yurt, rent-a-tepee, rent-an-RV, a horse camp, a fly-in camp, group camping areas, group cabin areas, and backpacking areas. I found myself interested in the rent-a-yurt business. It turns out that it's available only at DeGray Park, whose picture in the guidebook so enticed me. These circular, raised huts on a wooden platform out in the woods sleep up to six people and rent for about $45 a day, with equipment included. The horse camp is at Devil's Den State Park; ponies will cost you about $12 a day. You can rent an authentic tepee on a raised wooden platform near a lake at Petit Jean State Park. These accommodate up to six folks; for your daily fee of about $45 you get the tepee, the necessary equipment, and a canoe. You can rent your own recreation vehicle, mounted perma-nently, at two parks: Bull Shoals and Cane Creek. At the former, the daily rate is roughly $72, while at the latter it's about $65. For that you get a 29-foot trailer with heat, air-conditioning, and room for up to eight.

The state guide goes on to explain what's to see and do at each of the parks and museums. It outlines the fee structure for activities at each facility. And, of course, there's one final marketing tool: a letter from the director of state parks, who urges people to "come experience one of the finest systems of parks and museums in the nation."

But the best news for mature visitors comes near the back of the booklet. Winter discount rates are outlined, as are rates for senior campers. Arkansas state parks have determined that U.S. citizens sixty-five and over or those with Golden Age Passports from Uncle Sam will be admitted to state park campgrounds for half the regular price.

I have contacted all the states about their discount policies for sea-soned travelers. They have responded that there are financial breaks at state parks and other attractions, but the rules vary from state to state.

My advice is, when you plan to visit a state, contact its Department of Tourism or State Parks Division to learn how you might benefit financially from a walk in the park. If Arkansas is any guide, you will likely get some helpful catalogs featuring mouthwatering photographs that'll have you making reservations to visit state parks in many jurisdictions.

OUTDOOR ADVENTURE PROVIDERS

Millions of us love to explore the outdoors. Walking and hiking are popular pastimes for older folks as well as twenty-somethings. They're great ways to see a country's natural assets, get away from urban sprawl and pollution, and keep fit in the process.

There has recently been a merger of two leaders in the hiking vacation industry. After twenty years of providing walks to scenic and historic places in Europe, BCT Scenic Walking has become a partner with **Backroads,** a leading U.S. adventure trip provider. The combined entities offer a hundred expeditions to thirty-four places from Patagonia and Peru to Canada and Alaska, as well as destinations across Europe and as far off as New Zealand. Backroads goes beyond mere foot traffic, providing bicycling and other adventures as well as special considerations for single travelers and families. The best way to learn more about Backroads is to call (800) 462–2848 or hit the Web and type www.backroads.com or www.backroads.com/bctwalk.

Want to try a hike across China? **China Hiking Adventures, Inc.** (www.china-hiking.com) offers half a dozen trips across the nation: four hiking adventures, a Tibet and Three Gorges Tour, and a holiday tour specifically targeted to mature travelers.

American Wilderness Experience is another adventure vacation provider, sending folks out into the woods for a fun and rewarding time. White-water rafting, horseback-riding trips, canoe vacations, rock climbing, even mountain biking are all possibilities. The agency is a type of wilderness broker, planning trips in conjunction with many tour operators. Some of the trips are geared to the post-fifty crowd, so if you contact American Wilderness, be sure to inquire about discounts for the well seasoned. You can make contact with American Wilderness Experience at (800) 444–0099.

A similar service is offered for brave people who want to get back to nature way up north, in Alaska. A group called **Alaska Wildland**

Adventures will design a program just right for your age group. Rafting, yachting, birding, whale-watching, glacier gloating, and wilderness hiking are all possible. You can also get out into the deep woods for encounters with grizzly bears and other critters. Take your courage and plenty of bug spray. Contact Alaska Wildland Adventures at (800) 334–8730.

Overseas Adventure Travel offers nonsedentary global holidays to folks over fifty. This tour purveyor gives you an exotic destination but throws in a little luxury as well, which means upscale tent locations, inns and hotels, and lodges in the bush or the jungle. The trips range from moderately tough to difficult. The good thing about OAT trips is that groups are limited to eighteen, so you don't feel lost in a hiking horde of thousands. I have talked to several veterans of these excursions who have found them quite exciting and good value for the money. Overseas Adventure Travel is a member of the Grand Circle Travel family. Call (800) 597–2482.

Senior World Tours is what the name implies. Trips are more ambitious than a bus tour of France or a train ride across Canada. Senior World can send folks for snowmobile drives through Wyoming as well as walking trips in the United States, England, and France. Bicycle and rafting trips are also offered—though they're less heart stopping than trips for younger adventurers—down the Snake River in Idaho or along the Colorado River through the Grand Canyon. To see whether these tours might appeal to you, contact Senior World Tours at (888) 355–1686.

One of the earliest adventure travel firms designed for baby boomers and beyond is **Eldertreks.** It offers active, away-from-the-madding-crowd trips for groups of fifteen hardy souls to some fifty countries. Take a safari in Kenya, tour Mongolia by camel, go hiking in Patagonia's Torres del Paine, or explore the ruins of Angkor Wat in Cambodia. These trips focus on physical activity but also on exploration of nature and cultural interaction. Destinations range the world, from Borneo and Bali to Belize, and from Thailand to Turkey. Eldertreks' Trip Finder phone number is (800) 741–7956.

AFC Tours offers escorted trips for "our crowd" to North American and overseas destinations. Here at home, you can choose national park odysseys or trips to big cities. You can also opt to travel to London, Bangkok, or Hong Kong. AFC organizes cruises, train trips, and grandparent tours. There are a few extras with this group. As part of the package, AFC picks you up at home, delivers you to the airport for your outward journey, and then brings you back home upon your return. And if you are a single traveler who books four months in advance and a roommate cannot be located, the company waives the single supplement charge. Contact AFC Tours at (800) 369–3693.

Collette Tours can also provide enjoyable vacations to the senior set. It says that it's one of the oldest escorted-tour companies in the business. It arranges a hundred different excursions to more than four dozen countries and offers a "round-the-world" trip each year. Collette advertises that it offers travelers first-class hotels and tours at a leisurely pace. It now has trips that spend several days at one travel base, thus avoiding the need to pack and unpack, changing hotels every night or two. Collette's telephone number is (800) 832–4656.

For something completely different, try **RFD Tours.** I think this is a great idea and worth your consideration. This concept was developed years ago as a type of exchange program between American farmers and those from other lands. Later, it was used as a way to arrange flower and garden tours. Nowadays, it plans tours and trips for mature travelers to the United States and places overseas. You can do some exploring if you like, but the pace is a bit slower than other adventure vacations. Some of the tours are created with a view that older folks can take trips with their grandchildren. You can inquire about RFD Tours by giving the company a ring at (800) 323-7604.

The **American Hiking Society** has come up with vacation plans that combine two very important criteria: getting you into the great outdoors and giving you something meaningful to do while enjoying it. American Hiking Society Volunteer Vacations take you to magnificent backcountry locations where you build or rebuild footpaths, cabins, and shelters. In the process you meet new friends, hike peaks and valleys, sit around a roaring campfire at night, and come home from "vacation" recharged. These holidays cost only $100—but of course you are working for your supper, as they say. For American Hiking Society members, the fee is just $80. To find out more, hop online at www.americanhiking.org.

LONG-DISTANCE TRAILS

The United States has been remembering the extraordinary undertaking of Meriwether Lewis and William Clark, 200 years after their team made its historic journey from the Midwest to the Pacific Coast and back. This has engendered new interest in walking and hiking. Our country is endowed with some incredible scenic and historic trails that can be a hiker's nirvana. The granddaddy, or perhaps grandmama, of them all is the **Appalachian National Scenic Trail** along the East Coast. The most persistent among us have trekked the entire 2,174-mile trail from Springer Mountain, in northern Georgia, to Mount Katahdin, in northern Maine. The Appalachian Trail crosses fourteen states and is considered one of the most grueling hiking paths in the nation. It was developed by volunteers and opened as a continuous trail back in 1937; it became the first U.S. National Scenic Trail in 1968. Parts of it had fallen into disrepair, but nowadays some 4,000 volunteers contribute more than 185,000 hours of effort to maintain the Appalachian Trail each year. So successful has the AT been that the International Appalachian Trail has been developed, into Canada. It extends to the province of Newfoundland.

In the West the **Oregon Trail** evokes the struggle of 400,000 pioneers who traversed its crude network of rutted paths from the Mississippi River to Oregon in search of better lives and new opportunities. Interestingly enough, the Oregon Trail is just 4 miles shorter than the Appalachian Trail, measuring 2,170 miles.

THE AMERICAN DISCOVERY TRAIL

The American Discovery Trail is considered the great American trail because it runs from coast to coast, Delaware to California—some 3,000 miles. It connects towns, cities, and rural regions. The trail has currently been mapped but is still being connected. When finished, it will interconnect five National Scenic Trails, ten National Historic Trails, twenty-three National Recreational Trails, and local and regional pathways. It will be the enthusiast's Holy Grail. Get your hiking shoes ready.

Another emigrant route is the **Mormon Pioneer Trail,** which from 1846 until 1869 saw more than 70,000 Mormons travel from Nauvoo, Illinois, across the Great Plains to their new goal, the Great Salt Lake. It was there they created the state of Deseret, later to become Utah.

The **California Coastal Trail** stretches 1,200 miles from Mexico to the border with Oregon.

The **Great Western Trail** will be an even more ambitious border-to-border undertaking when it is completed: a continuous corridor stretching from Mexico to Canada, passing through some of the most spectacular scenic beauty in the western United States. Walkers will travel through Arizona, New Mexico, Utah, Wyoming, Montana, and Idaho. It will actually be more than one trail: The first will be apportioned to hikers, while another will be used by horseback riders, mountain bikers, and those with motorized vehicles. I'm not too crazy about that unless the noisy crowd is kept far away from the hiking crowd.

The **Old Spanish Trail** traces the route of earlier settlers who made their way to the American West. The trail starts in Santa Fe, New Mexico; turns northwest toward Castle Dale, Utah; then arches southwesterly through the desert to Los Angeles.

Those are the biggies. But if you love the great outdoors and wish to enjoy it more, below are some regionally focused long-distance trails that you might like to encounter up close and personal.

If you live east of the Continental Divide, there's the **Allegheny Trail** through Virginia and West Virginia, extending 330 miles through some rugged terrain in the Allegheny Mountain Range and meeting the Appalachian Trail in Monroe County, West Virginia. This pastoral path offers solitude in rural stretches, spectacular vistas, mountain streams, farmland, and interesting geology.

In the West the **Arizona Trail** traverses the Grand Canyon State's mountain ranges from Mexico to the state of Utah. This is no flat hike. The trail meanders from desertland in the south into forestland and mountain peaks up north. This route is best done in spring or fall, when it's not too hot in the desert or too cold and snowy in the Arizona mountains.

The **Bartram Trail** in the southeastern United States traces the footsteps of naturalist William Bartram as he walked through North Carolina, South Carolina, and Georgia. Those who have hiked it say the Bartram rivals the Appalachian Trail, though of course the latter's fame outshines the Bartram. Still, you can enjoy great views, plenty of wildlife, and excellent fishing along the trail.

The **Bay Area Ridge Trail** runs around San Francisco Bay in California; when fully operational it will connect public parklands and watershed areas for some 400 miles of Bay Area open space. Proponents say it will provide hikers exquisite views of nature and wildlife within urbanized Northern California.

To the Northeast next, and the **Northville-Placid Trail,** which passes through the Adirondack Mountains of New York State. It connects the southern foothills of northern New York's most famous mountain range with the High Peaks near the Canadian border. Aside from remarkable hills and valleys, there are abundant streams, ponds, and lakes all along the length of this trail. It is 133 miles long, but given the topography, hikers say it takes an average of nineteen days to get from end to end.

Sheltowe Trace is a 268-mile jaunt in the southeastern United States, passing through Kentucky and Tennessee in what is now known as Pickett State Park. If you hike this trail, you will walk along ground explored earlier by Daniel Boone and John Muir.

Tahoe Rim Trail is a complete loop around the Lake Tahoe Basin in Nevada and California. A new trail, it extends some 150 miles. Aside from walkers, horseback riders are allowed, and even cross-country skiers in winter. If you've been to Lake Tahoe, you know how breathtakingly beautiful it is. Imagine walking all the way around it.

Vermont's **Long Trail** traces the length of the Green Mountain State from Massachusetts to the border with Canada. Running 270 miles up Vermont's spine, it's one of the oldest trails in the nation and one of the East Coast's most rough and rugged hiking paths. If you complete the main trail, you might then want to explore the other 175 miles of side trails into the wilds of Vermont.

New York and New Jersey's **Long Path** runs from Fort Lee, New Jersey (just across the George Washington Bridge from New York City), up the Hudson River to Albany, the state capital. The Long Path is 325 miles now, but there are plans to make it longer, extending to the Mohawk River and into the Adirondacks. Once you get there, you can connect with the Northville-Placid Trail for an unending journey.

A WORLD OF HIKING

There are, of course, hundreds of less intense trails and paths throughout America. State and local governments maintain many hiking areas for dedicated walkers. Canada, too, offers an extensive network of hiking trails, most notably in the Rocky Mountains. There are long and memorable walks through Banff, Jasper, Kootenay, and Yoho National Parks, as well as through Mount Robson Provincial Park and Kananaskis Country. The thrills continue abroad, with trails through South America, Europe, Africa, Asia, and Australia.

Just recently I was in the tiny European principality of Liechtenstein for an installment of the television series. Liechtenstein is a very small place, the fourth-smallest country in Europe. It's only 62 square miles in total, about the size of Washington, DC, and yet one of its tourist lures is its extensive network of hiking trails. The principality maintains 250 miles of hiking paths, both on its flatter region, called Lower Liechtenstein, and in the mountains. Some of the mountain trails take hikers to the highest points of the country. Only determined hikers will make it to the highest peak, Grauspitz, at about 8,000 feet above sea level. There is no regular trail, but the Liechtenstein Tourism Division told me during my visit that many dedicated hikers make it their goal to hike to the highest point of each country in Europe.

Incidentally, perhaps some of you mature American hikers would like to accept that challenge as well. If you do, you're in for some magnificent times, in more ways than one. When you finish Europe, you could make

A HIKER'S ONLINE RESOURCE

I came across an interesting Web site that has information on trails virtually everywhere in the world. It also provides weather data, maps, information on huts and other lodging, even a link to equipment and a packing list for your next date with destiny. If you love to hike, this may be your ready-reference desk: www.traildatabase.org.

similar plans to hike to the highest point in each of the fifty states. I met a fellow from New York State recently who is part of a club that does just that. He's scaled the peaks in thirty states thus far.

If you are a so-so hiker, you can combine your walks with other diversions. A group called Adventure South, for instance, has devised a Midlife Adventure to New Zealand. It's a thirteen-day "active" holiday, so you can see the country and enjoy it in several ways. Your tour includes a sail on a chartered yacht through Auckland Harbor, an exploration of a private limestone cave with the family who own it, a trip through the volcanic region of Rotorua, a hike through trails near the base of Mount Ruapeha, a sea kayak adventure near Marlborough Sounds, a water taxi ride to Abel Tasman National Park and a hike through it, a walk on advancing glaciers, a flight to the bush, a bushwalk through New Zealand forestland, a jet boat ride, and more walking near Mount Cook before finally relaxing for a few days prior to your journey home. Everything is included, and the trip price (as of this writing) is $5,110; add $1,040 for single traveler supplement.

MORE IN THE OUTDOORS: SKIING

If hiking is not your passion, or not your idea of a good time, there are other outdoor experiences for mature explorers. Just because you're past fifty doesn't mean you have to give up things like skiing. Indeed, there are several ski clubs for the senior set. The **Over The Hill Gang** offers large discounts and varied ski trips to those who have passed the half-century mark. **GO50** is another club that allows members to save on trips to four dozen ski resorts in North America. The **Ski Atlantic Seniors' Club** has what it calls an affordable ski program for mature schussers.

Here's something even more incredible. The **70+Ski Club** has a membership of more than 15,000 people in their seventies, eighties, and nineties who participate in organized ski trips and other club events.

Ski resorts have recognized older skiers, and scores of sites provide special discounts on day and season passes for sixty-plus skiers. These slopes are located in California, Nevada, Arizona, Alaska, Oregon, Washington, Colorado, Montana, New Mexico, Utah, Wyoming, Indiana, Michigan, South Dakota, Wisconsin, New Jersey, North Carolina, Pennsylvania, Virginia, Maine, Massachusetts, New Hampshire, Vermont, and New York. Some of them offer free skiing to older folks.

In California, for example, skiers seventy and above go free at Boreal, Donner Ski Ranch, and Soda Springs. Nevada resort Mount Rose provides free skiing to those seventy and over, while at Diamond Peak you must be eighty and above for a free lift ticket. Oregon's Mount Bachelor has free skiing for folks seventy and beyond. In Colorado the post-seventy crowd skis free anytime at Monarch and Solvista, while at Copper Mountain and Winter Park, seventies go free Monday through Thursday. At Montana's Bridger Bowl, if you want to ski for free, you must be somewhere between 72 and 127 years old. New Mexico's Taos Ski Valley offers a free ski pass to folks seventy and higher. At Park City in Utah, free skiing is for those seventy and above, while at Powder Mountain you must be eighty or more.

Paoli Peaks in Indiana offers free ski runs to seventies and up. In Wisconsin, Devil's Head gives those seventy and above a free ride. At Shawnee Mountain in Pennsylvania, you ski for nothing if you are at least seventy. In New York the seventy-and-above crowd goes free at Gore Mountain and Titus Mountain. And in Vermont three resorts offer free lift passes to those seventy and older: Ascutney Mountain, Bromley Mountain, and Magic Mountain.

Aside from ski clubs, many travel agents and Web groups offer discounts to mature Americans for airfares, resorts, and lift tickets. Even most airlines offer ski packages, and the discounts include the cost of the flight. In the interest of one-stop shopping, there's a Web address that will provide brochures on most of the ski areas in North America and advise you of discounted ski packages: www.snowpak.com.

Many of you may be interested in expanding your ski horizon. There are ski packages galore to the European Alps. Among the first-class destinations are Innsbruck, Kitzbuhel, Lech, and St. Anton in Austria; Bormio, Cortina, and Courmayeur in Italy (home of the 2006 Winter Olympics); Chamonix and Val d'Isère in France; and Davos, Interlaken, St. Moritz, Verbier, and Zermatt in Switzerland. Beyond that, you can book ski trips to several resorts in Argentina and Chile, as well as to New Zealand.

GOLF

Perhaps golf is more to your liking upon entering your golden years. Here, too, there are ways to enjoy your sport without paying full price. Golf courses and resorts from coast to coast offer specials to mature golfers. In addition, there are deals at resorts in Europe and Mexico. Golf gurus now say Mexico has emerged as a leading golf destination.

Most folks would agree that golf is not a cheap sport at the best of times. On a recent trip to Bermuda for *The Seasoned Traveler* television show, I discovered that some courses there can charge a few hundred dollars for eighteen holes. Entrepreneurs to the rescue! **Golf Card** is a way to help duffers save big bucks on the cost of golf. Once you pay your fee and become a member, promoters say that some 3,800 courses offer savings for cardholders. You'll get a couple of free rounds of golf, and you'll save as much as 50 percent on golf links across the globe that are part of the program. Call for information at (800) 321–8269. The people who run this say the typical member is sixty-plus, has played the game a long time, and travels eight to twelve weeks per year, so a card with special privileges at golf courses around the world is even better to some than a credit card.

Golfers over fifty can join the **National Senior Sports Association,** which sponsors golf "tournaments" once a month at courses across the country. These are actually mini holidays and come complete with hotel accommodations, golf (of course), most meals, and things to do for the spouse who would rather shop, or die, than be subjected to golf. There are thousands of members who pay a yearly membership fee. You must pay for the trips to get you to the First Tee. Information is available at (800) 282–6772.

In addition, don't overlook the many stores, catalogs, and Web sites that offer reduced rates on clubs and other gear for seasoned golfers.

AMUSEMENT PARKS

If you're a grandparent, you may like the idea of taking your grandkids to an amusement park. Unfortunately, the largest parks in our country (Disneyland, Disney World, Universal Studios, and Busch Gardens) do not offer seniors reduced admission prices—but others do. The Six Flags amusement parks from coast to coast offer discounts to mature travelers, either fifty-five or sixty. Six Flags Kentucky Kingdom in Louisville allows folks sixty-five and above in for free. If you are planning to visit a Six Flags park in Atlanta, Louisville, Chicago, Dallas, Los Angeles, or Jackson, New Jersey, contact the park directly for local admission prices or go to www.sixflags.com to check prices. In addition, these places generally offer greatly reduced rates to children—and if the kids are short enough, they'll get in for free.

At Dorney Park in Allentown, Pennsylvania, mature funsters sixty and older get a 55 percent reduction on their admission for a one-day ticket during the summer. At the same time, little ones (shorter than 48 inches) are entitled to the same financial break. See www.dorneypark.com. In northern Ohio, Cedar Point in Sandusky—which has some of the most exciting roller coasters of any park in the nation—offers a "Funday" pass for seniors, a 32 percent discount. Cedar Point's electronic address is www.cedarpoint.com.

ECOTOURISM

Beyond the parks, trails, links, and slopes, there are other elements to the great outdoors that lure millions of older folks outside their homes. These people have decided to take "ecotours" both at home and abroad. Tour companies can now organize trips to China focusing on its natural beauty, architecture, or religion, as well as hiking trips through the world's most populous nation. Other groups will take you to the Australian Outback, the Barrier Reef, the unspoiled northwestern frontier of Australia, Lake Eyre, the Simpson Desert, or the Flinders Ranges. There are tours of the Sahara Desert, by camel or four-wheel drive, or both, leaving from Algeria, and including camping in the world's largest sand pit. You can even organize a trip to the top and bottom of the world, to the Arctic and Antarctica. If people want to see a place, there appears to be a tour operator willing to help them explore it, and there is no reason on earth why senior travelers should not be out there enjoying the best the world has to offer.

Closer to home, you can plan an independent exploration of the backwoods of Vancouver Island in British Columbia. It's amazing to realize just how little of that magical place is actually developed. Most of it is thick and spectacular backwoods, with few roads and fewer settlements. At the other extreme, British Columbia's mountains can provide stunning peaks, wetlands, hot spring mineral pools, and more wildlife than you'll ever see if you live on the North Side of Chicago.

For more information about ecotouring, along with specific tours to consider, see chapter 9, Voyages of Discovery.

CULTURAL HERITAGE TOURING

Older Americans are leading the charge in a new travel venture. The U.S. Department of Commerce reports seasoned travelers like us have created a boom in the cultural heritage tourism market. According to this agency, 46 percent of American travelers now visit some type of heritage site or go on a heritage tour. These include historic homes like the Franklin D. Roosevelt mansion in Hyde Park, New York, or the Martin Luther King Jr. birthplace in Atlanta; ethnic and cultural events celebrating the lives and contributions of the many groups who have made our society so rich and varied; fairs and festivals, including the ever-growing Folk Life Festival on the National Mall in Washington each year; music jamborees; and historical districts and towns that contributed to the growth and development of our nation, its economy, and its way of life. Many of these trips are taken to outdoor locations and venues. Baby boomers who seek a new level of enrichment, beyond purely leisure travel, are turning to such holidays. They are wide and varied in scope: American Indian history, black history, civil rights, the Revolutionary and Civil Wars, European immigration, the Voyage of Discovery by Lewis and Clark. History buffs can design their own itineraries or join a tour. There is much to see, given the 77,000 listings on the National Register of Historic Places. The National Park Service offers thirty regional trips designed by the National Register (www.nr.nps.gov/nr/travel).

The **Commerce Department's Office of Tourism** is helping to fuel interest in the phenomenon as well with its "American Pathways" tours.

There are more than a hundred such trips with various themes. One, for example, is called "Food for the Soul" and showcases ethnic cuisine; "Lady Liberty" highlights the immigrant journeys that so many of our relatives took to reach these shores. The Commerce Department says the excursions now travel to virtually all the states and are beneficial not only to the travelers who make the journeys but also to the local economies. Cultural heritage tourism generates some $164 billion for the U.S. economy every twelve months. So the next time you decide to take a cultural tour of Harlem, think about not only how much you are gaining from the educational experience, but also how much New York City's economy is benefiting from your visit. For more information: www.americanpath ways.com.

Many museums across the nation and nonprofit organizations have also gotten into the act. They sponsor study tours to places of historic and cultural interest. The **National Trust for Historic Preservation** and the **Smithsonian Institution** have organized tours of intriguing places. The National Trust can be contacted at www.nthp.org; reach the Smithsonian online at www.smithsonianjourneys.org.

National Geographic Expeditions (www.nationalgeographic.com/ xpeditions/) has created some interesting and informative getaways. One trip, cited in the *New York Times,* was an eight-day journey in 2004 that cruised from Jacksonville, Florida, north to Charleston, South Carolina, via the Intracoastal Waterway. It focused on the antebellum South, the wildlife of the region, and the natural beauty of the Southeast.

Sometimes a trip to the beach or a week of golf is not enough. When you get the urge to do something more meaningful in the great outdoors, a cultural heritage journey may be just right for you. There are plenty available, so find the one just perfect for your needs and desires.

And one last thought on this concept: Many of us older folks, who recall our own educational experiences, decry the education that our children and grandchildren are receiving. We wonder what they're learning in school when they seem to know so little about history, geography, literature, or culture. Seasoned travelers would probably do their children and grandchildren a great favor by taking them on these cultural heritage odysseys, not only in this country but overseas as well. Kids can learn more from trips like these than they're ever likely to learn from a textbook or a crowded classroom.

ADVENTURES AFLOAT

CHAPTER 8

Americans love to cruise. Millions have their own boats—sailboats for quiet, billowy glides through waves offshore, racing boats for high-powered skims across large lakes, small fishing boats that troll calm waters as occupants try to outwit the creatures below. Beyond these, Americans seem committed to larger cruisers, either for relaxation or for adventure. There are gigantic oceangoing vessels that transport passengers thousands of miles over the deepest oceans; river cruise ships that ply an expanding list of navigable rivers in the United States, Europe, North Africa, India, and China; and yachts that offer the ultimate in luxury, service, and cuisine.

There are also expedition cruises, which focus less on luxury and more on adventure, education, and exploration. You may study marine wildlife as you snorkel or scuba your way to the sea bottom or look for ancient ruins beneath the waterline; Alexandria, Egypt, comes to mind immediately. There are theme cruises on boats of any size, Christmas Markets cruises, musical tours, bridge tournaments, business meetings at sea. There are special alumni cruises, celebrity cruises, seminar cruises, fitness cruises, singles cruises, or senior cruises. You get the idea.

What I've learned over the past several months is that millions of mature Americans have taken cruises, both on the seas and on the rivers. I met a woman in Europe who had been on twenty-one cruises. I met a couple who cruise the rivers of Europe year after year. I encountered a man who had been on all kinds of cruises and found the ocean vessels too big and too bawdy. I know a couple who take two or three Caribbean cruises every twelve months, often returning to the same islands. They find comfort and convenience in those excursions.

BOOKING YOUR CRUISE

Seniors know about cruises, and they seem to know how to get a good deal in the process. But if you haven't hit the water yet, how do you know what's best for you, and at what price? You need to select a ship and a cruise that fit your requirements as well as your budget. At the same time, you need to look for ways to reduce your cost, if saving money is important to you. If you cruise in the off-season, you'll save money. Taking a European river cruise in November, with snowflakes falling and winds gusting, will cost less than in July. Taking an ocean liner to the Caribbean in the heat of summer or in hurricane season will also reduce your final bill—though it may raise your level of excitement if a storm threatens.

You can wait until the last minute to book your cabin and engage in bargaining with the cruise company. If the ship is less than full, the company may give you a deal. Ask about it. At the other end of the timeline, book very early and you're likely to get a discount for helping the shipping line fill cabins.

Deal with groups that specialize in short-term travel. Spur of the Moment, Stand Buys, and the Last Minute Cruise Club of Grand Circle Travel know what's available at the eleventh hour. Some of the largest travel organizations might offer you a break, given their extraordinarily strong buying power. They purchase rafts of rooms and want to get rid of them. Additionally, look for air–sea or sea–air packages. If you live in Eugene, Oregon, and want to take a cruise to the Caribbean from Miami, you'll need a deal on the round-trip flight to the East Coast and back, as well as on the floating vacation itself.

As with most things in our contemporary world, there are Web sites that may help you. Online bidding services sell cruises as a commodity product. You may consider this a bit esoteric, akin to trading pork bellies in the futures markets, and to some degree it is similar. The cyberstores act as travel consolidators and sell cruise inventory to the highest bidder. However, the highest bid may be paying well below the average rate for a cruise under normal circumstances. If you have the time, the stamina, and the patience to play this game, you may win in more ways than one.

Cruise companies themselves sell their wares, in this case rooms or suites, via online booking dealerships. One example is My Travel Company, which belongs to Carnival Cruise Lines. My Travel Company may sell rooms at a rate much lower than you'd get by calling the cruise firm directly. Once you climb aboard, you qualify immediately for a bargain on your next cruise. The bargain may entice you to travel again—the company certainly hopes you will. Most lines have a booking agent onboard, happy to take your reservation for the next sea cruise.

Business has been booming—so much so that, as of this writing, cruise companies had plans to introduce sixty-three new vessels over the coming months. Customers may have the upper hand. The firms will have a lot more beds to fill, and they are betting that demand for cruises will continue to rise. Since passenger manifests increased 73 percent between 1995 and 2000, cruise providers appear to have the numbers on their side.

In addition to regular bargains, seasoned travelers have other negotiating leverage. When dealing with various ship companies, seek your best reservation price and then ask about AARP, AAA, or other discounts. If you are a frequent traveler, ask about breaks for that.

KINDS OF CRUISES

Let's look at the differences between the two cruising experiences you can choose from.

Ocean liners are huge and provide a nonstop experience, food and drink all the time, and multiple diversions. The average liner has accommodations for 2,000-plus passengers, although Cunard's *Queen Mary 2* holds 2,800 riders and Royal Caribbean has four monsters: *Mariner of the*

MAJOR CRUISE PROVIDERS

If sailing is in your future, you should be familiar with these providers:

Abercrombie & Kent, (800) 323–7308; www.abercrombiekent.com

Carnival, (800) 327–9501; www.carnival.com

Celebrity, (800) 437–3111; www.celebritycruises.com

Crystal, (800) 446–6620; www.crystalcruises.com

Cunard, (800) 728–6273; www.cunard.com

Disney (if you're taking the family for a holiday), (800) 370–0097; www.disneycruise.com

Holland America, (800) 426–0327; www.hollandamerica.com

Princess, (800) 421–0522; www.princess.com

Radisson, (800) 285–1835; www.rssc.com

Royal Caribbean, (800) 398–9819; www.rccl.com

Star Cruises, (305) 436–4000 ext. 1105; www.starcruises.com

To select the right cruise for you, cast a wide net. Seek the advice of a travel agent, go online to travel Web sites, or contact the cruise companies above directly. If you belong to AAA or AARP, see whether they are offering cruise holidays. Talk to those who've been on cruises. Have them assess their various trips in terms of comfort, enjoyment, and value for money. Add it all up and then decide which cruise "rocks your boat."

Seas accommodates 3,807 passengers, *Adventure of the Seas* and *Explorer of the Seas* hold 3,840 folks each, and *Voyager of the Seas* welcomes 3,114 passengers. Now, that's a lot of neighbors.

If you are younger, fifty to sixty-five, you may prefer to be surrounded by new friends, even several hundred of them. There is always something to do on the big boats, from movies and shows, dancing and aerobics, to swimming and even casinos. People seldom get bored, but many get tired out.

Yachts and river craft, on the other hand, are smaller, more intimate. A yacht may hold 50 passengers, while a river ship tops out at about 150.

It's easier to meet people and make new friends. These ships are quieter places, with set meal times in one dining room, generally a single bar and lounge, a fitness center, and a library or other room for reading or games. There may be entertainment after dinner, but the show often ends at ten thirty and passengers retire relatively early.

Pick a river in Europe and there's probably a river ship carrying passengers. You can sail the Thames in England; the Seine in France; the Rhine, Mosel, and Danube in Germany and beyond; the Elbe and Po in Italy; and the Volga and Moskova in Russia and Eastern Europe. There are several options on inland waterways. You can ride barges, cruisers, sailboats, side-wheelers, and ferries. On a recent trip to Europe, I came to know the Big Four river cruise companies serving the region:

Grand Circle Cruise Tours has a fleet of more than a dozen vessels, carrying about 140 passengers each. For information, call (800) 597–2482 or visit online at www.gct.com.

Vantage Deluxe World Travel has a fleet of three river cruisers accommodating roughly the same number of passengers. Vantage can be reached at (800) 322–6677 or www.vantagetravel.com.

Viking River Cruises has a large fleet, and its ships can hold up to 150 passengers. The telephone number is (877) 668–4546; or check out its Web site, www.vikingrivercruises.com.

Uniworld, the other river-ride provider, has a fleet similar to the competition; its ship can carry up to 150 passengers. The phone line is (800) 360–9550, while online it's www.uniworld.com.

These companies also go beyond the European rivers, with trips to the Nile in Egypt. Another provider in that part of the world is **Oberoi Nile Cruises,** at (800) 562–3764 or at www.oberoihotels.com/oberoi. This is a great trip; we'll be doing an episode of *The Seasoned Traveler* from the Nile on a Grand Circle ship. River boats run through the Amazon in South America, the Ganges in India, and the Yangtze in China.

Here at home we mustn't forget **Delta Queen Steamboat Company,** which operates its trio of paddle-wheeler *Queens* as well as the *Empress of the North* on rivers in America. Call (800) 543–1949 or go online to www.deltaqueen.com. And there are other stateside cruises—on the Hudson River in the East; the Ohio, Mississippi, and Missouri in the Midwest; the Snake, Columbia, and Willamette in the West. While large liners can convey a sense of anonymity among the masses, it's harder to do that on small boats. There are fewer shipmates, and you see them most of the time. There are only so many places you and they can go.

Oceangoing craft get passengers away from it all, often for several days at sea, with nothing to savor but the sky and the sun. River vessels are on narrow bodies of water where there's always something to see. They stop regularly to visit towns, castles, vineyards, monasteries, or other sites. Passengers have the option of making the shore trip or staying onboard. When big ships dock, there is a carnival atmosphere because the vessel may have been floating for several days. But some of these behemoths are hard to dock, so small tenders must come out to transport passengers to shore. That's not the case with yachts and river boats, which can tie up easily at most ports of call.

Seagoing ships have experienced outbreaks of illness over the past few years, although the cruise lines say they have dealt with the problem (see the section titled Cruising and Disease Outbreaks, below). Riverboats have not encountered such problems; the companies say that's because they are smaller and easier to maintain and clean.

And this may be important for elderly women traveling alone: Larger vessels generally have single men aboard to dance with unescorted females. This is not always the case on river craft, unless the ship's captain or male members of staff take on that responsibility. On a recent river cruise, an eighty-one-year-old woman traveling alone told me she was disappointed that there were virtually no opportunities to dance on the ship. There wasn't much music played after dinner, and there were no men to dance with. There are plenty of chances on the big boats, however, with their nightly entertainment and paid hoofers.

So, you pays yer money and you takes yer chances. Younger, more active travelers may prefer the excitement and activity on the large liners. Older and less active passengers, or those who have made several sea cruises, might prefer the river trips.

THE CRUISING INDUSTRY

Americans who cruise know the half a dozen or so big names in commercial boating. **Carnival Cruise Lines** is one of the biggest concerns. It owns twenty ships sailing under the Carnival Cruise Line logo, three Cunard vessels, a dozen ships of the Holland America Line, twelve more

ships that make up Princess Cruises, as well as nine other lines under the Carnival umbrella.

Another big player is **Royal Caribbean Cruises,** parent of Celebrity Cruises and its nine ships, as well as Royal Caribbean International, which sails twenty vessels—including the four ships mentioned earlier that carry more than 3,000 passengers each. Then there's **Star Cruises,** which controls seven large ships under its name and eleven more bearing the Norwegian Cruise Line banner.

The next time you see an advertisement in the travel section of your newspaper, as I did, promoting a sale on several cruise lines, understand there are just a few monster companies that largely control the industry. The number of vessels may be increasing, but the number of corporate players is holding steady, or decreasing.

Some superships are colossal and classics at the same time. The *Queen Mary 2* is the quintessential cruise liner, at 151,000 tons. It houses its own theater, planetarium, and plenty of other diversions. The 2004 *Caribbean Princess* is more than 100,000 tons and has nineteen decks with accommodations for almost 3,800 passengers.

SMALLER LINES AND SMALLER SHIPS

But there's another marine option, smaller and possibly more enjoyable. American Cruise Lines is christening a new vessel called the *American Spirit*. It weighs less than 2,000 tons, has four decks, and welcomes ninety-two passengers. Some see this as the best of all worlds, a small craft for the high seas. If you like this idea, here are some companies and options for you to look into:

American Cruise Lines, (800) 814–6880; www.americancruise lines.com. The company that offers the *American Spirit* noted above has a total of three vessels in service carrying forty or ninety passengers from Maine to Florida and specializing in trips about history and nature.

American Safari Cruises, (888) 862–8881; www.amsafari.com. These yachts accommodate one to two dozen passengers. They can go off the beaten water-path, exploring islands, small coves, and inlets— which the supersize vessels can't negotiate or navigate. American Safari also traverses the West Coast on three vessels that ply the waters from Alaska to the Baja on wildlife and nature expeditions.

Celebrity Xpeditions, (866) 973–8466; www.celebrity.com. Two ships to worldwide destinations.

Clipper Cruise Line, (800) 325–0010; www.clippercruise.com. Four ships with itineraries to North America and beyond.

Cruise West, (800) 888–9378; www.cruisewest.com. Eight boats, each of which has maximum capacity of 114 passengers, transport travelers along the Pacific Coast from Alaska to Panama, for nature, wildlife, and adventure cruises.

Lindblad Expeditions, (800) 397–3348; www.expeditions.com. Five smaller vessels with a list of worldwide destinations.

Sea Dream Yacht Club, (800) 707–4911; www.seadreamyachtclub .com. Sea Dream has two yachts that hold 110 passengers each and ply the waters and the shoreline of the Caribbean and Mediterranean Seas, often making detours when the ship's captain spies a quaint cove. Because these captains know their areas so well, they are able to take passengers to places virtually unknown to most tourists, even well-traveled ones.

GREAT LAKES CRUISING

In the United States, **Great Lakes Cruise Company** can transport you to five magnificent waterways that form part of our northern boundary. To learn more, call (888) 891–0203 or visit www.greatlakescruising.com. **American Canadian Caribbean Line** offers itineraries from the Great Lakes to the Caribbean on two ships holding no more than a hundred passengers. You can reach the company at (800) 556–7450 or online at www.accl-smallships.com.

Seabourn Cruise Lines, (800) 929–9391; www.seabourn.com. Three suite-only ships, carrying 200-plus passengers to the Caribbean and other locations.

Silversea Cruises, (800) 722–9955; www.silversea.com. Four all-suite vessels, up to 382 passengers, travel to worldwide destinations.

Star Clippers, (800) 442–0551; www.starclippers.com. Star Clippers offers three traditional sailing ships that take on 170 or 227 passengers each and travel to the Caribbean, the Mediterranean, and places a bit farther afield, like Thailand or Singapore.

Windstar Cruises, (800) 258–7245; www.windstarcruises.com. Three yachts with motorized sails take 148 or 308 paying customers to the Caribbean, Central America, Tahiti, and the Mediterranean, emphasizing exotic locales.

If you are unfamiliar with these smaller adventures afloat, there are plenty of resources to help you learn more about the tiny ships. The Niche Cruise Marketing Alliance (www.nichecruise.com) can tell you about the different lines and travel agents who specialize in this kind of travel. Small Ship Cruises (www.smallshipcruises.com) has a wealth of information on these types of boats, generally on those sailing overseas

The industry is growing and prospering, despite the seeming obstacles of higher fuel costs, a sinking U.S. dollar, and an up-and-down economy.

CRUISING THE MAINE COAST

If you want to explore the fabulous coast of Maine, there's a resource for you: The Maine Windjammer Association represents a fleet of tall ships that help you see the state from the water looking in. The telephone number is (800) 807–9463, or visit www.sailmainecoast.com.

More ships are being built, more come into service each month, vessels get heftier in size, and there seem to be more choices. That could be good news for consumers, especially mature travelers. Sound travelers are also smart shoppers. Look around before you choose a cruise.

CRUISING AND DISEASE OUTBREAKS

You may recall reading about the Carnival Cruise Line boat *Fascination,* on which 190 passengers came down with a virus while sailing to the Bahamas in December 2002. Thirteen crew members were also felled by the malady. *Fascination* was not alone that year. Four consecutive cruises on Holland America's ship *Amsterdam* were affected by what appeared to be Norwalk virus; hundreds of passengers and workers came down with it. Norwalk virus was first detected on land in Norwalk, Ohio, three decades ago. It reared its ugly head away from land in 2002.

Two cruises of the liner *Disney Magic* were also victimized by Norwalk-like symptoms, and 450 folks became ill. Fourteen crew and four passengers were affected by illness aboard the *Seven Seas Mariner.* And on another ship, the *Oceana,* 200 passengers and fifteen crew members were put out of commission by a gastrointestinal illness.

The U.S. Centers for Disease Control and Prevention rushed in to investigate all of these outbreaks. Cruise companies began an immediate program of disinfecting their vessels. Affected passengers were compensated for illness or shortened vacations. Other voyages were canceled

until shipping companies could figure out what was happening and how to stop it. And, as is usual in America, lawsuits were filed on behalf of some passengers.

CDC eventually concluded that Norwalk-like viruses are common in confined spaces and can affect almost anyone. Illness can be spread from person-to-person contact or from contaminated food and water. Officials noted that an interruption of sailings, coupled with intensified sanitation efforts, would break the virus cycle. They advised travelers to wash their hands and limit hand-to-mouth contact. A CDC official even pointed out that outbreaks on ships occur several times a year, but on a smaller scale than noted in 2002. He added that virus outbreaks can occur just as easily on land.

Despite all the hand-washing, name-calling, and lawsuits from the most recent incidents, there's no guarantee against other outbreaks in the future. Cruises simply involve hundreds or thousands of people from all over the country and the world crammed together in a confined space.

So what can you do? Wash your hands often with a sanitizing hand cleaner; pack a disinfectant and treat your bedding, bathroom, and cabin furnishings; limit close contact with strangers—especially those who may appear sick. And if you come down with something while on a cruise, seek medical treatment immediately and isolate yourself so you won't infect other passengers and crew.

CDC also suggests that you check out your ship before you sail to determine if it is safe and sanitary. The Vessel Sanitation Program is meant to guarantee that cruisers are up to standard. You can learn the status of your intended vessel by contacting CDC online at www.cdc.gov or by writing to the Chief of the Vessel Sanitation Program, CDC, 4770 Buford Highway NE, Mailstop F-23, Atlanta, GA 30341-3724.

Millions of Americans take thousands of cruises each and every year, the vast majority of which are safe, secure, and enjoyable. But as with everything else in this complex society we live in, it's up to each of us to safeguard ourselves.

VOYAGES OF DISCOVERY

As much as we may like to stroll a sandy beach, hike a mountain trail, or snorkel a coral reef, lots of adventurers our age prefer to slow down a bit at times, to expand our minds instead of our calf muscles. Educational vacations are a priority. Some people take these trips at least once a year. There are many holidays that combine physical exertion with mental stimulation, providing the best of both travel worlds.

ELDERHOSTEL

Elderhostel is the country's first—and many would say foremost—educational travel organization for mature explorers. It has been around for some thirty years. The Boston-based agency calls itself the largest travel group of its kind in the world. Its 10,000 programs serve almost 200,000 people in any given year. You can travel to ninety or more countries to participate. Elderhostel's philosophy is simple: Learning is a lifelong experience that should go on long after the college degree or the PhD has been conferred.

The tours and trips are not just series of dry lectures in college class-rooms while the regular students are home for summer break. Elder-hostel combines education with destination. Want to learn more about Claude Monet? Take a trip to the villages where the impressionist master lived and worked, then view his paintings at a Paris museum. Care to trace the roots of American music? Take a Mississippi River ride from Memphis to New Orleans to learn about American blues, spirituals, and jazz. Would you like to walk in the very footsteps of Lewis and Clark 200 years after their Voyage of Discovery? There's an Elderhostel expedition to achieve that goal. And if these sound a bit dull to you, there's a more active component.

During a recent trip overseas, I met a couple from suburban Chicago. Bicycling fans, they have taken nearly a dozen Elderhostel bike journeys to Europe. They've ridden through East Anglia in England, biked Belgium and the Netherlands, and cycled through southern Germany. They love it because the trips allow them to travel some 35 to 50 miles per day while stopping for lectures, discussions, or other more cerebral pursuits along the way. On their excursions, this couple has met Nobel Prize winners, politicians, and just plain folks, thus managing not only to get plenty of exercise but also to engage in lively conversations on many topics. The riders range in age from fifty-five to well past eighty. My friends also chuckled about the few times their biker group got lost and about the time it rained so hard, they had to stop and ask a Belgian farmer to let them take shelter in his barn. In typical Elderhostel fashion, there's a cleverly named Web site to tout these tours: www.roadscholar.org. You'd expect that from Elderhostel, wouldn't you?

An Elderhostel catalog is chock-full of invigorating trips, among them dogsledding over wintry Minnesota trails, hiking through Peru, dancing to Moroccan music in the Sahara Desert, and much more. To learn more, call (877) 426–8056 or visit www.elderhostel.org.

That Web site provides overviews of all the trips it offers. One really caught my eye. It's called "Christmas and New Year in Central Italy: Assisi and Siena." The trip is directed by Trinity College in Hartford, Connecticut, and it examines the holidays from this most beautiful location.

The trip includes a bit of walking each day, up to 3 miles, and takes in several towns, museums, and archaeological sites. Christmas travelers fly to Rome, then head to Assisi for seven nights, Siena for six, ending up in Florence before returning home. In Assisi there are lectures about Umbrian civilization from Etruscan times to the present. There are talks about local music and field trips to the Basilica of St. Francis and the regional capital, Perugia. There are visits to ceramics centers and a performance of seasonal music, with a viewing of a living Christmas crèche. Then it's on to Siena for more field trips, a dining excursion to the Tuscan countryside, and perhaps the highlight of the trip: a New Year's Eve party, Italian-style, with dinner, music, and games. Not your father's Elderhostel.

MORE LEARNING ADVENTURES

Elderhostel's younger cousin, or perhaps competitor, is twenty-five years old and also based in New England. **Interhostel** was created as an international educational travel experience for the fifty-and-over crowd. Based at the University of New Hampshire in Durham, it offers what are called learning vacations in several countries around the world, from Austria to Australia and from China to the Czech Republic. There are more than sixty Interhostel learning vacations each year.

What's makes Interhostel different from, say, Elderhostel is its Familyhostel component. These are educational trips and programs for youngsters eight to fifteen, along with parents or grandparents. Some of the most popular summer jaunts are to England, France, Switzerland, and Austria. The idea behind Familyhostel, conceived in 1991, is to give families an opportunity to travel abroad and learn together about another country's history and culture.

Of course, if you don't want to be around a bunch of kids, you'll stick with Interhostel, which has trips for about twenty to forty adults aged fifty or better. Most trips last two weeks. To learn more about the organization, call (800) 733–9753 or visit www.learn.unh.edu/interhostel.

Not to be outdone by these East Coast groups, Southern Oregon University has developed the **Senior Ventures** program in Ashland, Oregon. This program is more limited in scope and involves a lot of theater and museum visits. One vacation might include three plays at the Oregon Shakespeare Festival and five dinners at local restaurants.

Another might be all theater visits, while a third might combine theater coursework with attendance at theatrical performances, followed by classes on jazz. The group has also organized several recreational and travel adventures across the West. Add to that the fact you are "studying" in southern Oregon or Washington State, near glorious Pacific Ocean beaches, breathtaking mountain peaks, and magnificent Crater Lake. Lifelong learners never had it so good. For information, call (541) 552–6378 or go online to www.sou.edu/siskiyoucenter/seniorventures.

For twenty-five years the group **TraveLearn** has been taking Americans on educational tours across the globe. It caters to small groups and involves a wide range of ages—from thirty to eighty and beyond. Lecturers and escorts for these overseas tours come from more than 300 U.S. universities, colleges, and associations. TraveLearn brags about the first-class accommodations and transportation it provides its seasoned students. You can venture from Ireland to Indonesia, Italy to Israel. The organization offers free information to subscribers on its TraveLearn Cybertravel Newsletter. It's delivered once a month and highlights a TraveLearn destination. You can contact the Hawley, Pennsylvania, group by calling (800) 235–9114 or going on the World Wide Web to www.trave learn.com.

One of the nation's premier centers for learning is the **Chautauqua Institution** in the Finger Lakes region of western New York. Located on Lake Chautauqua, this is a magnet for those who crave an active academic respite from the mundane chores of everyday life. Chautauqua has a continuing commitment to lifelong learning through its celebrated summer educational programs, including lectures by eminent people in combination with classes, seminars, and talks. It has an array of performing arts programs—symphony and chamber music, opera and dance, and theater. Chautauqua offers a wide variety of religious programs to guests, and there's a recreational element as well. It's a different kind of vacation experience. Some call it a retreat from the rat race, a renewal of the mind and soul, a place to visit year after year.

And the place itself is special, all 865 acres of it. The Chautauqua Institution is a slice of Victoriana, a National Historic District village. It has welcomed presidents and performers, inventors and thinkers. It could soon welcome you, too. Think of it as attending all the Ivy League colleges at one time, on a campus as lovely as most of the Ivy schools. To learn more about the programs, call (800) 836–ARTS or delve into its

AND NOW FOR SOMETHING COMPLETELY DIFFERENT: THE SEMESTER AT SEA

Did you know you can take a voyage of discovery in a floating classroom? It's offered compliments of the Semester at Sea program administered by the University of Pittsburgh. Every autumn and spring semester, some 600 undergraduate students and their professors sail to exotic places while engaging in a full academic course of studies. The vessel stops at ten ports along the way, where the academicians meet local university students and professors, go on field trips, and engage in volunteer work.

How does this affect mature travelers? Each term, some sixty nonstudent passengers are invited for the ride, mostly older folks. They can audit classes and take part in all the activities on the ship. By the way, the ship is the SS *Universe Explorer*, deemed a nonluxury liner by one passenger but very comfortable. The food, she said, was wholesome and well prepared, served cafeteria-style, which will remind you of your college days.

The mature students get a twin cabin on the upper deck, away from the student masses. There's no formal entertainment onboard, but student musicians often play after dinner. Courses offered include economics, history, art, literature, business, theater, and biology. There's a library and computer lab. Professors deliver lectures on the next port of call so students will understand its history and culture. Guest lecturers from other universities are often invited aboard. And when the ship comes in, you can visit the town as part of a group tour or on your own, adding to your educational experience.

I have not done this myself, but it sounds absolutely first-rate. Indeed, if the program still exists when I retire and have plenty of time, I would consider signing up for a Semester at Sea. If it interests you, contact the Institute for Shipboard Education at the University of Pittsburgh: (800) 854–0195 or www.semesteratsea.com.

In the "everything's not perfect" category, you may have heard or read about the scary night aboard the Semester at Sea cruise in January 2005. As the craft was sailing from Canada to South Korea, it was struck by a 50-foot wave in the Pacific Ocean at the height of a storm. Several students and two crew members on the ship's bridge were injured in the freak event. The massive wall of water broke the windows on the bridge, damaged equipment, and caused a temporary loss of engine control. Everyone survived the ordeal and no doubt discussed the "extracurricular" activity for days afterward. These kinds of things can, and do, happen—part of the overall travel experience.

Web site at www.chautauqua-inst.org. Programs generally run from late June to late August, a most wonderful time of the year in the Finger Lakes. There are also special weekend experiences for older visitors.

On a trip to Europe, I met a couple from Virginia who just love to travel to Germany and have been back countless times. He used to work for the Defense Department, and the couple was stationed in Germany years ago. They struggled through German, never really mastering the language, but in 2003 she decided to focus on becoming a fluent speaker; she's been studying ever since. If this sounds like you, you should know about **AmeriSpan,** which offers language immersion programs worldwide to mature adults. You can learn twenty languages. The organization is a dozen years old and has had 18,000 students immerse themselves happily in that time period. Once you learn to speak the language, when's the best time to show off your prowess? AmeriSpan says it's best to travel overseas from February to April and in winter to avoid the summer crush of college-aged students. AmeriSpan is headquartered in Philadelphia. To learn more about learning more about languages, contact (800) 879–6640 or www.amerispan.com/language.

The **Center for Global Education** in Minneapolis offers travel-study seminars to Latin America. These can be heavy-duty, focusing on unfamiliar cultures and contemporary challenges in a challenged part of the world. Some of the programs and itineraries include "Social Change in Mexico," "Nicaragua in Transition," and "Social and Political Realities in Guatemala." The center's toll-free number is (800) 299–8889; its Web address is www.augsburg.edu/global/triplist.html.

The **Academy of Lifelong Learning** is a Springfield, Illinois, group that offers continuous academic opportunities for those of us fifty-five and older. Lincoln Land Community College designs classes and other activities to suit students. If you live in the Midwest, you might want to consider it. Call for information at (800) 727–4161, extension 6-2477, or go online to www.llcc.cc.il.us/all.

SPIRITUAL EXPERIENCES

Religious tours and pilgrimages are extremely popular with older Americans, and there are many to choose from. You can follow in the footsteps of Jesus Christ, Muhammad, Martin Luther, John Wesley, or Confucius. You can witness the Oberammergau Passion Play in Germany

UNIVERSITY LEARNING PROGRAMS WHEREVER YOU LIVE

Take a look around and you'll find retirement learning centers at many major universities nationwide. While this may not be a complete list, here are some of the college campus opportunities:

- University of Oregon
- Duke University (North Carolina)
- University of Southern Mississippi
- University of Wisconsin–Milwaukee
- Northern Illinois University
- George Mason University (Virginia)
- Harvard University (Massachusetts)
- The American University (Washington, DC)

(the next one takes place in 2010) or visit sites commemorating the saints (St. Francis Xavier's quincentenary fell in 2005). You can appreciate the places where apparitions are said to have occurred, see the foundations of the Muslim faith, admire the temples of the Hindu gods, approach Buddhist shrines, and pray at the Wailing Wall in Jerusalem.

Christian pilgrimages seem the most popular. There are variations, depending on denomination. For Catholics, Portugal has become a favored destination. Various groups can arrange weekend or one-week trips to Fatima, site of an apparition of the Virgin Mary and now hallowed ground for Roman Catholics. But if you were to contact an organization called **Destinations Europe,** www.destinationseurope.com, you would see a tour three times as long. It starts in Portugal with a visit to Fatima, then moves to churches and other sacred places in Braga, Coimbra, and Santiago de Comostela. After driving through Spain, the tour takes pilgrims to Lourdes, France, where the Blessed Mother is said to have appeared to St. Bernadette. After a few days in the south of France, it's on to Turin to see the Holy Shroud, said to be the burial cloth of Jesus after the Crucifixion. The whirlwind continues with a trip to Padua to visit the Basilica of St. Anthony, later arriving in Venice and a tour of St. Mark's Cathedral. Next, visitors go to Assisi and the Basilica of St. Francis. Finally, the trek turns south to Rome and the Vatican. The tour even promotes a papal audience and a visit to the Sistine Chapel in St. Peter's Basilica and the Vatican Museum. Devout Catholics may think they have died and gone straight to heaven after that twenty-one-day journey.

The same travel company offers a Methodist heritage tour in England. It takes the faithful to the beautiful city of York, in northeast England, where the Methodist Society used to meet. The next day the coach carries folks to Osmotherley, to a stone meetinghouse said to be one of the oldest Methodist chapels in the world. John Wesley himself visited this chapel often and preached to the villagers. On another day the tour stops in Epworth, where Wesley was born. A day trip to Oxford explores the colleges and sites associated with John Wesley. (At the University Church of St. Mary the Virgin, for instance, Wesley made his first convert to Methodism.) The tour turns west toward Wales and goes to Bristol, the town where Wesley's great crusade began. Then pilgrims are transported to Wells Cathedral, where John Wesley preached, and to Glastonbury, where Joseph of Arimathea is said to have brought the Holy Grail after the death of Jesus. You also visit Bath, Plymouth, and Cornwall—where Wesley engaged in some of his most impassioned preaching. There are stops at Salisbury Cathedral and, finally, at London's Wesley Chapel and Museum of Methodism. This trip lasts more than two weeks.

Other voyages focus on other religions. Buddhists can journey to Mount Wutai, regarded as one of that faith's most sacred places. The six-day excursion takes passengers from Beijing to Datong in Shanxi province. Followers are transported to the Yungang Grottoes, the Huayan Monastery, Shanhua Temple, and the nine-dragon screen. On the third day, guests go to Mount Wutai, considered the principal Buddhist mountain in all of China and Southeast Asia. Beyond this experience, there are other Buddhist tours to Nepal and India.

There are some fifty Christian religious tour operators you might choose for your own pilgrimage, offering travel to the holy sites of Catholic, Orthodox, and other faiths, as well as trips to the Holy Land, which combines Christian and Jewish heritage. There are some two

dozen Islamic tourism organizations, many of which specialize in getting pilgrims to the Hajj in Mecca, the sacred religious gathering and one of the Seven Pillars of Islam, the requirements of faith for believers. There are up to four dozen Jewish tour operators, some taking the faithful to China and South America.

The easiest way to find a religious trip for your needs is to contact a travel agent or look online using keywords "religion tours," "pilgrimages," and/or the specific religion in which you're interested.

ECOTOURING

It's but a short step from remembering our faith to preserving our future. So-called ecotours have also become big business, especially among mature travelers. Ecotravel firms claim to bring people like us closer to nature, exotic cultures, untouched rain forests, bird and wildlife habitats, and much more. Their stated goal is to give those in the developed world the opportunity to see what's left of the undeveloped world. Let me state categorically that most of these companies take great care to transport hordes of adventurers through vast swathes of uninhabited land while working hard to maintain its unspoiled condition.

Still, it strikes me as a contradiction in terms. How can thousands of people tramping the Galapagos Islands, even if they are on their best behavior, not interfere with the fragile animal and plant environment of that unique island chain? How can more thousands of people riding on motorized safari vehicles through the forestlands of Africa not affect the animals, their movements, and their long-term future? If a population of people equal in size to a large American city visits and leaves its mark on the Florida Everglades every year, won't the marshland be affected negatively over time?

I am somewhat dubious about environmental tours because despite the best efforts of many, we may be killing pristine places as we purport to protect them. One-of-a-kind plant and animal species cannot long endure when hordes of camera-clicking, litter-leaving tourists continue to invade their territory.

With that caveat in mind, however, let me tell you that there are many ecotour groups and companies enabling you to travel where you can't normally go on your own. What follows is a listing of a few providers that will take you away from this world to a different world altogether. There are others; you can find them if you look.

Everglades Day Safari advertises itself as "Florida's Finest Eco-Tour." It's based in Sanibel, but you can catch cruises from Florida's east or west coast. You'll be taken on jungle cruises through mangrove swamps or on airboat rides through the east coast's River of Grass. You'll get to see plenty of wildlife along the way. Lunch is included, featuring alligator and other local delicacies.

In the American West, **EcoTours of Oregon** has a list of one-day trips in the Pacific Northwest. Based in Portland, the company can take environmentalists and others to the Columbia River Gorge waterfalls, to Mount Hood, to Mount St. Helens, whale-watching off the Oregon coast, on a Lewis and Clark tour of the Columbia, on a cultural tour of American Indian sites, to Oregon's wine country, and more. None of the trips that I've reviewed costs more than $100 per person; many are closer to $50.

In British Columbia, Canada, **SunChaser Eco-Tours** has provided wayfarers with wilderness expedition tours for the last quarter century. You can board a 40-foot sailboat for a chance to watch whales on your journey to Khutzeymateen Park, home of the grizzly bear—one of the most attractive (if fearsome) creatures in the wild.

FOR THE BIRDS

Bird-watching is a mega-million-dollar pastime. Enthusiasts amble off into the woods or across rural fields in early mornings or during afternoon feeding times, armed only with binoculars and cameras. They'll spend hours, in utter silence, trying to add a single species to their life lists.

Tour groups have taken note of this love of feathered friends, and there are now scores of birding trips you can take. Your research will tell you which tours are best for your needs and desires. The Web site Yahoo! lists some forty-five bird-watching tours available. They extend across the U.S. mainland to Africa and Alaska, to Central America and South America, and from Europe to Australia and New Zealand. While most of the providers tend to concentrate on one or a few areas, you can spread your own wings by hooking up with some of the companies that travel the globe:

- Field Guides Birding Tours Worldwide
- Victor Emanuel Nature Tours
- Wings Birdwatching Tours
- Eagle-Eye Tours

Several ecological expeditions are offered in Hawaii, many related to the waters surrounding the islands. **Ocean Eco Tours** in Kona, on the island of Hawaii, offers surfing, diving, and kayaking trips. There are also whale-viewing sails. The company will teach you how to surf or dive if you don't know already. The Kona dive takes you to see coral reefs, lava tubes, and lush marine life. These vacations are geared to beginners. On another island, **Maui Eco Tours** offers explorers of all ages paddle and snorkel trips.

If you have always wanted to visit the majestic Angel Falls in South America, **Angel Eco Tours** is for you. The company can arrange individual, family, and group tours of many areas in the southern hemisphere. Experienced guides will take hikers to Angel Falls—highest free-falling cascade in the world—and on to rain forests and jungles verdant with unique vegetation, more than 1,200 species of birds, and 250 different types of wildlife. The firm can also arrange trips to the Orinoco River, the Andes, and bird-watching jaunts or scuba dives in the Caribbean.

Farther afield, there's **Borneo Eco Tours** in Malaysia. This company specializes in nature-based experiences—wildlife river safaris, jungle trekking, white-water rafting, exotic plant and animal tours. It also operates a twenty-room "ecolodge" in the jungle. The Sukau Rainforest Lodge is situated on stilts and is completely self-sufficient in terms of water and power, using rainwater and solar energy. Each room has an attached bathroom with a solar hot-water shower; electricity comes from solar batteries. When the company takes you on a river safari tour, it uses electric motors to reduce noise, air pollution, and stress on wildlife.

Ecotourism is a booming trend in the travel industry. I have read about ecotours in Mongolia, Japan, Samoa, Australia and New Zealand, Belize and Ecuador, and South Africa and the Seychelles, not to mention polar bear tours in the far-northern reaches of Manitoba, Canada. There are even birding tours to Israel.

GARDEN TOURS

A popular escape for seasoned travelers—and one that is, I believe, less intrusive on wilderness areas and their inhabitants—is the garden tour. These excursions head straight to green space. Garden trips are academic experiences as well as breathtaking moments in the sunshine surrounded by a sea of color. Visitors can discover new plants and new procedures, ways to improve their own bit of greenery back home. Garden tours are easy on the legs, but exciting and challenging to the senses.

Since I live in Georgia, I'll mention Callaway Gardens in the west-central part of the state. It's a 14,000-acre weed-free wonderland with horticultural displays that delight all who visit. It also has miles of woodland paths and drives. It was created by wealthy industrialist Carson J. Callaway in 1952 and has become world famous in part for its native azaleas, many rare, which are more brilliant in color than cultivated shrubs.

I have visited similar lush gardens in many states, most of which were developed by the nation's industrial giants who, after making their fortunes, looked for ways to give back to their communities. A prime example is the Missouri Botanical Garden in St. Louis. It was set up by local businessman Henry Shaw, based on the gardens from his native

England, and opened to the public in 1859. Today it's a National Historic Landmark and a center for botanical research. There's a Victorian area, international gardens, and plenty of beauty all around.

Beyond our borders, countless thousands of garden lovers set their sights on Vancouver Island in British Columbia. That is where you'll find Butchart Gardens in Brentwood Bay, near Victoria. This fifty-acre site features a rose garden, Italian garden, and Japanese garden—but its claim to fame is the Sunken Garden, developed by the Butchart family in their depleted limestone quarry. It may be the most impressive bit of green space I have ever seen.

Garden enthusiasts now have more places to prospect, with the help of several tour companies. There are many close to home and even more in Great Britain, a bit of a horticulturalist's heaven, renowned for the massive Kew Gardens near London, the annual Chelsea Flower Show, and hosts of private and public gardens up and down the country.

Coopersmith's Tours says it is North America's oldest garden travel company. It offers small-group visits (five to twenty-two passengers) to California, Britain, Europe, and New Zealand. The company stresses the upscale nature of its trips and accommodations.

FLORA Garden Tours organizes trips to homes and gardens in eastern England, through Cambridgeshire and East Anglia to the Cotswolds, not far from Oxford and Stratford-upon-Avon. It will also arrange excursions to the north (Yorkshire and Northumberland) and offers special-interest garden visits to historical places and even prehistoric sites. **Cornish Garden Tours** will whisk you to the southwestern tip of Britain, the warmest and possibly wettest part of England. The influence of the Gulf Stream creates a climate conducive to the health and well-being of subtropical plants. The company ushers groups in April, May, and June to witness displays of magnolias, camellias, azaleas, and rhododendrons. It's also the time of year when hedgerows and woodlands come alive with wildflowers, primroses, and violets bursting forth.

Way up north, there are garden jaunts in the Highlands and the upper reaches of Scotland. **Northern Scotland Garden Visits** will help you see some terrific private and public gardens; some tours throw in a magnificent castle for good measure. Another major English tour provider is **Sisley Garden Tours,** which offers garden lovers' tours to secluded spots in Britain and Northern Europe.

Gaia's Gift offers customized tours of French gardens for those who speak English. The **Global Garden Project** has custom-garden trips through Europe, Asia, and Latin America.

And perhaps the new Garden of Eden is New Zealand, blooming in splendor way out in the Pacific. I've already mentioned that Coopersmith's organizes trips there, but so do many others. **Expo Garden Tours** can get you to New Zealand, as well as Holland (brilliant in tulip season). **Pacific Pathways** offers garden and other tours to New Zealand and Australia.

There are plenty of trips for green-thumbers. Try the World Wide Web for the most complete list of garden getaways.

EAT YOUR WAY AROUND THE WORLD

We have time for one last voyage of discovery—and this one tastes great. I'm talking about cooking vacations, another rip-roaring success in the travel industry. There are cooking trips across the United States, to Mexico, and to the gastronomical capitals of the world.

Here at home, consider the **Vintage Hudson Valley Inn-to-Inn Cooking Vacations,** which includes a stop at the headquarters of the

Culinary Institute of America in Hyde Park, New York, the town in which I grew up. Out west **Jane Butel's Southwestern Cooking School** will help you master that spicy and delectable cuisine. The gracious host of the public television cooking program will be your chef and counselor. The **Cooking School of the Rockies** in Boulder, Colorado, teaches you the basics of overall good food preparation. And in northern California try the **Apple Farm** at Philco in wine country, which advertises itself as a "house party with some cooking lessons thrown in." If Cajun or Creole foods awaken your taste buds, there's the **Cajun Country** class at St. Martinsville, Louisiana, taught by a leading authority on that cuisine. And a company called **Epiculinary,** based in Lake Bluff, Illinois, bridges the gap from domestic to international fare. It can not only send you to cooking courses in the United States and Mexico but also overseas, to "make tapas in Spain, bouillabaisse in France, handmade pasta in Italy or chili rellenos in Santa Fe."

The most popular globe trots are to the places we associate with great food and cooking. So you'll find trips to Tuscany and Sicily in Italy, which boast two very different styles of food preparation. Try **Carmelita's Cook Italy** and the **Italian Cookery Course.** Meanwhile the **Rhode School of Cuisine** in southern England offers cooking classes and gourmet cooking trips to France, Morocco, and Italy. You'll stay at villas in Provence, Marrakech, and Tuscany. **E&M Travel** organizes cooking excursions across France and to several regions in Spain and Portugal.

And just to show you how popular this trend has become, you can learn the art of Creole cooking at a mountain inn overlooking the Pacific Ocean in Costa Rica. It is available through **Acadian Farm.**

Many men and women love to cook. They do so regularly. Others have lost interest. Cooking can be a chore after a day of work and child rearing. But when we reach our golden years and have more time, cooking delicious meals can be a pleasurable hobby and a delight to devour. Seasoned travelers seem just the right group to discover (or rediscover) the culinary skills and treats of cooking tours around the world.

The next time you start to think about a vacation and the idea of another cruise just doesn't float your boat, look beyond the traditional holiday. A voyage of discovery vacation might be just what you need.

SHOPPING SPREES

CHAPTER 10

If you're like me, you hate to shop, and you especially hate malls and big-box stores. I don't enjoy pawing through bins of merchandise, differentiating the faulty from the gems and then buying those gems at just the right price. I don't want to haggle with vendors, either. Despite my underdeveloped acquisitive sense, however, I have had some memorable shopping experiences, both in the United States and overseas. Call it my latent romanticism if you will, but the quaint, the classic, and the homespun—shops with "character"—beckon to me because they are as much travel experiences as they are shopping excursions. So as contradictory as it may sound, I invite you to come shopping with me across America and the globe, for something new and different.

MY FAVORITE PLACES TO SHOP IN THE NORTHEAST

- Portland, Maine. On the city's working waterfront, the cobblestone Old Port Exchange is the place to go for fine art, antiques, and boutiques.
- Freeport, Maine. Home to L.L. Bean and scores of other specialty outlet shops.
- Portsmouth, New Hampshire. A treasure trove of shops, galleries, and microbreweries downtown.
- Boston, Massachusetts. Shop Newbury Street for high-end chic boutiques; the Marketplace in Faneuil Hall for down-to-earth eateries, fresh produce on Saturday, and local memorabilia; and Copley Square for its upscale stores and heady atmosphere.
- Cape Ann (Rockport and Gloucester), Massachusetts. Artists' colony atmosphere.
- Mystic, Connecticut. Discover colonial New England at Olde Mystick Village.
- Newport, Rhode Island. All across the central city.
- Wickford, Rhode Island. The town is midway between Providence and Newport, on the western shore of Narragansett Bay, with small, quaint shops.
- New York, New York. Fifth Avenue and Madison Avenue; in Lower Manhattan check out Greenwich Village and Chelsea Market on Ninth Avenue between 15th and 16th Streets.
- Hoboken, New Jersey. There are some fine shops in the center of town. And what a view across the Hudson to Manhattan.
- Philadelphia, Pennsylvania. The main downtown district along Market, Chestnut, and Walnut Streets; Rittenhouse Square and Rittenhouse Row.
- Pittsburgh, Pennsylvania. The Golden Triangle downtown; the Strip District, at the edge of downtown; and Station Square, across the river from downtown.
- Baltimore, Maryland. The Inner Harbor is the place to see and be seen.

- Alexandria, Virginia. Spend time in Old Town.
- Colonial Williamsburg, Virginia. Browse the craft houses on Market Square.
- Old Charleston, West Virginia. Capitol Street has shops and restaurants housed in nineteenth-century buildings.
- Lexington, Kentucky. Victorian Square downtown is a full block of restored nineteenth-century buildings.
- Berea, Kentucky. The Folk Arts and Crafts Capital of Kentucky.

MY FAVORITE PLACES TO SHOP IN THE SOUTHEAST

- Nashville, Tennessee. The District, a sixteen-block area of food, clubs, and stores downtown.
- Asheville, North Carolina. The Biltmore Village at the Biltmore Estate outside of town consists of restored English-type structures with shops and eateries.
- Charleston, South Carolina. The Old City Market in central Charleston.
- Atlanta, Georgia. On the northeast side of town, Buckhead remains the city's premier retail neighborhood.
- Savannah, Georgia. Stroll the streets along the Savannah River for the best shopping.
- Miami/Miami Beach, Florida. Get to the glitz at South Beach, especially along Collins Avenue.
- Tampa, Florida. Head to Centro Ybor, the city's Latin quarter on the edge of downtown.
- Fairhope, Alabama. Wonderful shopping and restaurants right in the middle of town.
- Natchez, Mississippi. Shop downtown and along the mighty Mississippi River.
- New Orleans, Louisiana. In the Vieux Carré, visit the French Market. Heading west, shop in the Garden District and at Riverbend near the University District.

MY FAVORITE PLACES TO SHOP IN THE MIDWEST

- Branson, Missouri. Downtown Branson has several dozen shops and hundreds of flea market stalls.
- Kansas City, Missouri. The Plaza's Spanish/Moorish architecture alone is worth seeing, along with its 150 shops on the west side of town.
- St. Louis, Missouri. Union Station in the city center has been transformed from a rail center to a retail shopping center.
- Austin, Texas. SOCO—short for South Congress Avenue—near Sixth Street is a district of galleries, boutiques, and eateries, about five blocks from the Texas State Capitol.
- Dallas, Texas. Neiman-Marcus has its landmark store downtown.
- San Antonio, Texas. Spend your time along the River Walk, the Paseo del Rio.
- Cleveland, Ohio. The Arcade downtown is among the first indoor shopping centers in the nation.
- Chicago, Illinois. Magnificent Mile, the high-quality district on North Michigan Avenue.
- Frankenmuth, Michigan. In this community settled by Germans, there are several shops in the center of a town brimming with Old World atmosphere and charm.
- Milwaukee, Wisconsin. Downtown is a shopper's haven. Small stores and ethnic specialty shops share the cobblestone streets with the Shops of Grand Avenue.
- Minneapolis, Minnesota. Nicollet Mall is a twelve-block pedestrian shopping street in the center of town, connected by interior walkways for winter shopping.
- Bloomington, Minnesota. Just a short hop from Minneapolis–St. Paul International Airport sits the nation's largest retail extravaganza. The Mall of America has more than 4 million square feet of shopping, dining, gazing at sea life in the aquarium, and having fun at the seven-acre amusement park. I visit not to shop but to gaze at the size and scope of this retail monster, as well as to watch the busloads of seasoned shoppers disgorged into it.

- Deadwood, South Dakota. The ex-gold-rush boomtown that lost its luster, then reclaimed it with gambling, has several shops along the main drag.

MY FAVORITE PLACES TO SHOP IN THE WEST

- Sandpoint, Idaho. The Cedar Street Bridge Public Market used to be a bridge over Sand Creek. Now the building has been renovated to look like the Ponte Vecchio bridge shops in Florence, Italy.
- Seattle, Washington. Pike Place Market near the waterfront and Pine Street downtown.
- Port Townsend, Washington. The downtown retains its Victorian-era charm. There's an eclectic selection of shops.
- Portland, Oregon. Pioneer Place and other shops downtown. At the northern end of the downtown is a bona fide tourist attraction: Powell's City of Books is said to be the largest bookstore in the nation. It takes up an entire city block and can take you hours to get through.

- Denver, Colorado. Downtown's 16th Street Mall, Larimer Square, with buildings restored from the time of the Civil War, and Historic Lower Downtown (called LoDo by locals) offer shopping, eating, and entertainment.
- Salt Lake City, Utah. Gardner Historic Village is a conglomeration of old structures from across Utah that have been converted to stores, selling collectibles, furniture, and more. Trolley Square, a trolley barn built nearly one hundred years ago, still contains a trolley or two, stained-glass windows, and old-time light fixtures. It also has shops and restaurants.
- Albuquerque, New Mexico. Old Town Plaza in the downtown area.
- Mesilla, New Mexico. A charming town in the south of the state near Las Cruces, with a long Mexican heritage. The Plaza is a place of regular cultural events; the surrounding buildings have been rejuvenated and now house shops and businesses.
- Santa Fe, New Mexico. Shop near the Plaza and the Cathedral of St. Francis of Assisi.
- Phoenix, Arizona. Biltmore Fashion Park on the northeast side is a place of good taste and better-quality shopping. In Scottsdale the Borgata is a shopping and restaurant complex whose design came from San Gimignano in Italy. Try Fifth Avenue and Fashion Square as well.
- Sedona, Arizona. Tlaquepaque resembles an upscale Mexican town, replete with specialty stores and good restaurants. It's just south of the center of Sedona.
- Tubac, Arizona. Midway between Tucson and the Mexican border, Tubac is a small blip in the huge Sonoran Desert, but it's crammed with quaint shops and galleries.
- Los Angeles, California. Rodeo Drive in Beverly Hills or Malibu for special stores and eateries.
- Carmel, California. The downtown district is chock-full of unusual stores and galleries featuring the works of local artists.
- Monterey, California. Cannery Row is another retail gem. It's the site made famous by author John Steinbeck.
- San Francisco, California. Union Square remains the heart of the City by the Bay's downtown retailing. On the waterfront go to Fisherman's Wharf and the Anchorage. The Japan Center and

Chinatown sell a wide range of items; for nostalgia purposes, drift on over to Haight Street, with shops that sell books, art, clothing, and the offbeat recalling the 1960s.

- Ketchikan, Alaska. The Creek Street boardwalk in downtown offers specialty shops and boutiques.
- Skagway, Alaska. The famous mining town has shopping geared to the gold and the good times that followed when prospectors struck it rich.
- Honolulu, Hawaii. The Ala Moana Center near downtown. Also check out Fort Street, a pedestrian shopping area downtown, and the Cultural Plaza in Chinatown.

MY FAVORITE PLACES TO SHOP IN CANADA

- Toronto, Ontario. Downtown's Path Underground, some 5 miles of walkways from shop to shop on Yonge Street. The Distillery Historic District, where liquor was once distilled, is a new shopping, cultural, and entertainment district. Bloor-Yorkville is not only Toronto's nightspot but has some serious upscale retailers as well.
- Montreal, Quebec. Place Ville-Marie runs nearly 20 miles beneath the city center with loads of shops to browse. Rue Ste-Catherine and Rue Sherbrooke are two of the city's most fashionable shopping streets.
- Vancouver, British Columbia. The original Gastown district downtown offers souvenirs, other kinds of shops, bars, and eateries. The city's West End, with tony stores along Robson Avenue.

MY FAVORITE PLACES TO SHOP IN EUROPE

- Dublin. Pedestrian-only Grafton Street for the upscale items, Temple Bar for the post-hippie items.
- London. Oxford Street for your average goods, Bond and Regent Streets for the upper crust. Burlington Arcade for a taste of shopping in the London as head of a sprawling empire. Carnaby Street for low-end clothes, Jermyn Street for the highest-of-the-high-end haberdashery. Shopping is also a big deal in Knightsbridge and Chelsea, along Kensington High Street, and on Portobello Road in Notting Hill.

- Brussels. The Upper Town is more expensive when you search for chocolate, beer, and other items. The Lower Town is cheaper. You can also browse some fine shops near the Grand-Place and near the Bourse.
- Paris. The Rue du Faubourg Saint-Honoré is where the trendy shop, while the Champs-Elysées is the place for tourists and mass-market sales. At the Palais Royal there are loads of boutiques; you'll also find plenty of shopping and creative dining on the Left Bank, south of Notre Dame.
- Amsterdam. Most of the streets in the center city are crammed with delightful stores and places to eat. But remember: Coffee shops or coffeehouses also sell marijuana legally. If you don't want to be bothered with that, go to a cafe; these are considered non-smoking in more ways than one.
- Rome. Posh shopping takes place near the Piazza di Spagna along the Via Borgognona and Via Condotti. The famous Via Veneto is also known for its upper-end shops, cafes, and hotels. Via del Corso is less upscale.
- Prague. The Old Town is one of the main places to shop in this most beautiful European city. The other area of note is Wenceslas Square.
- Vienna. There are four neighborhoods here known for good shopping. Head to Karntnerstrasse, the Graben, Kohlmarkt, and along the Rotensturmstrasse. Remember that *Strasse* means "street" in German.
- Salzburg. The famous Getriedegasse is the quaint, often crowded market street here, near the home where Mozart was born. (*Gasse* is German for "alley.") But there are intriguing produce and other markets through the alleyways one block south, along with some lovely little shops on Residenzplatz.
- Copenhagen. There are many small districts in this capital, but the bulk of the shopping takes place at the Royal Copenhagen Center.

VOLUNTEER VACATIONS

CHAPTER 11

I have heard many people over the years talk about their dreams and their desires. Travel can be both a dream and a desire. And for a lot of folks, vacations are among the most important events in their lives. They plan them diligently. After all, they'll tell you, "I need something to look forward to." They are anticipating beautiful sandy beaches, long walks through unspoiled forests, or a calming cruise to some exotic destination. They're leaving the work or retirement routine in the dust, paying good money to relax or to be active, while enjoying themselves. The thought of paying for the privilege of traveling far from home and working for others seems foreign to many.

But for a growing number of Americans, the term *volunteer vacation* has great meaning, including boundless opportunities and endless rewards. Some say those rewards overshadow the benefits of a typical vacation. From one end of the nation to the other, volunteers of all ages are making changes in their world. They do so by building roads and bridges in national parks, by caring for sick children in orphanages, by teaching foreigners to speak English, or by helping to prevent the extinction of animal species. Many older people have done well, have been treated kindly by life, and have seen many interesting places. Now they choose to give back to others less fortunate.

Such undertakings are a booming trend, and seasoned travelers are once again leading the charge as volunteers. To be sure, there are lots of teens and twenty-somethings who join the Peace Corps or take a summer off to help others, but mature Americans often constitute the majority of volunteers. And why not? After all, we have time to give and don't have to worry about money or security. The senior set has the wherewithal to help out, and we help out often.

Still, some of the well-heeled profess surprise when they learn they are not only giving their time and energy for a good cause, but also have to pick up the tab for the honor as well. Most, if not all, working vacations require participants to pay virtually all their costs: transportation, lodging, and meals. If travel to a remote venue is required, a volunteer agency will sometimes cover that expense, but you'll still have to cough up the costs of getting to the scene of the action and staying there for your time of dedication. The reason is often simple: If the volunteer groups covered all such expenses, they might not have enough money to continue their mission.

Vacation volunteers are not only about building bridges, they are also about bridging the gap between disparate nations and cultures. Human interaction is often a potent by-product of the connection of volunteer to recipient.

A volunteer assignment is no walk in the park. It can be strenuous, challenging work. Depending on where you go and which agency you deal with, you may have to resign yourself to primitive living conditions and lackluster cuisine. If you plan on a vacation helping clear forest trails in Wisconsin, with meals prepared over a campfire, you won't expect a room at the Ritz and a four-course dinner. That's in part the reason some volunteer groups discourage the term volunteer "vacation." The fear is that folks may arrive to find the work so demanding and so difficult, they become disillusioned and disenchanted, not only with the group they're helping but with volunteering in general.

If this kind of "holiday" appeals to you, it requires a complete understanding of what's involved on each and every trip you contemplate. First, be certain you are dealing with a reputable and responsible volunteer agency. Make sure it will provide what it promises, allowing you to make the contribution you intend. If possible, talk to others who have made these journeys. You'll find that most are delighted and fulfilled by their contributions. There are books, articles, and Web sites that describe volunteer trips completely; they can help you decide which volunteer opportunities are solid undertakings and which verge on the fly-by-night. These feel-good trips can last from five days to several weeks, so you need to feel comfortable with your potential choice long before you can feel good about it.

You'll need to be certain that all will go smoothly, that you *will* make a difference, and that you'll feel glad you made the commitment. I can imagine few things more painful than a month in some remote place where nothing seems to be going right and you feel you are wasting your time, talent, and money.

THE VOLUNTEER EXPERIENCE

When you sign on for this labor of love and dedication, understand that you will be part of a small but select group of perhaps ten or twenty people who all set out to achieve something remarkable. Volunteers tell me they also accept the challenge because it allows them to meet new people and make new friends, share ideas and ideals, learn more about other cultures, and at the end of the day feel good about the work they've done.

You can expect to pay from $500 to $2,500 or more per week for your excursion, depending on where you go and what your work entails. The fee normally covers room and board; transportation costs are extra. Some groups allow adults to bring children or grandchildren along to help out, but there's a charge for the little ones as well. You need to be sure the volunteer opportunities are both appropriate for, and beneficial to, youngsters.

Volunteer trips often require participants to be "people" folks. After all, you'll not only work *for* the people you are serving, but you'll likely labor *with* a group of other volunteers, nearly all of them strangers. Your work is often performed in close quarters under less-than-ideal conditions for weeks at a time. This can test your diplomatic and humanitarian skills. The more people-oriented you are, the better things will be for everyone.

Despite these minor tribulations, the vast majority of volunteers seem to love the endeavor from start to finish. They often say they believe they get more from these trips than they give. I saw a piece on Fox News about volunteer vacationers Robert and Jane Roach, both seventy-three. They said they were avid travelers but found many trips lacking. The Oregon couple noted that when they went on package tours, the guide would show them one historic building and then move quickly to the next attraction. The Roaches often felt deprived—they came home knowing very little about the country they'd just visited or about its people. But that changed when they went on volunteer vacations. They got to know the local people and learned more about their countries and customs. For the Roaches, volunteer trips made all the difference.

Some people set aside one vacation period every year for the privilege of making a difference. One year they might teach young children in rural Africa, then help prevent animal extinction in Asia the next. A third year might be spent here at home repairing hiking paths at a national park. Such trips can be physically tiring but emotionally exhilarating, instilling in participants a new sense of energy and elation that they have completed such an important task.

There are roughly a dozen kinds of volunteer enterprises:

- Caring for abused animals
- Helping scientists with environmental research or other projects
- Teaching English or other courses to students young and old
- Engaging in archaeological digs or restoring older structures
- Helping at camps for special-needs children
- Building infrastructure in impoverished communities
- Constructing homes for the homeless
- Providing health services in rural regions
- Caring for orphaned or abandoned children
- Helping a family farm continue to operate
- Clearing trails in the wilderness
- Working on park improvements

A few volunteer holidays pay a small stipend if you are involved for a long time. Most assignments, as I've noted, cost you money. Accommodations can range from a tent in a national park or monument, to a hostel in remote regions of Africa, to a very acceptable hotel room on Nantucket Island, Massachusetts.

You'll get plenty of research information before you depart, so you'll know what to expect on your trip and what's expected of you. You'll learn about the people and the place you're visiting. When you arrive, you'll be met by a qualified escort who will take you from the airport or train station to your assignment site. Volunteer groups provide security during your stay, and you'll get on-the-job training for your occupation once you have settled in. There will be a volunteer coordinator nearby, and you'll be guaranteed medical attention should it be required. That's in part what you are paying for; the rest goes to the good cause itself: schools, hospitals, parks, communities.

You may qualify for a tax deduction for the fees and travel expenses incurred, but you'll need to discuss this subject with the volunteer group and your own tax preparer. For example, the volunteer enterprise must be registered with the Internal Revenue Service as a legitimate, tax-exempt, nonprofit organization known as a 501(c)(3) group. While there are a few exceptions, this is the general rule, so investigate your options thoroughly.

While nearly anyone can volunteer for nearly any kind of work activity, some opportunities have specific requirements and job descriptions. If you are rebuilding paths along the Appalachian Trail, you need to be a fine physical specimen. If you are planning to teach environmental science classes to students in Belize, you must understand science and ecology. If you want to help construct irrigation systems for farmers in Malawi, you might need to know something about the fundamentals of such projects. In general, the volunteer organizations will make sure you're not shocked when you arrive on site. In fact, these groups won't let you register for volunteer ventures unless they consider you compatible and qualified for the task at hand.

VOLUNTEER VACATION PROVIDERS

You can opt to do good at locations across the United States and in scores of countries overseas.

Earthwatch Institute is credited with initiating the idea three decades ago that volunteers could improve the world. It organizes some 130 trips and expeditions to forty-seven nations. Earthwatch is a leader in scientific field research and education with a goal of creating a safe and sustainable environment. It has programs in many countries, and you can learn much more about this group from its Web site: www.earth watch.org.

Long recognized as a leader in this field, **Global Ventures** promotes what it calls service learning. By its definition, volunteers travel, sign up to help others, and, in the process, learn more about where they are and the people who live there. In business for two decades, this group was created to establish partnerships between people who want to help and those in underserved areas trying to become self-sufficient. Global Ventures will send you to projects within the United States or to nations abroad. Programs extend for one, two, or three weeks. There are 150 service teams in ninety places on five continents. The overall program runs throughout the year, which is a boon to seasoned Americans, many of whom are retired and can travel on almost any of the 365 days a year. You could provide child care, tutoring, or health care. You could take part in conservation, construction, or repair work. Global Ventures says no specialized skills are required. To learn more about the opportunities and the attendant costs, contact www.globalventures.org.

Because I live in Georgia, I am especially mindful of the Georgia-based group **Habitat for Humanity** and its Global Village program. I am also aware of the care and guidance it has received from a fellow

Georgian, former president Jimmy Carter. Habitat has been building homes for needy families around the globe for years. You can join one of these construction junkets, helping either your own neighbors here at home or the homeless in other lands. Habitat takes volunteers on two-week trips and charges you up to $2,000 for the experience; still, many carpenters come running, and some are probably singing "If I Had a Hammer." Contact the group at www.habitat.org.

Another highly rated volunteer vacation group is **Cross-Cultural Solutions,** which operates more than a dozen volunteer pilgrimages to Brazil, China, Costa Rica, Ghana, Guatemala, India, Peru, Russia, Tanzania, and Thailand. It sends some 1,500 people out to change the world every year. The agency's two-week journeys can cost participants around $2,000, but that includes food, lodging, and in-country transportation. You can learn much more on the Web at www.crosscultural solutions.org.

The **Sierra Club** offers outdoorsy types volunteer wanderings from coast to coast. The National Outing Program, for example, contributes some 27,000 hours of work to state and federal land agencies, restoring wilderness areas, maintaining trails, cleaning up campsites and trash, and removing nonnative plants that have been introduced into many natural habitats but don't belong. You could also take some time to help preserve an archaeological site in Hawaii or protect wildlife at Mammoth Cave in Kentucky. Once again, you have to pay for this honor, and you also have to shell out for your lodging on site. Details from www.sierra-club.org.

Along that same trail, the **American Hiking Society** builds and preserves pathways in some of this country's most amazing and treasured woodlands. This is rough work, but somebody wants to do it. Volunteers even continue to rough it after a day's toil. Participants are asked to bring their own tent, sleeping bag, and hiking equipment. There are other charges tacked on, so read the group's Web information carefully. Go to www.americanhiking.org.

I have researched many volunteer groups, and one that's really caught my eye is **Travel with a Challenge** (www.travelwithachallenge .com), an umbrella Web site seeking seniors with helping hands and hearts. Among the offerings for mature travelers is one called "Realise New Zealand" (that's the British way of spelling *realize*). Hardy volunteers help with reforestation, wildlife surveys, plant propagation, or park maintenance. Guest workers can also spend time at the Maori cultural center to learn about the history of this indigenous New Zealand group. Further information can be yours at www.realisenz.co.nz.

Travel with a Challenge also offers projects restoring a Buddhist temple in Mongolia and carrying on archaeological programs in the Four Corners region of the southwestern United States. Having just prepared a television program on this vast and rich chunk of our national real estate, I thought some of you might enjoy this kind of trip. After all, the very first Americans lived in this part of our world, some arriving as early as 10,000 B.C. The Four Corners is a repository of some of the most significant archaeological material this country has. It is rich in history, from the earliest Anasazi, to the Puebloan people, the Basket Makers, and finally to contemporary Indian tribes—the Navajo, Hopi, Apache, Ute, Zuni, and more.

Another venture likely to warm the tender hearts of animal lovers invites volunteers to Central America. In the Mayan Mountains of Belize, workers trudge the jungled foothills to a sixty-acre private reserve that rescues and rehabilitates endangered wildcats. The vacationers learn about Central American jaguars, pumas, ocelots, margays, and jaguarundis even as they work to help them survive. The **LiFeline Center** was created to conserve cat species and save their natural habitat, while studying the felines' behavior. Many of the animals have been abused by humans and need nurturing before they can be released into the wild. A week of work there will cost volunteers about $1,000, which includes lodging, meals, and training. This group states that volunteers aged forty to sixty-five will find such an endeavor particularly worthwhile. Information is available at www.li-feline.com.

If you have plenty of time to spare, **i-to-i Ventures** may be just your cup of tea. Projects with this coordinating agency can last from four to twenty-four weeks in two dozen countries worldwide. You can choose to teach English or work in conservation, health, media, construction, or related endeavors. For further information, try www.i-to-i.com.

If you have an even grander goal in mind, consider **Volunteers for Peace,** which sends out vacationers on projects to foster international education and friendship. Go to the World Wide Web to learn how you might work for world peace. The address is www.vfp.org.

Another senior-friendly opportunity is with **Orangutan Foundation International,** the only organization trying to preserve these wonderful creatures in their dwindling natural habitat. Orangutans live on just two islands, Borneo and Sumatra, the latter of which was affected by the 2004 earthquake and tsunami. This group sends volunteers to the front lines in the fight to save the species. British conservation tour operator Discovery Initiatives manages the program and notes that 60 percent of those who volunteer are mature travelers. For information: www.orangutan.org.

The **Archeological Institute of America** has an online directory of fieldwork opportunities across the world. There are more than 200 study sites on the list, and each entry describes the archaeological work involved, age and skill requirements, accommodations offered, and fees charged. If you dig this kind of vacation and would like to dig for a worthwhile purpose, go online at www.archeological.org.

Dealing with more contemporary problems is the goal of **Amizade, Ltd.,** which fosters community service in urban and rural regions alike. Volunteers cater to human needs and work to improve the local environment. Amizade promotes cross-cultural exchanges by arranging a schedule of work and recreation at several spots worldwide. The group says half of the helpers are seasoned travelers. Check this one out by going to www.amizade.org.

The **Orphanage Outreach Project** is a Christian-based organization that takes an interdenominational approach to the issue of parentless children. The group supports orphanages in the Dominican Republic and sends volunteers to provide educational opportunities to the children, while others build and maintain facilities. Orphanage officials say about one of every three volunteers is an older American. To discover more about the Outreach effort, go online to www.orphanage-outreach.org.

For citizens of the world, an agency called **Global Citizens Network** works with people committed to sharing values of peace, justice, tolerance, cross-cultural understanding, and global cooperation. Sounds almost superhuman in its scope. The seven- to twenty-one-day trips allow up to a dozen volunteers to work with villagers on projects that benefit local communities. About half the volunteers in any given year are older Americans. To learn more, log on to the agency's Web site at www.globalcitizens.org.

The **Oceanic Society** is a nonprofit group that sponsors Oceanic Society Expeditions, aimed at protecting marine life and the marine environment through research and ecological education programs. As a volunteer you might be called on to band wild birds or measure sea turtles.

Three of every five volunteers are seasoned travelers. And we could certainly use more efforts to protect the marine environment. This was made abundantly clear to me on a recent visit to the Florida Gulf Coast. There I learned of efforts by developers in Destin to take over a bird sanctuary along the harbor and convert the sand dunes to condominiums. For further information, visit www.oceanic-society.org.

American groups are not alone in providing volunteer opportunities. The **Land Conservancy of British Columbia** is a charitable trust with a mission to protect significant environments as well as properties with historical, cultural, scenic, or recreational value. TLC works in Canada's westernmost province and offers prospective volunteers weeklong conservation holidays at one of eight properties in British Columbia, ranging from small islands to large ranches or forests. The cost is moderate and includes accommodations (tents or cabins), meals and snacks, and a day off in the middle of your vacation so you can reward yourself with a little sightseeing. Visit TLC at www.conservancy.bc.ca.

There are other volunteer groups based beyond North America. **Archeology Abroad,** for example, is based in London and seeks volunteers for some 1,000 historical sites across the globe. For detailed information, drop by www.britarch.ac.uk.

Also in England is the **National Trust Working Holidays,** part of the country's National Trust. The agency cares for 1,250 species of wildlife, more than any other animal charity in Europe. The Trust also controls the important lands and buildings of Britain, making it the nation's largest private landowner. It has a monumental task, and it performs it magnificently. The Trust organizes 450 working holidays in England, Wales, and Northern Ireland each year. It welcomes overseas volunteers, like us Yanks, between the ages of eighteen and seventy. For older workers, the Trust suggests you consider the Oak, Oak-Plus, or Archeological Holidays, which are less rigorous physically. If you are an active baby boomer, however, go for the gusto and work yourself silly. These trips are inexpensive, include food and hostel accommodations for volunteers, and are well worth your consideration. For more information, go to www.nationaltrust.org.uk/volunteers.

You get the idea. There are plenty of places worthy of your good efforts. New ones emerge on a regular basis. Aside from accessing the World Wide Web, you can read up on these endeavors by going to bookstores or

RSVP

Lest I forget, allow me to take time to recognize the fine work of a ground-breaking program in which older folks can give back to their communities and their country. The Senior Corps operates the very successful **Retired and Senior Volunteer Program,** known more commonly as RSVP. In case you don't know about RSVP, it offers a nationwide network of programs that provide mature Americans a chance to apply their life experiences to meeting the needs of many communities. RSVPers mentor young people, organize Neighborhood Watch programs, test drinking water for pollutants, help provide social services, teach English to immigrants, and much more. Nearly half a million folks fifty-five and over donate four hours per week on average to help some 65,000 local organizations. While volunteers are not compensated for the actual work, some sponsoring agencies may reimburse volunteers for costs incurred. Local agencies offer training, and RSVP provides insurance coverage. This is just one of the programs under the Senior Corps umbrella. It also coordinates the Foster Grandparent and Senior Companion programs. Some two million Americans help other Americans each year in these three programs. For more information, contact www.seniorcorps.org.

your local library to search for the most appropriate way to spend your next vacation doing good.

Just think about it. Rather than returning to the Alps for another ski vacation, you could be teaching English in Paris, studying Buddhism in Tibet while helping to restore a temple there, living and working with families engaged in organic farming, helping residents of Guatemala get access to clean water, saving elephants from lawless hunters in Africa, and so much more. The ski trip might pale in comparison.

If you believe you should see and help America first, there's a multitude of opportunities to roll up your sleeves and get to work. Selfless volunteers are working wonders, improving conditions on Indian reservations in the western United States, minding children in large cities whose parents have to work but who can't afford day-care services, and rehabilitating several National Park Service sites as that agency copes with federal budget shortfalls. For others, there are abundant experiences outside our boundaries. Some are trying to protect the pink river dolphins in Peru from being wiped out by fishermen. Others are lending a hand to scientists trying to preserve the coral reefs in Fiji, harmed by agricultural runoff and galloping development. Still others travel to Uganda to work with the Jane Goodall Institute, maintaining the health and safety of chimpanzees. Some will jet off to Hong Kong to conserve the wetlands and waterfowl of eastern China, and still more will travel to Costa Rica, working to maintain and restore the lush primeval cloud forests.

These volunteers will give of themselves for a week or two, perhaps a month or more, paying for the chance to work. They often work with people who are just half their age but have the same goals in mind: to make things right with the world. Some older folks relish the chance to work with younger volunteers, exchanging ideas and life stories, while others prefer co-workers of roughly the same age. The simple fact is this: There are thousands of projects that help countless people, and they cannot be done without volunteers. More and more retired people, and boomers as well, have been infected by the volunteer bug. It gets them involved helping other people. It is a match made in heaven.

TRAVEL JOURNAL: WHERE TO GO AND WHAT TO SEE

CHAPTER 12

It's time to travel, whether in an RV, an SUV, or a CRV. Millions of mature Americans like to spend quality time seeing as much of the United States as possible. They drive their cars, trucks, or tanks from state to state and to our neighbor nations, north and south. At other times, seasoned travelers want to cross borders or cross oceans to learn about other countries and other cultures.

If you are an experienced explorer, you may think you've seen and done it all. Indeed, some folks find themselves in an occasional tourist rut, traveling to the traditional destinations over and over. Here at home, there's Florida, California, the Grand Canyon, and New York City. Some drive into Canada or fly to a Mexican resort village. Or they'll go to England, France, and Italy in Europe. I have begun encountering more and more mature Americans who are venturing beyond this traditional travel envelope, however, either on their own or with tour groups. Some of these seasoned travelers don't miss a thing, but others may overlook beautiful or important places. They are either pressed for time or they don't know enough about the destinations they are visiting.

An informed traveler is a satisfied traveler. So, in this chapter, let me tell you about some of my favorite places across this grand country of ours. As a bonus, I'll give you my Top Ten places beyond the boundaries of the United States. To see more, you need to know more. I'll tell you about some wonderful places in each and every state and also how to get additional information about each of the states.

ALABAMA

There is more to Alabama than moonshine and the Crimson Tide. It's an easy state to get around in, too, although the poor quality of its roads may make you scream.

If you are in northeast Alabama, drop by **Anniston,** a pleasant town with an interesting Museum of Natural History and the Berman Museum of World History. It has a lovely, tree-lined main street that feels warm and welcoming. Because I live near Anniston, I like it for one very special feature: the local dairy on the outskirts, where my wife and I get fresh butter and cheese, not to mention milk and ice cream made right on the premises.

Farther north look for **Fort Payne** and one of the neatest natural wonders in this state. Little River Canyon National Preserve is 14,000 acres of woodland splendor, offering a wide variety of outdoorsy activities. My family likes to swim in the cool waters of the rushing Little River on a hot summer day. And there's a terrific loop road through the canyon. Drive slowly, stop often, take lots of pictures.

Birmingham is the largest city in the state, and its Museum of Art is very impressive for a city its size. Spend some time in the Wedgwood exhibit. Best of all, there's no admission charge. Drive through town to

---

SPECIAL SPOT IN ALABAMA

Jasmine Hill, north of Montgomery. The gardens and outdoor museum are called "Alabama's Little Corner of Greece" because the site features acres of classical sculpture recalling Greek gods and Olympic heroes. There's a full-scale replica of the Temple of Hera in Olympia, Greece, birthplace of the Olympic Flame.

get to the statue of Vulcan (the Roman god of fire), one of the world's largest iron figures and a tribute to Birmingham's past as an iron city, the "Pittsburgh of the South."

In the south of the state, Bon Secour National Seashore and Wildlife Refuge is near the town of **Gulf Shores.** The beach is quiet, and there are no high-rise condominiums packed together at the water's edge. I have spent time on this sandy stretch when there were only about a dozen people sharing the beach.

On Mobile Bay's eastern shore, **Fairhope** is one of my favorite towns—attractive and well run. Fairhope was founded on utopian ideals and employed a single tax system, which remains in effect today. Residents lease their land, and that money goes to the single tax colony, which pays for services. Civic pride runs rampant throughout the town, which boasts a lovely downtown full of shops and restaurants and a wonderful marina on the bay. Fairhope has attracted artists, writers, and retirees. Authors Winston Groom and Fannie Flagg live here.

Mobile is a great old port city whose claim to fame has to do with partying. It held the first Mardi Gras celebration in this country in 1703, predating New Orleans. The party in Mobile is more family-friendly than events in the Big Easy. Mobile retains the charms of its past, brought by settlers from France and Great Britain. It's a town of quaint squares downtown and some marvelous old homes.

Tuscumbia, in the northwestern portion of Alabama, is where Helen Keller was born and bred. It's also the town where the Muscle Shoals rock-and-roll sound was born and is the home of the Alabama Music Hall of Fame.

For more information: www.touralabama.org or (800) ALABAMA.

ALASKA

It's so big, brawny, blustery, and breathtaking that one trip does not do justice to the Last Frontier. But here's a start at what to see. **Anchorage** is a pleasant place to begin, and—given the importance of the Inuit cultures—you should take in the Alaska Native Heritage Center. It profiles the five regional Native groups that live in this largest of the United States.

To the north is a place most visitors try to tread, **Denali National Park and Preserve,** home of the 20,320-foot Mount McKinley, tallest peak in North America. Natives call the mountain Denali; the National Park Service uses both names. This is a paradise of forests, valleys, scenic views from the hilltops, and glaciers, not to mention nearly 170 species of birds and some 40 mammals. It's one of the few places Americans can see grizzly bears in person, if not necessarily up close.

Glacier Bay National Park and Preserve is said by many to be one of Alaska's most scenic spots. That's like saying there are a few people living in New York City. This three-million-plus-acre park in the southeastern edge of Alaska is home to fantastic glaciers that flow from the snowcapped mountain summits.

Juneau, the state capital, sits on the edge of Glacier Bay Park and is an island unto itself. The capital is accessible by air or by sea. There are no roads from the rest of the state. In this land of glaciers, Juneau boasts a Glacier Gardens Rainforest Adventure, which takes visitors to a lush forest at Thunder Mountain. The famous Mendenhall Glacier is here, too, part of the Tongass National Forest. This blue baby is a dozen miles long and a mile and a half wide.

Ketchikan is the state's southernmost point and is situated on stilts in the Tongass National Forest. If you like rain, this is your place. With up to 160 inches of moisture each year, Ketchikan may be the wettest town in North America.

Nome is so far from anything else, it beckons the experienced traveler. It's way out west near the end of the Seward Peninsula. Nome has two things going for it. It's the end of the famous Iditarod dog race at one end of the year and the Midnight Sun Festival commemorating the summer solstice at the other. The festival goes on for days (because there are no nights) and includes the Nome River Raft Race. By the way, the Iditarod is more than just a bunch of mushers in the dead of winter. It recalls a diphtheria epidemic in 1925. The necessary medical supplies were delivered by heroic dog teams; the tradition continues to this day.

> **SPECIAL SPOT IN ALASKA**
>
> Gates of the Arctic National Park and Preserve, way up north almost in Barrow. I've never been, but I'm told this monster park (eight and a half million acres) is so rugged and so austere, few people go. If you ever get there, and I certainly hope I do, you'll have a park four times bigger than Yellowstone just about to yourself and the caribou.

Along the southeast part of the forty-ninth state, **Sitka** is considered by many its most beautiful town. It is surrounded by large mountains, a series of islands, Sitka National Park, and the Alaska Raptor Center.

Skagway may be the most fun place in the big state. In 1897 crowds of prospectors poured into the region, seeking their fortune in Klondike gold. Many struck it rich, and many others did not; the rush didn't last long, and many miners moved on. The town has retained some of its late-nineteenth-century look. There's a great train ride through White Pass to the edge of Canada.

For more information: www.travelalaska.com or (907) 929–2200.

ARIZONA

Arizona is one of about a dozen states I've lived in, and it's hot but, of course, it's a dry heat. (When people from Chicago say that, I want to scream because a hundred degrees is blistering, dry or damp.) This state is also more diverse than many visitors realize, with dry deserts and rugged pine-forested mountains, huge lakes and rugged rock formations.

Benson, southeast of Tucson, is home to the state's newest park and one of the world's few so-called wet living caves open to the public. Kartchner Caverns State Park is a seven-acre cave system first discovered

SPECIAL SPOT IN ARIZONA

Mile High Ranch in Ramsey Canyon, south of Sierra Vista in the southeastern corner of the state. This is a "weigh station" for hummingbirds as they travel from north to south and back again. Plan to spend part of a day watching these clever creatures—and if you're a true bird fancier, look into renting a cabin in the canyon so you can really commune with the hummers.

in 1974. One column within the cave is 54 feet tall. I couldn't wait for this park to open; it's very popular. People have discovered it on their journey along Interstate 10.

Bisbee nearly died, but the locals are trying to keep it alive. In the far southeastern corner of the state, Bisbee is the copper version of Skagway, Alaska. It's a mining town that around 1900 became prosperous enough to rival San Francisco for sin and culture. When the mine closed, Bisbee had virtually no reason to live; still, residents worked to preserve it. Critics of the effort called Bisbee "the town too dumb to die," a takeoff on Tombstone up the road a piece. Today the downtown district called Old Bisbee is replete with small shops, and tours of the Copper Queen mine are offered.

In extreme northeastern Arizona, **Canyon de Chelly National Monument** is a national treasure. On the Navajo Reservation, its red sandstone walls can rise 1,000 feet, and magnificent cave dwellings are located along the 26 miles of the canyon. You must see the White House. To get there, you have to hike 1.5 miles down into the canyon, then get yourself back up to the parking lot. The White House Trail is the only one open to the public. Navajo guides can take you into the depths of the canyon. The place gets crowded in the summer so go visit in February, when almost nobody's around except the Indians who live down in the canyon itself.

Chiricahua National Monument near the Arizona–New Mexico border is the former homeland of one of the most famous of the Apache tribes. Cochise was based here and led his followers in staunch resistance to white settlers. The rocky area provided plenty of places for the Indians to hide and harass the interlopers.

At the very southernmost part of the state is **Coronado National Memorial,** significant because it's the place Francisco Vásquez de Coronado first entered what is now the United States as he led his forces in search of gold from the Seven Cities of Cibola. It's a very quiet park nowadays, not overrun with travelers.

Grand Canyon National Park inspires me every time I go—and I have been there more than half a dozen times. Try to visit in late autumn or in winter when the snow flies. A nice change of pace is the North Rim, which is generally less packed in the summer, although it's a long way around if you're driving up from Flagstaff. And in any season, be sure to be on the rim when the sun is rising or setting.

Monument Valley is surreal and so beautiful, but it's hard to reach. Way up in the far northeastern part of Arizona (it extends into Utah), it's chock-full of red sandstone monsters, some reaching 1,000 feet into the clear desert sky. Some folks say it's a mystical or religious place. Others call it a terrific bunch of rocks to climb. Most people just stare at the odd shapes and take lots of pictures.

Along Interstate 40 in northern Arizona, **Petrified Forest National Park** is a 93,000-acre showplace for magnificent petrified logs. Five sections of the park have large selections of this stonelike wood.

Phoenix gets bigger every time I visit. It looks more like Los Angeles and its population is soaring, but there are three places well worth your time. The Heard Museum downtown has assembled one of the most impressive collections of Indian art and culture anywhere. You could spend a day there. The Desert Botanical Garden is a great place to become acclimated to the flora and fauna of this dry, dusty region. And the Phoenix Zoo is quite a good one, with special sections on southwestern and African animals.

Phoenix and neighboring Scottsdale are home to some fabulous hotels and resorts. But one of my favorites is the Arizona Biltmore Resort and Spa, conceived by Frank Lloyd Wright and the only Wright hotel still standing. It's a magical place, and if you visit in the low summer season, room rates are on sale. Nearby is the upscale Biltmore Fashion Park shopping center. **Scottsdale** itself is an upscale Phoenix suburb, with some fine shops and art galleries, and some marvelous hotels, resorts, and spas. It has become a classy destination for the jet set, looking to relax.

The Red Rocks of **Sedona** in north-central Arizona are magnificent. My only complaint: Sedona's been "discovered," and the hotels and housing developments are springing up fast and furious. Get there before the view of the rocks is spoiled forever.

Down south, **Tombstone** is "the town too tough to die," a former lawless mining town, and the place where Wyatt Earp kept the peace. The O.K. Corral, site of the infamous shoot-out between the Earps and the

Clantons, is a popular attraction, as is Boothill Graveyard on the outskirts. The rest of the town is a tourist trap, but people from North Dakota seem to love it.

Tucson is a lovely city, with strong Mexican influence, but it, too, is growing feverishly. You'll love the fact it's virtually surrounded by mountains and home to the Old Tucson Movie Set and the Arizona–Sonora Desert Museum, both west of town. Saguaro National Monument (east and west of the city) preserves the stately saguaro cactus found only in this region. And the University of Arizona is an important part of the community. South of Tucson, visit the artists' community of **Tubac;** below that is the **Tumacacori National Historic Park,** a preserved mission built by the Jesuit priest Eusebio Francisco Kino in 1691 to convert and serve the Pima Indian community.

Williams is in northwestern Arizona and is the gateway to the Grand Canyon. Smart people who don't want to drive to the canyon and fight for a parking space will park in Williams and take the Grand Canyon Railway to the park.

And when you pass through **Yuma** on the way to California, stop for a look at the old Arizona Territorial Prison. It's a hellhole on earth—a place prisoners wouldn't want to be sent twice.

For more information: www.arizonaguide.com or (866) 298–3795.

ARKANSAS

The Natural State is relatively small, but it has a few big things. In the northwestern corner **Eureka Springs** has been drawing in tourists who take the waters, allegedly containing medicinal powers. Native Americans began the practice, and Caucasian Americans picked up on a good thing around 1850. The springs are not the thing nowadays, but there are country music shows that attract the faithful. Each January, too, the annual eagle-watch is a magnet for thousands of birders. The town, also called the "Little Switzerland of America," is home to the Great Passion Play.

Helena is a neat little river town with a unique feature and some famous natives. It's on the Mississippi River, so it's Arkansas's only link to the sea. The town has some lovely old homes to visit and is the hometown of lyric soprano Frances Greer, country singer Conway Twitty, and blues singer Sonny Boy Williamson. Every October, Helena celebrates its musical heritage at the annual King Biscuit Blues Festival.

Bill Clinton fans will want stop at **Hope** in the southwest. His boyhood home is in the town.

The best thing about Arkansas for my money is **Hot Springs National Park** in the western part of the state, reflecting the "American Spa" glory days. Portions of it are surrounded by a good-size city. The waters here

are magnificent: rainwater absorbed into nearby mountains then taken 5,000 feet below ground, where the earth's heat increases the water temperature to 143 degrees. It emerges as Hot Springs. The tour guides say the process takes 4,000 years to complete—mind-boggling but worth your attention. You can take the waters here, and prescription baths are permitted but only with a doctor's order. Hot Springs is also a charming town. Be sure to stop and see it.

Little Rock is the state capital and not overly distinguished. But it is called the City of Roses because of the large number of fragrant flowers in gardens and yards across the city. The locals made big plans, and a big deal, about the new Bill Clinton Presidential Library, which opened in November 2004.

Mountain View, in the Ozarks, has a lively cultural heritage. The annual Arkansas Folk Festival sets up here each April, as does the Southern Regional Mountain and Hammer Dulcimer Workshop and Contest. The Old Time Fiddlers State Championship Competition heats up each September, while the Fall Harvest Festival is held in mid-October. The Ozark Folk Center is also in the town.

Murfreesboro is the state's former diamond center at Crater of Diamonds State Park. You can look for the gems yourself but are unlikely to find any. Hundreds of prospectors came before you. They found the first diamond in 1906; more than 70,000 have been excavated since then.

For more information: www.arkansas.com or (800) NATURAL.

CALIFORNIA

I could write a book about the Golden State . . . but many others already have. Millions of folks live in California, and millions more visit each year. I'm more partial to the state's northern reaches, but I'll start where most California dreamers dare to tread, SoCal.

Death Valley is hot and low—the lowest place on the face of the lower forty-eight states. When it does rain here, however—as it did in early 2005—Death Valley comes alive with desert vegetation blooming madly until the weather warms. When it's cool, this is a remarkable place to visit and to hike.

Los Angeles is big, spread out, traffic laden, and exciting. I'm partial to Santa Monica, which has the ocean and the hills and seems less spoiled than the rest of the big city.

San Diego and **La Jolla** are towns almost too good to imagine. The bigger city is blessed with balmy weather, beautiful beaches, and appealing neighborhoods (at exorbitant prices). La Jolla is a fabulous enclave of beachy splendor and a first-class university. The first time I visited the pair, I took an instant dislike. But so many others told me how much they loved these towns that I went back, and back, and back. I finally got it. These cities are magnificent and absolutely magnetic.

When you get to the coastal area from **Carmel** to **Monterey,** some folks say you've died and gone to heaven. I find this area very special, especially driving along the coast. The weather is idyllic. It's not hard to understand why people are so charmed to call the region home.

SPECIAL SPOT IN CALIFORNIA

I'm a fan of the town of Solvang, in the Santa Inez Mountains above Santa Barbara. What could be a tacky re-creation of Old World Europe is done more tastefully than some other American clones of European villages. It's still a tourist trap, though, so try to savor Solvang in an off-season.

Lake Tahoe is huge and hugely attractive. It's clear and blue and enticing, stretching 22 miles along the border with Nevada. And it is deep, the third-deepest lake in the United States, with a maximum depth of 1,645 feet below the surface. It's so deep that it could cover the whole state of California in a foot of water. But when you consider that the lake water is nearly 100 percent pure, some people might not mind a bit!

San Francisco is, of course, San Francisco. People keep going there and falling in love with it. Many of us like the idea of leaving our hearts there. I can never get enough of Fisherman's Wharf, Chinatown, Haight-Ashbury, or San Francisco Bay. I even like the idea of trekking up those hills, just to go down the other side. It's also, in my opinion, one of the best restaurant cities in America.

San Luis Obispo is an attractive city with an enchanting mission by the same name. **San Simeon** appeals to the journalist in me, or at least the Hearst Castle does. It just goes to show what yellow journalism can buy: in this case a 165-room palace with three guest houses and 127 acres of prime estate land, once enjoyed by newspaper magnate William Randolph Hearst.

Yosemite National Park is certainly one of the most impressive places in the U.S. park system. Its valley is awe inspiring, its waterfalls impressive, and its scenery truly breathtaking. I'm contemplating going back; I don't think a single visit can do Yosemite justice.

For more information: www.visitcalifornia.com or (800) 462–2543.

COLORADO

Rocky Mountain high is still a thrill in this square state with so much to offer. Eastern plains end abruptly, bumping up against the majestic Rocky Mountains, headquarters for some of the finest snow skiing this nation has.

Aspen is one of those ski resort towns that have become exquisitely famous. A failed silver mining town, its celebration of winter, called Winterskol, is one big toast in mid-January. And Maroon Bells is perhaps one of the the most photographed mountainscapes in the nation.

Central City is the site of Colorado's first gold discovery, ten years after the Sutter strike in California. People flooded into Gregory Gulch— named for John Gregory, who found the mother lode. A town grew up on the steep gulch, and it became known as "the richest square mile on earth." More than $67 million in gold was extracted. The true mining bonanza, however, was **Cripple Creek.** This ranching village was changed forever when gold was found in early 1891. Within months the town became known as "the $300 million cow pasture." Its yield far surpassed that of Central City.

Colorado Springs is blessed with multiple natural wonders, from Pikes Peak to a Garden of the Gods (where the Great Plains meet the Rockies), to a Cave of the Winds (and twenty lighted chambers to visit, at a chilly fifty-four degrees). The Springs is also home to the U.S. Air Force Academy, with a spectacular setting and a campus that is some-times closed to the public. This is one of my favorite places in the state.

Denver, the state capital, is a city that has arrived, although it has become a victim of its own success, with mega traffic and polluted air. It boasts some compelling museums (the Museum of Nature and Science, the Colorado History Museum, and the Denver Art Museum). Its zoo and Ocean Journey are first-rate. But my favorite place in town is the Hammond Candies factory on the north side of town. Tours are offered each day to the site where old-fashioned chocolates and other confec-tions are made.

Durango, in the south, is home to a narrow-gauge railroad that takes passengers through the mountains in San Juan National Forest on its way to Silverton. The nine-hour ride is normally packed with tourists in the summer. Consider a visit in May, early June, or October when all the families are either back at work or back in school.

I've always been partial to dunes along the seashore, so the sight of the **Great Sand Dunes National Monument and Preserve** in the middle of prairie land is even more arresting. The sand is so heavy here, it cannot be blown away by the winds, so it has settled over the past fifteen millennia into a 30-square-mile area of shifting sands.

Mineral Springs is famous for its hot spring pool—and this is not your average pool. At two blocks in length, it's one of the world's largest outdoor thermal pools. The water temperature remains at 90 degrees, with a nearby therapy pool containing water of 104 degrees. Think about relaxing in that on a chilly winter day.

> **SPECIAL SPOT IN COLORADO**
>
> Dinosaur National Monument, in the extreme northwestern corner of the state, stretches into Utah. It's said to be one of the world's largest concentrations of fossilized dinosaur bones from the famous Jurassic period.

Leadville is said to have one of the most colorful histories in the nation; it also claims to be the highest incorporated city in the United States, sitting 10,000 feet above sea level. And it has a rich, if tawdry, past as a gold-mining community from 1860 onward. The National Mining Hall of Fame is downtown while Colorado's highest peak, Mount Elbert, sits just south of town in its 14,433 feet of majesty.

Mesa Verde National Park, in southwestern Colorado, is a major archaeological preserve with nearly 5,000 sites, including 600 cliff dwellings. Mesa Verde ("green table" in Spanish) is a large forest on the top of the flat rock. There is also abundant wildlife here. My friends call it the most awesome of the ancient cliff sites in the Four Corners region.

Rocky Mountain National Park is all about Being Big. It encompasses nearly 266,000 acres, but what's most impressive is that within the park there are seventy-eight peaks 12,000 feet high or taller. And there are incredibly sheer drop-offs, some of them falling 3,000 feet down to rocky gorges.

Vail is a Bavarian-style town that has become a key ski center in winter and another of those fun-loving places all year. The Colorado Ski Museum and Hall of Fame are here.

Along with Aspen and Vail, there are many other ski towns across Colorado. Residents of Utah would disagree, but many folks swear the

Colorado mountains provide the best skiing and snowboarding in America.

For more information: www.colorado.com or (800) 265–6723.

CONNECTICUT

The Nutmeg State proves the old adage that good things come in small packages. The third-smallest state offers some postcard images in its northwestern hill towns and quaint communities along its stretch of sea—actually the Long Island Sound. Its Quiet Corner in the northeast takes visitors back to another time in New England.

East Haddam offers Gillette Castle State Park on the edge of the Connecticut River. This twenty-four-room mansion is the former home of actor and playwright William Gillette, best known for his performances as Sherlock Holmes. Gillette adapted designs from German castles for his own Connecticut country home. I enjoyed visiting this place when I lived in New England.

West of Hartford, **Farmington** is a kind of time capsule, an elegant, upscale community of wealth and culture that hasn't changed much in a couple of hundred years or so. There are several aristocratic homes to see and visit. One of them is now the Hill-Stead Museum, set on 152 acres. Look for impressionist paintings on the inside and a lovely sunken garden outside.

The state capital, **Hartford,** doesn't have a great deal to offer travelers, but you'll probably enjoy the homes of two notable neighbors in a swank part of town called Nook Farm. Mark Twain's nineteen-room Victorian house was the author's home for seventeen years. Now a museum, it contains 50,000 items from Samuel Clemens and his family. Nearby is the restored home of Harriet Beecher Stowe, where the author of *Uncle Tom's Cabin* lived for twenty-three years. Make a day of them.

Ledyard, at the southeastern edge of the state, personifies two extremes of American Indian culture. The Mashantucket Pequot Museum explores the history of the Pequot tribe and neighboring Indian settlements. The Foxwoods Resort Casino shows the contemporary tribal reality, with 6,500 slot machines waiting for some coins to drop.

At the other end of the state and far more to my liking is **Litchfield** in the northwest. The town is nearly 300 years old and still shines, with many fine colonial homes, including the residence where Harriet Beecher

Stowe was born. Litchfield typifies what I love so much about New England villages. There's a real sense of place, of history, of beauty, of contentment. You'll want to drive through all of this part of the state—there are many other towns just like Litchfield.

Mystic is about the sea and about creativity. Once a thriving artists' colony, it is known today as home of Mystic Seaport, seventeen acres of period homes, shops, and other structures that explain life in a seaport of another era, the mid-nineteenth century. The Mystic Aquarium with its 3,500 sea creatures is also worth a visit.

SPECIAL SPOT IN CONNECTICUT

Stonington is a quaint coastal town, the last protected harbor on Long Island Sound. Once controlled by the Pequot Indians, the area was taken over by English settlers. Massachusetts and Connecticut both claimed it, and Stonington was attacked by the British not once, but twice, during the Revolution and the War of 1812. Its days as a sealing and whaling center are long gone, but its charm remains in abundance. Drop by and look for a place to enjoy seafood.

Old Saybrook is a lovely little community on the Long Island Sound, one of many havens for retired people. The town's roots go back to Dutch and English settlers. Many people have told me that the one thing visitors should not miss is the Clam Hash at a restaurant called Pat's. Next time I'm in Connecticut, I'll be there.

For more information: www.ctbound.org or (800) 282–6863.

DELAWARE

We move now from the third-smallest state to the second tiniest. Still, I have spent many wonderful days in the First State. **Delaware City** is at the northern tip of this slender state, on the Delaware River. Just offshore on Pea Patch Island is the impressive Fort Delaware State Park. You can get to the 280-acre park only by ferry, and once you arrive, you are greeted by a circa-1859 fort, nature trails, and observation areas to view avian wildlife.

In the middle of Delaware, you'll find its small state capital, **Dover.** Its Old Historic District centers on Dover's Green, with some older churches and Wesley College in the vicinity. On this green in 1787, officials from Delaware became the first of the original thirteen states to ratify the U.S. Constitution. This is also the hometown of an astronomer named Annie Jump Cannon, who developed a type of telescopic photography that allowed her to define some 400,000 stars while she worked at the Harvard University Observatory. Contemporary Dover focuses on stars of a different type: The city's population nearly triples when the big NASCAR race takes place each year at Dover International Speedway, attracting some 100,000 race enthusiasts.

Lewes (pronounced *Lewis*) was founded in 1631 by Dutch settlers. Its strategic location at the mouth of the Delaware River led to Lewes's becoming a center of the whaling industry. Today it is the home of the Marine College of the University of Delaware; it's also the spot where you catch ferries to the town of Cape May, New Jersey. Take a stroll down the town's Fisherman's Wharf.

Odessa is a quaint community in north-central Delaware. The town was named for the Russian grain port, after farmers began bringing their grain to Odessa for shipping. There's a section of town commemorating well-preserved homes and other buildings from the eighteenth and nineteenth centuries. Stop the car and take a walk along its shady streets.

SPECIAL SPOT IN DELAWARE

New Castle. I love this town on the Delaware River. William Penn actually arrived here first and set up a Quaker colony. It has been run by Holland, Sweden, Great Britain, and the United States. Once a trading center, the town's business district was destroyed by fire in 1824. Still, some of its classical homes remain, and the town has the look and feel of New England. Come for a stroll; visit the green and some of the older homes, on view to the public; walk near the river and enjoy colonial and Federal architecture that still looks magnificent today.

Rehoboth Beach is my favorite beach town in the First State. It's popular with the Washington, DC, crowd because it's the closest ocean town for the bureaucrats in the nation's capital. Folks desert the humid swampland of DC and head to the breezy, beachy town of Rehoboth, even though it can get quite crowded in summer. That's odd because *Rehoboth* is a biblical word meaning "room enough." Bethany Beach and Fenwick are also excellent places to enjoy sand, surf, and sun.

Wilmington could be just another small, undistinguished city—except for one treasure. Settled by the Quakers, in the early 1800s it attracted a man by the name of du Pont, along with his family. They became one of the leading gunpowder producers in the new nation. The town became wealthy and cultured. Later du Pont switched from explosives to chemical manufacture, and it remains a vital part of this northern Delaware city. But the family left behind two exquisite heirlooms. First is the Winterthur estate, 6 miles from downtown. This English country estate of Henry Francis du Pont may hold one of the finest collections of American decorative art. The nearly 1,000-acre estate also has some amazing gardens. And even better gardens are farther out of town, actually across the state line in Pennsylvania. Longwood Gardens was a summer hideway for Pierre du Pont and has some of the most incredible grounds of any garden in the Northeast. When the weather cools, take the children or grandchildren to Longwood for the expansive display of Christmas lights. It is superb.

For more information: www.visitdelware.com or (866) 284–7483.

FLORIDA

Now to the Sunshine State, a stretch of seemingly endless beaches on the Atlantic Ocean and the Gulf of Mexico. People come here, of course, for winter warmth and fun in the sun. Millions have decided to stay here, even though the summers can be blisteringly hot and humid. A Florida study concluded that 40 percent of those who come to Florida to escape winter's wrath will eventually settle in the state for good.

The **Everglades** is a gloriously exhilarating swampland that can also be a bit intimidating. In fact it's a freshwater river, meandering along in no particular hurry. Be sure to go deep into the Glades to see some of its million and a half acres and 350 species of birds. Boat tours are essential to seeing the Everglades National Park.

At the southern tip of the long peninsula, the **Florida Keys** are examples of life about as good as it can get. Stretching more than 110 miles from Key Largo, the longest of these islands, to Key West, the southernmost community in the continental United States, they are sunbaked beauties luring millions of visitors every single year. The drive along U.S. Highway 1 is alone worth the trip. And the wonderment doesn't stop at Key West. You can hop a boat or seaplane and travel 65 miles farther west to the Dry Tortugas National Park. Its remote location means it can be less crowded than the Keys.

Fort Lauderdale is a wonderful residential community with miles of lagoons, canals, and beachfront. There's plenty of old money here for you to envy. The Bonnet House and Gardens along the north Lauderdale beach is worth a visit. And in a place known for training future tennis and swimming sensations, Fort Lauderdale is the home of the International Swimming Hall of Fame. It's a town of canals and was the first Florida community I ever visited. Some friends of my parents retired there and bought a lovely house. They chose one of the canals because they were boaters. I spent a week with them and learned about the good life.

Fort Myers is a great beach town at the southwestern tip of the Sunshine State, where royal palm trees line the streets. This warm Gulfside town has attracted the famous and the unknown for years. Henry Ford and Thomas Edison both escaped their northern homes and wintered in the Fort Myers area; their homes are now on public view. What I find so appealing about Florida's west coast is the long string of islands off the shore, with superb beaches, parkland, fine homes, and some excellent shopping.

Farther up the west coast is **Homosassa Springs** and a state park that hosts manatees, Florida's most endangered animal. In winter these gray giants congregate in the Homosassa and Crystal Rivers. The 2,000-pound critters have no natural predators, but pollution, development, and boat propellers are their worst enemies. See them soon, because they could disappear for good.

Lake Wales is in the center of the state, just below Orlando, and the Historic Bok Sanctuary is its chief attraction. Frederick Law Olmsted (who developed Boston's Fens and New York's Central Park) created this 250-acre garden masterpiece. The bell tower and gardens were dedicated to the American public in 1929 by Edward Bok, a Dutch immigrant. This is really quite special; don't miss it.

Miami and **Miami Beach** are Renaissance cities. Reversing decades of decay and dismay, they have become travel jewels once more. The world seems determined to beat a path to the art deco splendor of South Beach in Miami Beach, which has become one of the hippest, slickest locations in all South Florida. Dine and be seen in the posh neighborhood. More sedate and extravagant is the Italian Renaissance treasure known as Vizcaya Museum and Gardens in Miami.

Up north, **Ocala** is the home turf of Florida's Thoroughbred business. It's horsey country with stately old homes in town and massive horse farms out in the country. Ocala is trying hard to rejuvenate its old down-town area, which would be a plus to the community. Outside of town, one of Florida's wonders: Silver Springs, said to be the largest formation of clear artesian springs anywhere in the world.

Orlando has become the world's entertainment capital. The central Florida farming town has been transformed into a massive metropolitan playground. You've probably been to Walt Disney World, Disney's Animal Kingdom, Epcot Center, Sea World, or Universal Orlando. After all, nearly everyone from this country and Europe has likely visited.

St. Augustine is, of course, a true historical gem. The oldest con-tinuously inhabited European set-tlement in these-here-parts has been preserved to give us the flavor of the Spanish influence on this region from 1513, when Juan Ponce de León stumbled across the area while in search of the Fountain of Youth. The Old City is being restored to its colonial days and is worth every minute you can spare.

> ### SPECIAL SPOT IN FLORIDA
>
> It may seem corny and old-fashioned, but the Weeki Wachee water springs are worth a special trip. Aside from its celebrated "mermaid" underwa-ter show, enjoy the ride on the Wilderness River Cruise as you learn about the flora and fauna of west-central Florida.

St. George Island, in the Panhandle, is perhaps one of my favorite places in this big state, despite having the same name as mine. It's a place where high-rise condominiums are absent, and many homes and cottages occupy places in the Florida sun. And it shows you that while many tourists seek out the Atlantic beaches and the Gulf from St. Petersburg to Naples, some of the best beaches are way up in the far northwestern extreme of the state.

Sarasota is a gorgeous upscale city on the west coast and hometown of the circus kingpin. Today tourists can see the John and Mable Ringling Museum of Art, the couple's 1920s estate. There are wonderful islands and beaches west of town, and Sarasota has even fostered an Amish com-munity, east of the downtown area. It's where the sect spends winter months, when conditions become chilly in Pennsylvania and Ohio.

Tampa–St. Petersburg are night and day. Tampa has a wonderful old Cuban district called Ybor City, but it's really all about gleaming new structures in the downtown area. The popular Busch Gardens amuse-ment park is on the city's northern edge. St. Petersburg maintains its older exteriors and its cultured past. It's also closer to the beach areas; my favorites are Pass-a-Grille and Fort De Soto Park.

For more information: www.flausa.com or (888) 735–2872.

GEORGIA

This is my current home state, and in some places, it's bulging at the seams. Georgia is growing fast, as are other Sun Belt states. Atlanta has become the capital of the New South, one of the most important corporate and business centers in America. What's most interesting to me about the Peach State is how big and diverse it is. Georgia is, in fact, the largest state in area east of the Mississippi River, and it teems with things to see and do, from its northern mountains to its southeastern beaches.

Andersonville, in the center of this state, is a tragic reminder of man's inhumanity to his fellow man during wartime. In 1864 the Andersonville Prison was opened by the Confederacy, twenty-six acres in size, but impermeable. At one time it held 32,000 Union prisoners, in space meant for 10,000. Its main source of water became contaminated, leading to illness and death. Andersonville was the most feared and infamous Civil War prisoner-of-war camp. It's still a chilling place to visit today.

SPECIAL SPOT IN GEORGIA

I'm partial to the town of Madison, some 50 miles east of Atlanta. Its antebellum houses remain intact and are magnificent. It has a thriving downtown, full of shops and eateries. Madison has spawned a great Civil War story, which some say is a myth. The story goes that in November 1864, Union forces under General William Tecumseh Sherman approached Madison. They found the town so appealing, they decided to spare it, even while destroying other Georgia communities. Others say that this never happened; it's just a means of promoting the town. Either way, seeing Madison's mansions is a good way to spend a day.

Athens is home to the University of Georgia and a very nice college town. But what I most recommend about Athens is the State Botanical Garden, located at the edge of the city. It's a 313-acre facility with several gardens and 5 miles of trails. Best of all, there's no admission charge.

Atlanta is home to more than a dozen major corporations, the world's busiest airport, and Civil War memorabilia; it's also the birthplace of the civil rights movement because it's where Martin Luther King Jr. was born and bred. Things to see: the Atlanta Cyclorama, a marvelous 360-degree depiction of the Battle of Atlanta; the Margaret Mitchell House and Museum, which remembers the author who made so much of that battle in literature; the Atlanta Zoo, one of the few places anywhere housing giant pandas; the World of Coca-Cola; and tours of CNN Center, where cable news got its start and made its mark. Hotlanta, as it's called (especially in summertime), has some fine restaurants and excellent shopping. But it has plenty of traffic congestion, too, so consider using MARTA, the public bus and subway system.

Outside Atlanta, **Stone Mountain** is worth a side trip. An 825-foot granite slab is a gigantic work of art. Action figures of Confederate president Jefferson Davis, General Robert E. Lee, and General Thomas "Stonewall" Jackson rise as high as a nine-story building. The work was started by Gutzon Borglum, who later crafted Mount Rushmore. But a dispute with the United Daughters of the Confederacy, who sponsored the work, forced Borglum to abandon the project. Augustus Lukeman led a team of chiselers who finished the mountain, the most popular attraction in Georgia.

Dahlonega was a gold mine of a town, literally. A federal mint built there in 1838 made more than $6 million in coins. Visitors can still pan for the precious metal. Not far from here is Amicalola Falls State Park and the starting (or ending) point of the Appalachian Trail, which runs clear up to Maine.

On to the seashore and the **Golden Isles,** a series of barrier islands along the Atlantic. There are some beautiful, pristine islands. St. Simons and Jekyll Islands are the busiest. Some are off-limits to people, reserved for wildlife. My favorite is **Cumberland Island National Seashore,** the largest of the bunch. Access is by ferry only; once you get there, no cars or bicycles are permitted. There's limited camping, one hotel, and miles of beach. Best of all, wild horses and other critters roam Cumberland. You might actually meet them.

Helen is up north, in the mountains, and it looks a great deal like an Alpine village 4,000 miles to the east. Many people find it tacky, while others love it. Helen's annual Oktoberfest seems to run for many months.

Pine Mountain is home of Callaway Gardens, Resort, and Preserve. This is one of the largest and most extensive gardens I have ever seen. It covers 14,000 acres—and that's a lot of flowers and shrubs. Callaway also has hotels and golf, sailing and tennis. And come Christmas, millions of lights brighten the green space.

Plains is the hometown of Jimmy Carter, Georgia's only president. From humble beginnings Carter rose to the White House and a Nobel Peace Prize. After he left office, he returned to Plains and remains active in the tiny community. Carter was a peanut farmer, and there are many in the area. Plains is a great place to buy fresh peanuts.

Rome is home to Oak Hill, where Martha Berry lived. This cotton farmer's daughter became something of a saint in northwest Georgia. She brought literacy to the region by teaching rural children in the one-room schoolhouse that eventually became Berry College.

Savannah is Georgia's first community and its grandest. James Oglethorpe and his band of settlers came ashore in 1733 and claimed the land as England's last colony. He created twenty-four squares in the city, with fine homes built around green space. Twenty-one of the squares survive. Savannah grew and prospered with cotton at its core and today retains it elegance and charm. Juliette Gordon Low was born here, later founding the U.S. Girl Scouts. And I'll leave it for you to decide whether Savannah or Charleston is the more elite of the old southern charmers.

Warm Springs is a quaint community in western Georgia with some wonderful little shops on the main drag. But the curative powers of the springs themselves brought many people here after 1832, when the town became a health resort. One of these visitors was Franklin D. Roosevelt, who visited in 1924 after contracting polio. He later established the Warm Springs Foundation to help others and bought a cottage nearby in 1932, where he spent a great deal of time as both a private citizen and president of the United States. Roosevelt died in the Little White House on April 12, 1945.

Waycross is at the far southeastern end of the state. The Okefenokee Swamp is here, a massive wildlife area well worth a visit. Nearby is the Southern Forest World Museum, on the history of forestry in the South.

For more information: www.georgia.org or (800) VISIT–GA.

HAWAII

I've been to these magical islands only once, and I'm virtually certain once is not enough. So I've turned to others for help in extolling the virtues of our fiftieth state. Many visitors go to Honolulu and don't stray too far from there. That would be like visiting California and never leaving Los Angeles. We'll start our tour on the Big Island, Hawaii.

Hawaii Volcanoes National Park is on the southeastern edge of the island; both Kilauea and Mauna Loa volcanoes are situated here. Mauna Loa, by the way, is the biggest volcano in the world, rising some 13,600 feet above the Pacific. Given the active nature of the Hawaiian volcanoes, this should be a highlight of any trip here. The park is open twenty-four hours, so you can marvel at the wonders of nature both day and night.

> **SPECIAL SPOT IN HAWAII**
>
> Akaka Falls State Park is located on the Big Island near the town of Honomu. Despite being overshadowed in many ways by the raging volcanoes to its west and south, this park can claim two waterfalls, one of which plummets 420 feet into a stream below. The vegetation is so thick in the park, sunlight never reaches the ground. It's a strenuous walk but well worth it.

Hilo is the Big Island's capital. The waterfront area, virtually destroyed by tsunamis in 1946 and again in 1960, has now been rehabilitated with parks, gardens, and other facilities. The town has resorts and hotels, which can serve as a base to explore the rest of the island. Hilo is also the center of Hawaii's orchid industry.

Kailua-Kona is the oldest resort region on the Big Island. It was a charmed spot, frequented by royalty when Hawaii was ruled by kings. And it is here that Hawaii grows and brews its rich Kona coffee, an $11 million business. There are just 3,400 acres of beans, perhaps explaining why such a rich coffee is so rich at the store. Some say it's worth every penny.

Waimea is also called Kauai and is near that other active natural wonder, Mauna Kea. The Kamuela Museum gives you a sense of local history, with an extensive collection of Hawaiian artifacts.

Now it's on to the island of **Kauai,** called the Garden Isle due to its lush vegetation and agricultural wealth. Historians think this island was inhabited before the others. And there's a caution: Many of the beaches here are considered dangerous due to strange currents and strong undertows.

Haena is a village at the very top of this island, said to be breathtakingly beautiful. It must be so, as *South Pacific* was filmed here. There are two state parks here, and some captivating beaches. But swimming and wading are discouraged from September through May because of unpredictable water conditions. **Hanalei,** not far away, is steeped in colorful history. Through history its life centered on trading, fishing, and whaling, and later on the sugar industry. Its beaches can be treacherous, so try kayaking or horseback riding instead of swimming in the Pacific. **Kapaia** is the site of Wailua Falls, some 80 feet high. Former Hawaiian leaders would prove their manliness by diving from those cliffs. In more modern times those same cliffs were used in the opening scenes of TV's *Fantasy Island.*

In **Kilauea** you should visit the Na Aina Kai Botanical Gardens and Sculpture Park, an incredible twelve-garden tapestry in paradise. There are nearly seven dozen bronze statues scattered through the park and gardens, as well as a variety of gardens, ranging from desert landscape to tropical fruit orchard, bog to beachland.

Waimea, at the southwestern edge of the Garden Isle, is significant as the site where Captain James Cook first landed in Hawaii in 1778. The town offers many activities to equal its natural beauty, but the Waimea Canyon State Park proves that nature is generally superior. The park's rim looks out over a marvelous canyon below. At 3,400 feet, the Canyon Lookout provides a glimpse of 10 miles of gorges cut through Alakai Plateau.

Lanai is the island James Dole purchased in 1922 to grow and market pineapples. Today it's owned to a large degree by Castle and Cooke, Incorporated, which has managed its growth. It is the least visited Hawaiian island, which means seasoned travelers might want to stop by to avoid large crowds. But understand that good roads are hard to come by on Lanai. Be sure you have a good four-wheel-drive vehicle. Hulopoe and Manele Bays on the south shore offer white, sandy beaches, the best swimming and bodysurfing, as well as diving to the underwater coral.

Lanai City is the main community on the island and its business center. On the outskirts are the Luahiwa Petroglyphs, inscribed boulders that can be reached only on foot. North of town the Garden of the Gods shows what erosion can do to create a series of buttes and pinnacles inside a canyon. They're best viewed around sunrise.

Next comes **Maui,** the second-largest island in the chain, also known as the Valley Isle. The Valley has been discovered; resort development has accelerated in recent years. One of Maui's highlights, in more ways than one, is **Haleakala National Park,** or the House of the Sun. Haleakala itself is considered an active mountain, though it's not erupt-

ing. The top of the mountain looks like a crater but is, in fact, more a valley that has suffered the scourges of erosion.

Hana, at the eastern tip of Maui, is a very beautiful place. The Hana Highway runs through ravines, forests, fishing villages, and waterfalls. There is hiking along the thoroughfare. But the road is curvy, with five dozen one-lane bridges—and there's not a gas station for miles. If you have rented a car, you won't be allowed to drive the Hana Highway. It's amazing but very taxing.

Kaanapali is a beach town on the west coast, part of the burgeoning resort area. Locals say it has the best beach on the Valley Isle. **Kahului** is the island's principal port and has the only airport big enough to welcome tourists. Its beach contains white quartz stones, which some unwitting visitors have mistaken for diamonds. **Wailuki**—the twin city of Kahului— was the site of the island's leading sugar producer. It's hard to tell where one of the towns ends and the other begins.

Kihei, on the southwestern edge of Maui, is another hot resort area, with white sand beaches that attract folks from the world over. **Lahaina** is a busy place on the western coast. It is home to the Maui Theatre, which offers a traditional Hawaiian production of music and acrobatics called *Ulalena*. A traditional luau is served at the town's Cannery Mall.

Maaleaea is on the south shore and home to the island's aquarium, the Maui Ocean Center. It's one of the best ways to become acquainted with the marine life of Hawaii.

Next, the island of **Molokai.** This is Hawaii before it was "discovered"; it's the island with the largest percentage of native Hawaiians. To some degree Molokai suffers from its history as a leper colony, a place of no return. Those days are gone, of course, and for travelers seeking less hustle and bustle, Molokai is the island for relaxation. **Halawa** is at the eastern tip of this island and retains several ruins of Hawaiian buildings and burial places. They were affected by a tsunami that swept over this region in 1946. Halawa is isolated, with only one road leading to it.

Kalaupapa National Historic Park on Molokai's north coast is an isolated area; it was the place of exile for those with leprosy, starting in 1866. Seven years later a Roman Catholic priest arrived at the settlement. His name was Joseph de Veuster, although he was known as Father Damien. He was expected to stay in Molokai just a few months but actually remained for sixteen years, taking care of victims of what we now call Hansen's disease. Father Damien died from the malady, but his good example brought others to minister to the sufferers. Modern medicine has virtually eliminated the disease. There have been no new cases admitted to Kalaupapa since 1969. Given the spot's removal from the rest of the world, getting here even today is a struggle, achieved by air or on foot.

Kaunakakai is the "big city" of Molokai, with a small business district and a long wharf into the ocean for fishing and boat mooring. There are some scenic roads running east and west along the ocean, but they are poor in quality; use a four-wheel-drive vehicle.

Maunaloa is a town on Molokai's western front and a former pineapple plantation processing center. This area's biggest event is nearby. Aloha Week, which is actually weeks long, begins on the second weekend in September and continues for the next six weeks as the various islands celebrate their heritage. One highlight: outrigger canoe races from Molokai to Oahu.

Pukoo, in the southeast, exemplifies another part of Molokai's past. Above the town lies a heiau with a platform roughly 60 feet high. It is the largest on Molokai and one of the biggest in the fiftieth state. What was it used for, you ask? Heiaus may have been used for human sacrifices.

Now to the "gathering place," **Oahu.** Eighty percent of Hawaiians live here; the state capital is located here as well. Oahu is the center of government, industry, and tourism, visited by more outsiders than any other island. King Kamehameha I discovered Oahu and conquered it in 1795. His trade with other nations brought outside attention, and the rest, as they say, is history.

Honolulu is a thriving city of nearly 400,000 people of Polynesian, Japanese, Chinese, and European heritage. The city's name means "protected harbor." It's best known for Waikiki Beach and nearby Diamond Head, King Kamehameha's statue, the Punchbowl Cemetery, and the Pearl Harbor memorial above the USS *Arizona.* Shoppers head to Ala Moana Center, while sun lovers flock to the beach. And you can still enjoy the traditional luau, a lively picnic of food and dance, at various locations around town.

Driving around Oahu is a treat, so let me recommend you hire a car and do the circle, making at least three stops. **Hanauma Bay** is east of Honolulu, a lovely nature reserve and beach. **Laie** is on the northern tip and is home to the Polynesian Cultural Center, a large preserve that will tell you the fascinating history of the Hawaiian people. **Waimea** is home to some sparkling water, providing some of the best surfing on the islands. There's also an Audubon Center nearby. Just south of town, stop at Waimea Falls Park, a nature park, botanical garden, and arboretum, with some 6,000 types of plants.

For more information: www.gohawaii.com or (800) 464–2924.

IDAHO

This is a state with big rewards. There's magnificent scenery from the desert of the southwest to the towering Sawtooth Mountains in the middle, to the Snake and Salmon Rivers farther north, and on up to the border with British Columbia. You don't travel to Idaho for urban enjoyment, even though the capital city is delightful; it's all about nature.

Boise is the state capital, a city of trees in the high desert and protected from harsh winters by the Owyhee Mountains. People are flocking to Boise for its fine quality of life, low cost of living, and big tax breaks. It's a very pleasant city, especially in winter. If you are taking kids on a trip, take them to the Discovery Center of Idaho. Older kids might enjoy the World Center for Birds of Prey and the World Sports Humanitarian Hall of Fame. This is a fine place to call home; retirees are moving in all the time.

Blackfoot is the showcase of the state's important potato industry. At the Idaho Potato Expo, you'll come across the world's largest potato chip—measuring a salty 24 by 14 inches. And all visitors get free potato products.

Coeur d'Alene is the biggest town in the slender northern strip of Idaho. It's a popular resort area located on a lake of the same name. It claims to have the longest floating boardwalk on the face of the earth, at 3,300 feet. In summer the "Lake City" comes alive with swimming, boating, waterskiing, parasailing, fishing, and even houseboats dotting the water.

Craters of the Moon National Monument is near Ketchum, in the state's center. This public land is said to contain more basaltic volcanic impressions than any other place in the United States, from activity dating back thousands of years. There's a nice loop road to take you through it all, late spring to November.

Hell's Canyon National Recreation Area is in the west-central part of the state. Its 653,000 acres straddle the imposing Snake River Canyon. This magnificent country is made even more breathtaking by the rushing water of the Snake as it surges northward to meet the Columbia River and head to the Pacific. This is heaven for hikers, backpackers, boaters, and floaters. White-water rafting is a big deal in this region of Idaho.

SPECIAL SPOT IN IDAHO

Shoshone, in the south-central part of the state. In a land of many caves, there are some special ones here. The Shoshone Indian Ice Caves are north of town and maintain a temperature hovering around twenty degrees; they stay cold no matter how warm it gets outside. If you drop down for a visit, even in summer, bring a coat. It's almost a mile to get to the world of ice, and you could get chilled to the bone in the process.

Kellogg, up north, is the Silver Valley's biggest community and another formerly prosperous mining town. At one time gold, silver, lead, and zinc were hauled out of the ground in this region, making millionaires of many. The Crystal Gold Mine is still open, for tours. Miles away, **Lava Hot Springs** in extreme southeastern Idaho is home to some famous hot mineral pools, with a constant temperature of 110 degrees. The town's been a popular health and fitness resort area for years.

Idaho also abuts Yellowstone National Park. Drive through it and enjoy the grandeur.

For more information: www.visitid.org or (800) 635–7820.

ILLINOIS

The Land of Lincoln is one of my favorite states, largely because of Chicago—a city I love. I lived there for only a year and, despite a few bitter cold spells in winter, it was a wonderful 365 days. Here are some of my favorite places.

Brookfield is near Chicago, and while I don't care for zoos as a general rule, the facility here is outstanding. That's because it houses a wide and varied collection of creatures, all left uncaged. The zoo staff has created environments replicating the animals' natural habitats. From what I could tell, every major region in the world is represented. To do it justice, an all-day visit to Brookfield Zoo is required.

Chicago is an arts, cultural, theater, dining, festival, and parkland supercity. It's compact, it's comfortable, and if it were located 500 miles farther south, its population might be twenty million, as opposed to just under three million now. After you've sussed out the best restaurants and Chicago-style pizza palaces to nourish your body, there is plenty to occupy your mind. The Adler Planetarium, the John G. Shedd Aquarium, the Field Museum of natural history and sciences, the Art Institute of Chicago, Grant Park, and the Navy Pier are all within one small section of town. The Loop-area shops and the Sears Tower skywalk are just west of that. And the world of fashion, design, and good living is north of the Chicago River on the Magnificent Mile of Michigan Avenue, Old Town, and along the Gold Coast. The famous Museum of Science and Industry is on the South Side, near the prestigious University of Chicago. And you might want to visit another zoo, in Lincoln Park. I have fond memories of a day many Decembers ago when my family went to sing Christmas carols to the animals. It was bitter cold. The hot coffee didn't help much, but we had a warm feeling in our hearts.

Chicago is a city of neighborhoods, and you might want to take one of the many tours to fully explore the vast mosaic that is the Second City. By the way, the Second City improvisation comedy show still packs them in on North Wells Street and still makes people laugh out loud. Chi-town is an arts extravaganza, too, with symphony and opera, jazz and blues (try

SPECIAL SPOT IN ILLINOIS

Petersburg, northwest of Springfield. Lincoln's New Salem Historic Site is near the town. It's a reconstruction of the old community of New Salem, where Mr. Lincoln lived from 1831 to 1837. The only original structure is the Cooper Shop, where the future president studied law at night. The rest of the town is brought back to life—a school, sawmill, gristmill, shops, and the Rutledge Tavern. It completes your Lincoln pilgrimage.

Rush Street for that), and theater galore. And it rivals New Orleans for festivals, with a calendar that is mightily impressive. There are ethnic and arts festivals, antiques fairs, the Chicago Blues Festival, an international film festival, and the nation's biggest auto show (even surpassing Detroit itself). It's my kind of town, and it could be yours, too.

History buffs or lifelong admirers will want to travel to the small town of **Dixon,** due west of Chicago, to visit the boyhood home of Ronald Wilson Reagan. The house has been restored to look as it did when Dutch was just a boy.

Galena is a charming Mississippi River town, exhibiting some of the best mid-nineteenth-century architecture in the Midwest. Just seeing some of the old homes might make you envious. There are representatives of Federal, Greek Revival, Italianate, Queen Anne, and Second Empire styles. Home tours are normally offered in June and again in September. And Galena is home to another president: Ulysses S. Grant's home is in the town and contains many of this general and president's possessions.

Libertyville is another Chicago suburb, but the Lambs Farm stands out. This nonprofit group provides housing and vocational support to developmentally disabled adults. There's a bakery, pet shop, store, restaurant, and much more, all operated by residents. Children will enjoy the farmyard, petting zoo, train ride, and merry-go-round.

Naperville can show you how Illinois looked in the nineteenth century. The Naper Settlement re-creates a rural community in the pioneer and Victorian times. The homes and other buildings are decked out for holidays. My family and I went for pre-Christmas festivities and enjoyed it immensely.

Oak Park has fostered many important literary and creative figures. Ernest Hemingway and Edgar Rice Burroughs were both born here, and architect Frank Lloyd Wright lived and worked here for two decades.

Oak Park boasts twenty-seven Wright creations. There are tours of the Wright stuff as well as the birthplace and a museum of Hemingway.

Springfield is the state capital and a contemporary city, but it will always be the town of Abraham Lincoln. His home, museum, and tomb are in town or near it. And every American who values liberty and equality should visit.

Urbana, in east-central Illinois, is home of the University of Illinois, and if you are old enough or wise enough to enjoy march music, you may want to visit. The John Philip Sousa Archives for Band Research are in the band building, including some of the maestro's own instruments.

For more information: www.enjoyillinois.com or (800) 226–6632.

INDIANA

Indiana is a state where cars are an important contributor to quality of life. Still, there's more to the Hoosier State than the famous Brickyard. If your travels take you to the heartland, Indiana is worth a stop or two.

Auburn is in the northeastern tip of the state and is home to the Auburn Cord and Duesenberg Museum. The Auburn Automobile Company in 1930 developed three luxury cars: the Auburn, the Cord, and the Duesbenberg. This museum, in the art deco factory showroom of the former company, now displays a hundred classic cars dating from the nineteenth century to now. But most of what you'll see are the three vehicles made here in the 1920s and '30s. Some younger folks have probably never heard of, let alone seen, an Auburn, a Cord, or a Duesenberg.

There's a different kind of history in **Battle Ground** on the western edge of the state. A monument marks the spot of the Tippacanoe Battlefield of 1811. Here General William Henry Harrison, governor of the Indiana Territory and later the ninth president of the United States, attacked Native Americans led by a man called Prophet, the brother of Tecumseh. The battle is described at the museum's interpretive center.

Columbus is quite the place. In this otherwise sports-dominated city, architectural design has been taken to new heights. Local buildings have been designed by the crème de la crème: Robert Trent Jones, I. M. Pei, Eero and Eliel Saarinen, and others. Half a century ago a philanthropic group developed a program to pay the architectural fees for creation of new public buildings. Nowadays Columbus City Tours takes you to see the architectural gems.

SPECIAL SPOT IN INDIANA

On the southern shore of Lake Michigan, at the top of the state, the Indiana Dunes National Lakeshore extends for some 15,000 acres. That these dunes exist at all, here in the middle of the nation, is remarkable. The largest dune, Mount Baldy, actually moves— about 4 feet away from the lake each year. There are also bogs, swamps, marshland, and lots of trails for walking. Tread lightly and enjoy.

Fort Wayne has an illustrious past and a cherished present. The early trading center became prosperous because of its location on the Wabash/Erie Canal, the longest in the nation at the time. The early wealth was put back into the community. Now Indiana's City of Attractions has nearly a dozen museums and historic sites near its downtown core. John Chapman is buried here, better known to most people as Johnny Appleseed. His final resting place is fittingly in Appleseed Park. And because the town is on the so-called Lincoln Highway, a coast-to-coast roadway planned in the early 1900s, Fort Wayne has its own Lincoln Museum in the center of town.

Indianapolis is the state capital, high-tech and pharmaceutical business center, and home of the granddaddy of racing events. It boasts a low crime rate and a high degree of cleanliness. It's also the home of Benjamin Harrison, America's twenty-third president. His sixteen-room mansion is open to the public. There are dozens of attractions here, including the excellent Museum of Art, which has undergone a complete renovation. But Indianapolis's legitimate claim to fame in the Motor Speedway, built in 1909 by Carl Fisher and site of the Indianapolis 500, NASCAR's Brickyard 400, and the Formula One Grand Prix.

Within the 2.5-mile oval is the Hall of Fame Museum, celebrating the drivers and their precious vehicles. Tours of the Brickyard are available. And speaking of sports, you can also visit the NCAA Hall of Champions, honoring college sports teams, players, and coaches. In the metropolitan area, the Conner Prairie is located near Fishers. It's a living-history museum recounting the life and times of pioneer William Conner, showing his estate and Prairietown, a typical Midwest town of the 1830s.

Yes, Virginia, there is a **Santa Claus,** at least in Indiana. It's in the southern part of the state, near the Ohio River and Abraham Lincoln's boyhood home in Dale, where he lived from 1816 to 1830. Santa Claus has the Holiday World Theme Park, with several sites related to Christmas but also to Independence Day and Halloween. There's an amusement park attached, with rides, games, and shows for children of all ages.

South Bend is legendary, especially if you're Irish or an Irish wannabe. The home of Notre Dame University also has a history center, the College Football Hall of Fame, and the Studebaker National Museum, displaying both horse-drawn and motorized Studebaker vehicles. Despite Detroit's current prominence, Indiana was once a center of auto assembly; it saw many of its brands go out of business as the industry changed and consolidated.

For more information: www.enjoyindiana.com or (800) 759–9191.

IOWA

Corn, cattle, and culture come to mind when I think about Iowa, along with the first caucuses in presidential election years, not to mention bridges in one celebrated county and a famous ball field in another. Iowa is special because it has the mighty Mississippi on its east edge and the Missouri on the west. It was the first state to allow riverboat casino gambling, back in 1991. And it's home to some very friendly people.

History comes alive at **Amana Colonies** in eastern Iowa. A group of German religious immigrants settled near the Iowa River in the mid-1800s. The colonies are actually seven villages, a type of commune amid the corn. The Germans started their own business making beverage coolers in a shed, and so was born Amana Refrigeration, now a leader in its field. Visit the Amana Colonies today and you'll be transported back to those earlier times, with old-fashioned shops and restaurants and places to spend the night. Folks in the Hawkeye State called the colonies an Iowa treasure. See what you think.

Cedar Rapids has an artistic past and a business present. Artist Grant Wood hailed from here, and so did lots of Czechoslovakians, who developed their own historical village in the southwestern part of town. Grant Wood left something behind in his hometown: the large stained-glass window he designed in the Memorial Coliseum. In 1930 he painted *American Gothic*. The town is today a leading manufacturing center and a major distribution center for Iowa's abundant agriculture. There are several museums in town, including the National Czech and Slovak Museum and Library.

Des Moines is the center of it all, in more ways than one. It's in the middle of the rectangular state, as well as the government and agricultural center. One of its jewels is the Des Moines Art Center, with an impressive collection of twentieth-century masterpieces. There are more than 3,000 pieces of art in the center.

Elk Horn, in the southwest, is to the Danish what Cedar Rapids is to the Czechs. The tiny town was settled by Danish farmers who are remembered even today. The Danish Immigrant Museum depicts Danish life in America; the Danish windmill was actually built in the homeland and shipped to Elk Horn.

Grinnell is just east of Des Moines. It exists today thanks to Horace Greeley, who uttered the famous words, "Go West, young man, go West and grow up with the country." Josiah Bushnell Grinnell did just that, setting up this town in 1854. He also donated land for what is now Grinnell College.

In the north of the state, **Mason City** is another beneficiary of architect Frank Lloyd Wright's work. The Stockman House was created by the clever Chicagoan. But there's more: It's also part of popular culture. Mason City was the hometown of Meredith Wilson, who used it as his model for the town in *The Music Man.*

McCausland is the place where Buffalo Bill Cody was reared. The limestone home is open to the public, while buffalo and longhorn cattle roam the property.

SPECIAL SPOT IN IOWA

Dyersville came to life as the "farm toy capital of the world" and still holds a National Farm Toy Show each fall. It's the site of the National Farm Toy Museum, showing off some 30,000 farm toys, trucks, and banks dating from the early twentieth century to today. And it's the movie site of *Field of Dreams*, the 1988 film about a baseball diamond in a cornfield that was more special than most. As corny as the film was, I'll admit I enjoyed it—and I'll bet you did, too. By the way, the field has free admission; you can bring along baseball equipment if you like.

Amana Colonies may have developed the refrigerator, but **Newton** is the birthplace of the washing machine. F. L. Maytag perfected a hand-powered washer. A motor came later, as did the cylinder washing machine that is the precursor of what we use today. Newton is called the "washing machine capital of the world."

The Dutch settled in **Pella,** leaving religious intolerance behind. Pella Historical Village reveres those pioneers and remembers the region from more than a hundred years ago. Wyatt Earp's boyhood home is located right inside the village. Each May, Pella celebrates Tulip Time and the town's Dutch heritage.

On the eastern side of the state, **West Branch** is home to Herbert Hoover, the thirty-first president of the United States. The Hoover National Historic Site is a few miles north of town. And on the other side of Iowa lies **Winterset** in Madison County, which is near six of the nineteen famous covered bridges of Madison County. Winterset is famous for a favorite son: Actor John Wayne was born here in 1907. His home and mementos are now available for public inspection.

For more information: www.traveliowa.com or (800) 345–4692.

KANSAS

Midway across America, you'll discover the Sunflower State, which may surprise you indeed. There's a lot more to Kansas, Toto, than many people think. You can start with the wild and crazy town along the Old Chisholm Trail that fostered a future president. Near the center of the state, **Abilene** attracted cowboys in the latter part of the nineteenth century as they herded cattle past the town. Wild Bill Hickok was the marshal of this community in 1871. Visitors today can still see signs of the old Abilene and can visit the boyhood home and presidential library of Dwight David Eisenhower, our thirty-fourth chief executive and a distinguished World War II military commander before that. In my youth I tried to visit all the presidential libraries, and I enjoyed this one.

Atchison is home to another famous American. Pioneer aviatrix Amelia Earhart was born here in 1897. The northeast Kansas town's International Forest of Friendship honors its native daughter and other aviation pioneers, including the Wright Brothers, Charles Lindbergh, and those who died in the U.S. space program.

If Abilene was considered wild, **Dodge City** was truly wicked. In fact, it was deemed "the wickedest little city in America" from the late 1800s onward. Cowpokes, cattlemen, railway workers, gunslingers, and gamblers all descended on this town in the southwestern corner of Kansas. Boot Hill was the final resting place for those who died with their boots on. The town still earns its revenue from cattle and agriculture, but few forget its inglorious past. It seemed a bit tame to me, though; I almost wish I could have visited when lawlessness was the rule of thumb.

Emporia is home of the famous *Gazette,* first published by William Allen White, who influenced national affairs from his tiny town in middle America. The Sage of Emporia, as the journalist came to be known, won a Pulitzer Prize in 1922.

Greensburg, in south-central Kansas, has an unusual claim to fame that caught my eye: The Big Well is said to be the largest hand-dug well in the world. It is 109 feet deep and 32 feet across. You can walk down a long flight of steps to the bottom. That means, of course, you have to reclimb the 105 steps back to the top, but the notoriety alone is worth the effort.

Head to **Hutchinson** in the center of Kansas for something really out of this world—the Cosmosphere and Space Center. It traces the history of rocket science and is said to contain one of the largest collections of Russian space artifacts outside Moscow.

Leavenworth is the oldest city in Kansas. Its Landing Park, on the Missouri River, recalls the city as the Gateway to the West 150 years ago. **Newton** is noteworthy as the largest Mennonite settlement in the United States. The Kauffman Museum near Bethel College shows the history and contributions of this religious sect. **Scandia** was settled by Swedish and Norwegian immigrants and retains its roots even today—local stores still sell Scandinavian crafts and products.

In the northeastern corner the state capital, **Topeka,** boasts a very fine Museum of History, from early times to the present. **Wichita** is the state's most populous city and a center of arts and culture. The southern Kansas city's science museum is worth a visit, as are the Wichita Center of the Arts and the Old Cowtown Museum.

For more information: www.travelks.com or (800) 252–6727.

SPECIAL SPOT IN KANSAS

Independence. It's the home of playwright William Inge (*Splendor in the Grass* and *Come Back Little Sheba*), but this is also the town where author Laura Ingalls Wilder lived for a few years. If you are a fan of *Little House on the Prairie*, come here as well as to her homestead in South Dakota. And isn't it amazing how many places this woman lived? I have lived in twelve states, but she seems to be everywhere.

KENTUCKY

I have never called My Old Kentucky home, but I have visited often and enjoy the state immensely. There's something about the smell of genuine mint juleps and the sight of real Kentucky bluegrass.

One of the neatest towns is **Bardstown,** Kentucky's second-oldest city and a social center of the state. The north-central town is also a distilling center, and some of the largest bourbon makers are nearby. My Old Kentucky Home State Park houses a mansion where it's believed Stephen Foster wrote the song that has become Kentucky's trademark. A musical about Foster's works is presented during summer evenings in the park's outdoor amphitheater. Bardstown is also home of the Oscar Getz Museum of Whiskey History, a must-see for serious imbibers. Finally, take a ride on the Dinner Train, which also serves lunch. You'll ride through the countryside in restored dining cars from another era and enjoy a delightful meal. I love coming to Bardstown and nearby **Loretto,** headquarters of the Maker's Mark Distillery, one of the nation's premier bourbons, and the Gethsemane Monastery, whose monks create some memorable fruitcake (replete with bourbon), wonderful cheese (alas, no bourbon), and chocolate (laced with you-know-what).

Car lovers will love **Bowling Green,** where the Chevrolet Corvette is built. In fact, the National Corvette Museum is located directly across from the GM Corvette Assembly plant. It traces the history of the muscle-car from its 1953 introduction and houses the one millionth Corvette ever made.

Speaking of bourbon, **Clermont** is near Louisville and is the home of the Jim Beam family, pioneers in the whiskey business. The Bernheim Arboretum and Research Forest is also in Clermont, some 14,000 acres holding some 5,000 plant varieties.

Cumberland Gap National Historical Park is a rugged place reminiscent of the early days of American expansion. Daniel Boone created the Wilderness Road in these parts in 1775, and the gap played an important role in the Civil War.

Elizabethtown, south of Louisville, has a penchant for odd history. The Schmidt Museum of Coca-Cola Memorabilia has hundreds of items of Coke-lore, probably surpassed only by the World of Coca-Cola in Atlanta. Elizabethtown's other museum is Swope's Cars of Yesteryear, with an impressive collection of American cars from the 1920s and after.

Most of us know **Fort Knox** as the place where the gold is stored. Unfortunately, the U.S. Bullion Depository is closed to mere mortals, for reasons you can probably understand. But open to the public is the Patton Museum of Cavalry and Armor, outlining the history of armored vehicles from the First World War through the most recent conflicts.

In Kentucky's capital, **Frankfort,** the local cemetery holds the graves of Daniel Boone and his wife, Rebecca; seventeen Kentucky governors; and the names of those who've paid the ultimate price in war. It's an impressive sight.

Harrodsburg marks the spot of the first permanent English settlement west of the Allegheny Mountains and the first in what is now Kentucky. The town was founded in 1774, and the Old Fort Harrod State Park is the site of that settlement. Today an outdoor drama called *Daniel Boone—the Man and the Legend* is staged from June until late August. And nearby is the largest restored Shaker village in the nation at Pleasant Hill, east of Harrodsburg.

Near **Hodgenville,** in the center of the state, Abraham Lincoln was born in 1809 and lived until he was seven, when his family moved away. There's a Lincoln Museum in town at Lincoln Square.

In the southwestern corner of the state, **Land Between the Lakes National Recreation Area** is 170,000 acres of woods, hiking trails, horseback-riding areas, a nature station, and a planetarium. Get the RV in gear and drop by.

Lexington is a lovely city, home of the University of Kentucky and bluegrass capital of the world. This is one of the first towns I discovered when I took my inaugural solo trip at age fourteen. The horsey ambience here can be every bit as enticing as a mint julep. I'll never forget my first visits to the Kentucky Horse Park and Keeneland Race Course, which evoked the equine splendor for which Lexington is celebrated. You can take a tour of the Bluegrass Nation, of course, but there's much more to the city. Ashland is the home of Henry Clay, the great statesmen of our nation's early days, as well as Mary Todd Lincoln, one of the sixteen children of Robert Smith Todd. She would later become first lady.

For most of the world, **Louisville** is synonymous with Churchill Downs, site of the renowned Kentucky Derby. Be sure to see the racetrack, but also take time to visit the Louisville Science Center and Zoo and Locust Grove, the retirement home of George Rogers Clark, an American pioneer and general in the war for independence from Great Britain.

In the south of the state, **Mammoth Cave National Park** is perhaps Kentucky's most visited attraction. It is monstrous indeed, with some 350 miles of caverns and underground tunnels. Officials call it the longest cave system in the world.

Paducah is a little gem found at the point where the Tennessee River meets the Ohio. The town has an illustrious past and has become an arts and antiques center, retaining some of its yesteryear charm. It's a great place to spend a day or, better yet, a weekend, strolling the streets and shops.

For more information: www.kentuckytourism.com or (800) 225-8747.

SPECIAL SPOT IN KENTUCKY

Berea is a tremendous little community south of Lexington, notable for Berea College, which accepts only students who need financial aid and puts them to work in a variety of jobs to help finance their education. Beyond that, Berea is known as the Folk Arts and Crafts Capital of Kentucky, and, indeed, it teems with artsy-craftsy types. You can't go wrong spending some time in this town.

LOUISIANA

Letting the good times roll is not the way of life in just New Orleans; much of Louisiana follows that dictum as well. This state blends the cultures of American Indians, French, Spanish, English, and Africans as deftly as a Louisiana chef prepares a fine roux. Louisiana exemplifies the good life along the Gulf Coast.

Avery Island is a hot place indeed. It's where Edmund McIlhenny first dreamed up a spicy pepper sauce that is still burning tongues today. You can tour the Tabasco factory and dream about heartburn past and future. While you're on the island, drop by the Jungle Gardens, a few hundred acres of beautiful flowers, along with an abundance of birds, deer, even alligators.

Baton Rouge is the state capital, home of Louisiana State University, and a gambling center, in boats on the Mississippi River.

There are many historical plantations in Louisiana and across the South. One of the more interesting, at least to me, is the Crystal Rice Plantation in **Crowley,** which is in south-central Louisiana. For generations, one family farmed this place and still does. When you visit and go on the aquaculture tour, you'll see how the owners grow two crops, rice and crawfish, at the same time on the same land. It's really quite something.

In the delta city of **Houma,** seven bayous come together. It's a place where tourists can hop on boats to travel deep into the swamp country of southern Louisiana—Cajun country at its wildest and its best.

Natchitoches is the first permanent settlement from the Louisiana Purchase. And don't try to pronounce the name as it looks. There's a national historic park nearby, Cane River Creole, with older homes and plantations on public view. It's also a fine town to walk through. And in case you're wondering, the locals say *NAK-a-tish*.

SPECIAL SPOT IN LOUISIANA

Vacherie, near New Orleans. Visit Laura: a Creole Plantation. This plantation is a bit different from most others in the South, focusing instead on Creole traditions from before the Civil War. The former sugarcane farm was also the reputed birthplace of the Br'er Rabbit tales written by Joel Chandler Harris. The stories are thought to have originated in the slave quarters.

Most of us have no trouble pronouncing **New Orleans,** although Louisianans prefer *NAW-lins.* Here in the city that care forgot, there's a festival or party every single week of the year. Mardi Gras is the most famous, but the good times seem to roll every single day. Most visitors tend to congregate in the Vieux Carré, the French Quarter, and there's plenty to see, hear, and do. But I think there's a lot more to the Big Easy than the Quarter. Hop the St. Charles Street trolley and visit the Garden District. Tour several of the famous cemeteries, found in every quarter of the city. These are some of the most interesting elements in this truly interesting town. Explore Audubon Park and Audubon Zoo on the west side, too, and take in the Botanical Gardens in the City Park near Lake Pontchartrain. Enjoy local music in myriad places. Take a bus tour around the entire community and then search out quality neighborhood restaurants away from the tourist traps. And let your sense of history and pride show forth by visiting the D-Day Museum before you leave town. New Orleans is a unique urban experience; be sure to savor it in its entirety, not just a small part.

South of the big city is **Jean Lafitte National Historical Park and Preserve,** created to save some of Louisiana's richest natural and historic resources. It includes the Acadian Cultural Center, the Chalmette Battlefield and National Cemetery, and other Acadian treasures. The park is named for Jean Lafitte, a smuggler in the early 1800s who spurned British advances of friendship and later helped General Andrew Jackson defend New Orleans against British forces.

St. Martinsville, south of Lafayette, extols the legends of Evangeline, made famous by author Henry Wadsworth Longfellow. There's an Evangeline oak, one of the most photographed trees in the nation; the Longfellow-Evangeline State Historic Park; and an Acadian Memorial.

For more information: www.louisianatravel.com or (800) 334–8626.

MAINE

Way up north to one of the most beautiful states in the nation. Maine is also a state of mind, not just a natural wonder. Its coastline is craggy and magnificent, with unique waterfront villages. Its inland reaches are equally spectacular.

Acadia National Park juts out into the Atlantic Ocean for some 50 square miles. Much of Mount Desert Island is tree studded, and memorable roads skirt its edge, showing off coves and cliffs and the ocean below. Acadia is the easternmost of all our national parks and worth the drive to get to it, more than halfway up the coast. The town of **Bar Harbor** stands at the entrance to the park. Don't pass it by too quickly. It's worth savoring.

Most folks know the Maine between Bar Harbor and the New Hampshire line, even though there is much more of the Pine Tree State. **Bath** is a quaint city near Portland with a long tradition of shipbuilding. The Maine Maritime Museum is a must for those who love the sea and the vessels that sail her.

Blue Hill is one of my favorite places in Maine. It's along the coast, not far from Acadia. Formerly a shipbuilding, seafaring, and lumber-harvesting town, its tastes have now turned to arts and crafts. Potters and others have moved in and given the community a new feel. Small hotels and restaurants keep people from leaving too quickly. Oh, and there really is a Blue Hill nearby, more than 900 feet tall.

Another glorious port town is **Boothbay Harbor,** with shops and restaurants, hotels and cruises, and a railway village with a narrow-gauge steam engine train.

Brunswick is home to Bowdoin College and another of those small ever-so-Maine communities. My wife and I used to spend weekends just driving through these towns; we never got bored.

If you like the communities mentioned above, you'll likely love **Camden** and **Rockport,** whose charms attracted the wealthy and famous, including poet Edna St. Vincent Millay. This year-round resort area has plenty of stores, hotels, B&Bs, and restaurants.

My family and I once stayed a week at a house in **Castine,** another priceless coastal community. It's small and charming and relaxing and gorgeous. Consider a meal or lodging at the Castine Inn. **Freeport** is known for the L.L. Bean Company and scores of other outlet stores. It is also home of the Desert of Maine, an area of sand dunes that have grown and percolated for more than a hundred years.

In the rural north of this state, you'll find **Moosehead Lake,** where people who don't like the coastal crowds come each year. **Greenville** is the center of this region of swimming, boating, hiking, canoeing, white-water rafting, and mountain biking.

Kennebunkport is the town the Bush family put on the map; members of the clan still spend summers here. It's a lovely little place to spend the day, whether you want to see a president or not, and it has a good assortment of shops and hotels.

Monhegan Island is off the coast near Camden. It is one of the most beautiful islands I've ever set foot on. Friends used to have a summer cottage at the top of a hill, with a view that seemed to extend forever. Its cliffs are the highest on the New England shore. I remember picking wild berries near the hilltop. The lobster boat used to come in at five o'clock each afternoon, and by six, I recall eating fresh lobster on the breezy front porch of a clapboard cottage in paradise. The Wyeths lived here, too, creating some of the family's most memorable works of art—and when you see Monhegan, you'll understand why.

SPECIAL SPOT IN MAINE

Mount Katahdin. In the northern wilderness in Baxter State Park, the state's highest peak is magisterial and mighty. It is often snowcapped and a marvel to view from a distance. It's the end of the Appalachian Trail, which begins in north Georgia. The Allagash Wilderness is up here, too, and if you like rural, this is about as good as it gets in the East. While you are up this far, visit Aroostook County—one of the largest counties in the country and another wilderness wonderland—and take in the towns of Presque Isle, Caribou, and Fort Kent.

Ogunquit is an Indian term for "beautiful place by the sea," and it lives up to the name. There's a pleasant downtown and a wonderful walkway along the shore. It's not far from Portland. **Pemaquid Point** is another one of those uniquely Maine places, a long peninsula pushing out into the ocean, with a protective lighthouse at the water's edge. This is prime picnic country.

Portland is a city that has restored its harbor area and attracts many visitors each year. The Portland Museum of Art is a worthwhile site if you visit. Portland is also the embarkation point of the overnight ferry to Nova Scotia.

Some people call **Wiscasset** the most beautiful town in Maine. It's another coastal place, with fine homes and several museums. And don't miss the international collection of music boxes at the Musical Wonder House.

For more information: www.visitmaine.com or (800) 533–9595.

MARYLAND

Its shape has always beguiled me: broad along the Atlantic coast, slender at its western extreme. Maryland is many states, from shore to mountain slope. There's no better place to begin your journey than **Annapolis,** the state capital and home of the U.S. Naval Academy. The city center takes you back hundreds of years to the colonial and post-colonial periods. After all, it was settled in 1649 by a group of Puritans from Virginia. Annapolis is a compact city, so it now suffers from the influx of crowds. The old homes and public buildings command your attention, especially near the State House.

Baltimore is the center of Maryland, a revitalized city that draws travelers to see its famous attractions. The Inner Harbor has become the magnet for tourism, with the USS *Constellation,* the Passport Voyages of Discovery, the Maritime Museum, and many stores and eateries. Baltimore is also known for its Art Museum, Maryland Science Center, Baltimore Zoo, Johns Hopkins University, and Pimlico Race Course, a venerable oval and the site of the second leg of racing's Triple Crown. The Preakness is run on the third weekend in May. Baltimore is a city of distinguished neighborhoods like Federal Hill and Mount Vernon Place, as well as some classy suburban communities. Long overshadowed by Washington, DC, just down the pike, Baltimore is nowadays a city unto itself.

SPECIAL SPOT IN MARYLAND

In northeastern Maryland are two towns often missed by tourists: Chestertown is on an inlet a few miles east of Chesapeake Bay. It's a lovely little town, with fine homes and good places to east, as well as being the home of Washington College. Farther north, Chesapeake City is on the C&D Canal (running from the Chesapeake to the Delaware River). What a wonderful place to shop or have Sunday brunch.

The Fort McHenry National Monument and Historic Shrine is also found here. It was the city's sentinel from the time it was finished in 1803, guarding against the unwanted. It became a trophy for British forces during the War of 1812. And it became a symbol for the new nation when Francis Scott Key, while watching the bombing of Fort McHenry, penned the poem we now know as "The Star-Spangled Banner." Later set to music, it became the national anthem 119 years later, on March 3, 1931.

The **Chesapeake Bay** is one of the most celebrated waterways in the nation, famous for crabs and for the charming communities that hug its shores. Some of Maryland's most lovely towns are on the eastern and western edges of the bay: **Crisfield** is said to be built on oyster shells and has several restaurants to sample this prized seafood. Offshore are **Smith** and **Tangier Islands,** old communities where the water is a way of life; **St. Michael's** on the Eastern Shore was a shipbuilding center but is now a quiet resort area with a historic area convenient to the Chesapeake Bay Maritime Museum; and near the Western Shore is **St. Mary's City,** the first capital of Maryland and now a select community with its own historical district. **Wye Mills** is a tiny town near the bay, known for upscale homes and fashionable resorts.

Heading west, the city of **Frederick** is famous from the days of the Civil War when it was held by both Union and Confederate forces. Even though the Rebel troops were advancing through the area during the Battle of Antietam, a woman named Barbara Fritchie held an American flag aloft and dared the Confederate soldiers under the command of General Stonewall Jackson to shoot her dead. They did not, of course, and she was immortalized in a poem by John Greenleaf Whittier. Today Frederick lures visitors with museums and battlefields, a national shrine to St. Elizabeth Ann Seton, covered bridges, wineries, and the famous "clustered spires" in the historical district.

Way out in western Maryland, near **Oakland,** is Deep Creek Lake, which attracts those interested in water pursuits. Across the state **Ocean City** attracts beachcombers to its Atlantic shoreline. This is a favorite area of Washington, Baltimore, and Annapolis residents for summer fun in the sand and surf. **Salisbury** is the largest city on Maryland's famed Eastern Shore and the second-largest port after Baltimore. Visit its historical district, called Newtown, and if you are a hunter or art aficionado, spend some time at the Ward Museum of Wildfowl Art, replete with decoys as well as some fowl paintings and sculptures.

For more information: www.mdisfun.org or (800) 634–7386.

MASSACHUSETTS

Although I was born and grew up in New York State, my second home was Massachusetts. I have lived in the commonwealth twice and have grown to love it, despite its flaws, among them high taxes and shady politics.

I'm very partial to **Amherst,** the five-college community in the west of the state, although only three schools are actually in the town (Amherst, the University of Massachusetts, and Hampshire College). Smith and Mount Holyoke are nearby. This is an estimable college community with beautiful hilly surroundings, the best of both worlds.

Amherst is near the **Berkshires** in western Massachusetts, one of the most delightful regions of the Bay State. Folks flock here for the summer, the Boston Symphony concerts at Tanglewood, and the lovely country towns like Lee, Lenox, Pittsfield, Stockbridge, and Williamstown. This area is also magnificent in fall, when those leaves drain their green and don their brilliant autumn colors. And, of course, you can ski here in winter.

One of the finest old towns in the Bay State is **Deerfield,** due north of Amherst. Historic Deerfield has more than a dozen old homes and historic sites, retracing a settlement that dates back to the 1660s.

Boston has been one of my most favorite American cities since the day I first set foot in the Hub of the Universe to attend college. I love the history—along the Freedom Trail, the Old South Meeting House, the Old North Church, and Faneuil Hall. America's history is tied to this city's past. In contemporary Boston I love the inner-city beauty, from the Public Garden to the fashionable homes of Beacon Hill and Back Bay. And I admire the vibrancy of the place, stuffed with arts and culture, museums, galleries, and fine restaurants, not to mention the sixty-odd colleges and universities in Beantown and beyond. Visitors must see the Museum of Fine Arts and the Isabella Stewart Gardner Museum, the Museum of Science and the New England Aquarium along the rejuvenated wharf district. You must walk through the Italian North End and browse the newly gentrified South End. Recall the life and works of a former president at the John F. Kennedy Library, and take a ride on the MBTA (Massachusetts Bay Transportation Authority), which the locals refer to simply as the T. Take a train to Charlestown to view the USS *Constitution,* said to be the oldest commissioned ship in the world. And then climb Bunker Hill to relive one of the earliest conflicts of the War for Independence. Hop the T to Cambridge, home of Harvard University

and the exciting Harvard Square, or to the Massachusetts Institute of Technology. I spent years in Boston and never got bored.

Beyond the big city, go to **Concord** and **Lexington,** two very appealing New England towns that are also part of this nation's early history. The Minute Man National Historic Park pays tribute to those brave colonists who were roused by Paul Revere and took up arms to preserve their province. Concord is also a literary jackpot, home to the likes of Ralph Waldo Emerson and Louisa May Alcott. The Sleepy Hollow Cemetery is a Who's Who of writers and artists: Emerson, the Alcotts, Nathaniel Hawthorne, Henry David Thoreau, and Daniel Chester French.

On the northern coast of Massachusetts there are three towns worth a visit. **Gloucester, Rockport,** and **Newburyport** are old fishing and shipbuilding villages that have diversified. The fishermen still come and go, but now artists, crafters, and storekeepers operate side by side. These towns feature eclectic shopping and some delightful old neighborhoods. A beauty of a town is **Salem,** also north of Boston. Nathaniel Hawthorne's House of the Seven Gables is on Turner Street; there's a Pirate Museum; and be certain to see the distinguished Peabody Essex Museum, with a phenomenal collection of art and architecture in some thirty galleries.

Still, most people know Salem as the site of the witch trials that began in 1692. There's a museum for that as well.

Lowell is a depressed city in the north of the state, near the New Hampshire line. But the Lowell National Historical Park commemorates the days when the town was prosperous, for Lowell, you see, was a textile center for early America and a pioneering community in the Industrial Revolution. The American Textile History Museum is also in Lowell.

As much as I enjoy the western edge of this state, I can't say enough about the extreme eastern end, **Cape Cod.** The towns along this arm into the ocean try to maintain the old values despite the drive for development. My favorite places are those farthest out: **Truro, Wellfleet, and Provincetown.** The Cape Cod National Seashore is humbling, and the beaches and dunes are extremely inviting. Provincetown is a hoot and a happening, especially in summer. But for older travelers who might be offended by overt activities by gays and lesbians, this may be one town to avoid.

South of Boston, the town of **Plymouth** is steeped in history, from the famous Pilgrims' rock and *Mayflower II* in the city center to the authentic Plimoth Plantation south of town. This is an area to enjoy as you remember the trials and tribulations of those first settlers in this region.

SPECIAL SPOT IN MASSACHUSETTS

You need to leave the mainland and take a ferry to Martha's Vineyard and Nantucket. The former is larger and more crowded, especially when the famous fly in for their summer hols. Nantucket is smaller, quieter, quainter, and utterly enchanting. No visit to the commonwealth is complete without a visit offshore. You will enjoy both of these charming islands.

Basketball fans will race to **Springfield** for the Basketball Hall of Fame, which is actually quite well done.

If you love Norman Rockwell's work, and who doesn't, head to **Stockbridge** to visit the Rockwell Museum. It is fascinating, and its location on thirty acres of gardens and hills will thrill you just as much.

Old Sturbridge Village in the town of **Sturbridge** is a re-created rural New England town from 200 years ago. It's a captivating place and draws huge crowds in the summer.

For more information: www.massvacation.com or (800) 447–6277.

MICHIGAN

I have only been to Michigan a few times, but each time I go methinks it is a place of great wonder, unknown to most Americans. I like it so much, I have planned to do an episode on Michigan in the second season of *The Seasoned Traveler* on TV. The other thing you need to remember is that there are two Michigans, the Lower Peninsula and the Upper Peninsula, or UP, as Michiganders call it.

Ann Arbor owes its existence to the University of Michigan and shows its gratitude in many ways. Several museums, a botanical garden, and an arboretum grace the community; the arboretum is only proper given the town's name.

There's a sight worth seeing in the town of **Baldwin,** in western Michigan. A man named Raymond Oberholzer has immortalized the pine tree in the Shrine of the Pines. He chiseled artworks from tree stumps and other bits of pine cut in the late 1800s. Among the pieces are beds, chairs, candlesticks, even a 700-pound table.

Battle Creek is the cereal capital of the nation, and Kellogg's Cereal City is one of the highlight attractions in this town west of Detroit.

Speaking of the Motor City, **Detroit** is attempting a comeback. The Renaissance Center downtown is a symbol of the attempts by the city to rebound from a period of blight and decay. The Detroit Institute of the Arts houses an impressive collection of Dutch, Flemish, and American masters. In suburban **Bloomfield Hills,** the estate of former *Detroit News* publisher George Booth has become a major cultural center for the community. The Cranbrook Estate is open to the public, as is the Cranbrook Museum, bringing various displays to the community. Nearby **Dearborn** is not only the headquarters of the Ford Motor Company and its large production plant, but also home of Henry Ford's Greenfield Village. This hundred-acre park is not just about cars; it's also a tribute to American ingenuity and creativity. Various displays show advances in transportation, communications, agriculture, and industry. It is called the largest indoor–outdoor museum in the nation and is certainly one of the most visited places in the country. And if that's not enough, Dearborn is also the home of the Automotive Hall of Fame, near the Henry Ford Museum.

If you get to the Upper Peninsula, there are two special places: **Fayette** has its Historic Townsite, an authentic industrial village founded in 1867 by Fayette Brown, manager of Jackson Iron Company. The

SPECIAL SPOT IN MICHIGAN

I'm partial to Ishpeming, which is hard to pronounce, and which historians say means "heaven." It was once an iron-producing city but has found a new life as a ski center. The sport began here in 1887 when a group of locals formed a ski club; things grew from there. Today Ishpeming is headquarters of the U.S. National Ski Hall of Fame and Museum, which remembers the best skiers America has produced. The community is way up north in Michigan's Upper Peninsula, which gets boatloads of snow every year.

operation shut down less than three decades later, but the site has been saved for history buffs.

And beyond the UP, **Isle Royale National Park** is the largest island in Lake Superior and one of our least visited national parks because of its remote location. It's a place of dense forest, wildflowers, and wildlife, including loons, moose, and wolves. You can get to the park only by boat or seaplane, and you should probably make reservations. If you make it to Isle Royale, you might also want to be captivated by Pictured Rocks National Seashore along Lake Superior. This is a stretch of colorful cliffs rising a few hundred feet high.

Down south, **Frankenmuth** is a small piece of southern Germany in southern Michigan. Bavarian ministers settled in the United States in 1845. The town retains its German roots today in its history museum, while Bronner's Christmas Wonderland, which claims to be the world's largest Christmas store, is a hit with visitors from near and far.

Near the northern tip of the Lower Peninsula, **Gaylord** is a large community with a connection to Switzerland. The town is also where you'll find the Call of the Wild Museum, with some 150 copies of North American birds and animals.

Grand Rapids in the western end of the state is home of the Gerald R. Ford Museum, recalling the life of America's only nonelected president.

While Frankenmuth is German and Gaylord is Swiss, **Holland** is unabashedly Dutch. Each May the western Michigan town throws a big party, also known as its spectacular tulip festival. It's a great time to visit, even if there are thousands of other folks trying to see the floral displays along with you.

One of the most memorable places in Michigan is **Mackinac Island,** a magical speck of land in Lake Huron that transports you back to quieter times. Don't try to bring your car to the island, which permits only horse-drawn carriages, bicycles, horses, and walkers. Grand Hotel is an institution. Be sure to visit Mackinaw City on the mainland when you're in the area.

Sault Ste. Marie, on the upper end of the Upper Peninsula, is the oldest town in the state. The first Europeans arrived here in 1620, and the French and British took advantage of the fur trade in the area. The first American lock was built here in 1855. You can still take a boat tour of the locks today.

For more information: www.michigan.org or (800) 543–2937.

MINNESOTA

It is a land of exquisite beauty, the epitome of efficiency and good manners, and a place of humility. The Gopher State claims it is the "Land of Ten Thousand Lakes" when, in fact, scientists say there are probably closer to 15,000 such bodies of water across this northern plain. Minnesota is also a place of deep snow and extreme cold, all of which residents seem to take in stride and get the best of.

The people of **Apple Valley** are proud of the Minnesota Zoo, 500 acres big and 2,300 animals rich. Of particular interest is the Minnesota Trail, which highlights the wild animals inhabiting this region. **Austin** is famous as the home of Hormel Foods, after George Hormel opened a butcher shop here in 1887 and it became a national brand. The town is often called Spam Town USA because of its famous food product.

I've mentioned **Bloomington** before, in chapter 10, Shopping Sprees, but I'll note it again. The Mall of America is a true phenomenon, the largest mall and entertainment complex in the country. Right up there with it is Knott's Camp Snoopy, which claims to be the largest indoor family theme park in the nation, sprawled over seven acres with twenty-five rides, including a roller coaster and log flume ride—and don't forget the LEGO Imagination Center and its several thousand square feet of models.

Blue Earth is at the bottom of the state near the border with Iowa. It is famous for two quite extraordinary things: The ice cream sandwich was invented here, and a 55-foot statue of the Jolly Green Giant resides here, symbol of Green Giant Seneca Foods.

In northeastern Minnesota, **Duluth** is at the mouth of Lake Superior and boasts a place called the Depot, an old railroad station that has been revitalized as a series of museums. Depot Square has been rejuvenated to look at it did one hundred years ago, complete with two dozen stores and a trolley line. The town of **Ely** is even farther north and east and is a popular fishing and camping resort area. It's also where you will find the International Wolf Center, dedicated to the preservation of wolves. Not far away in the frozen recesses of northern Minnesota is **Eveleth,** home of the U.S. Hockey Hall of Fame celebrating the sport, including the 1980 Olympic miracle when the U.S. hockey team defeated Russia in Lake Placid, New York.

SPECIAL SPOT IN MINNESOTA

Chanhassen, west of Minneapolis, has one of the finest dinner theaters in this nation and is worth a visit. Outdoors, the Minnesota Landscape Arboretum is a 900-acre green space with ponds, a waterfall garden, a rose garden, and more than 6 miles of walking trails.

International Falls is often called the coldest place in America, although other spots get just as frigid. It is the gateway of the **Voyageurs National Park,** dedicated to the early French Canadian settlers of this region. There are boat tours of the park in summer and early autumn.

The Twin Cities are not identical twins. **Minneapolis** is tall skyscrapers, arts and culture, corporate headquarters, and upscale shopping. **St. Paul** is older and more sedate, government-centered, less brash. Both are delightful communities. In the bigger town, Minnehaha Park holds the first frame house built in Minneapolis, while Minnehaha Falls was made famous by the Longfellow poem "The Song of Hiawatha." I've always thought of the Twin Cities as leaders in local arts, and the Guthrie Theater is the local repertory troupe, with a tradition of excellence. The Minneapolis Society of Fine Arts Complex and the Walker Arts Center are some of the other sites worth seeing while here.

Rochester is a famous medical community. You can tour the headquarters of the Mayo Clinic, founded by the Mayo brothers, Drs. William and Charles, one hundred years ago, and the first private group practice in the United States.

Walnut Grove is famous for one of its resident daughters, Laura Ingalls Wilder—the children's author who seemed to move around quite a bit. She lived for a time here, and a museum here in town recalls the lives of the author and her family, along with the history of the town. In the very southeastern tip of Minnesota, **Wykoff** is home of the Mystery

Cave, a series of caves, underground walkways, and cave pools.

For more information: www.exploreminnesota.com or (800) 657–3700.

MISSISSIPPI

The Magnolia State is another one of those places often overlooked by travelers, as some sort of southern swampland where nothing much happens. We know better. To start with, there's **Bay St. Louis** at the western end of Mississippi's brief shoreline. The Gulf Coast is one of its attractions; another is the John C. Stennis Space Center, a massive research and testing facility for the space shuttle program and for space, environmental, and oceanographic studies.

Travel east along Route 90 and you'll come to the state's glitter gulch, **Biloxi.** This resort and fishing town has now become a gambling center, with ten casinos stretched out along the waterfront and more planned. Biloxi also has a sense of history in Beauvoir, the last home of Jefferson Davis, U.S. senator, secretary of war, and president of the Confederacy. The home and a Confederate museum occupy the sprawling grounds and tell the story of the rise and fall of this celebrated statesman. Biloxi is also home of the Maritime and Seafood Industry Museum, where you can still go out on a shrimp boat—although it's a tour, not the real thing. My other favorite towns along the Gulf Coast are **Ocean Springs** and **Pass Christian,** both of which are attracting legions of retirees to their residential ranks.

In the northwest, **Clarksdale** is a musical legend in its own right, home of the Delta Blues Museum, which tells of the influence of this type of music on the state. Across Mississippi at its very northeastern tip, **Corinth** is a relic of the Civil War. It was occupied by both Confederate and Union forces, and an 1862 battle here is deemed one of the fiercest engagements of the conflict. Nowadays the town recalls that period at the National Park Service's Civil War Interpretive Center.

In a land of cotton, **Greenwood** remains one of the largest cotton markets in the United States. It is right in the middle of the Mississippi Delta.

Jackson is the Magnolia State capital and full of museums, among them the Mississippi Agriculture and Forestry and National Agricultural Aviation Museum. It's a long name for a big place, some thirty-nine acres

highlighting the economic and technological events that shaped contemporary America. You'll also find the Mississippi Museum of Art and the Museum of Natural History, as well as the state's Sports Hall of Fame and Museum. There are other arts and culture venues in this city of grace and government.

Speaking of grace and charm, **Natchez** relives its glorious past three times each year in pilgrimage tours of the many marvelous antebellum homes. This Mississippi River town became wealthy on the backs of cotton workers, and plantation owners erected spectacular edifices in town for a respite from rural life. Natchez remains an attractive city to this day; there are many mansions worth your time and energy.

Oxford is a jewel in the north of the state, home of the University of Mississippi and spawning ground of noted southern authors including William Faulkner. His Rowan Oak near the town square is the home where the author died in 1962. The recently renovated estate is open to the public. To the west is the town of **Tupelo.** The King of Rock and Roll hailed from here, and the white house where Elvis Presley was born is now open for public viewing. The town is also headquarters of the Natchez Trace, the historic trade route heading north, to Nashville.

While Biloxi is the queen of on-land gambling, **Vicksburg** is a place where riverboat casinos appear in abundance. It's another wealthy riverfront town that holds annual pilgrimages to show off its upper-crust homes. The Vicksburg National Military Park recalls the Civil War siege of this community in 1863, one of the most significant battles in the War Between the States. The Vicksburg campaign produced a slew of war heroes who are honored by more than 1,000 memorials and markers in the park.

> **SPECIAL SPOT IN MISSISSIPPI**
>
> Gulfport, next door to Biloxi and home to the Lynn Meadows Discovery Center. This is an unusual museum to take the grandchildren, a place of discovery with a twist or two. You can create your own work of art, broadcast in the news center, take a trip to China, or try to fathom the mysteries of science. Children of all ages should enjoy this place.

For additional information: www.visitmississippi.org or (866) 733–6477.

MISSOURI

The Show-Me State has much to offer, and I wish I knew it better, having been there only three times; it's not enough. Here's what is hot.

Branson has come from nowhere to join the ranks of the leading travel attractions in Missouri. In the southwest of the state, on the border with Arkansas, it reminds me of a mini Nashville or a country-and-western Las Vegas. It wasn't always so. People used to come here for the rural solitude of the region after reading a book called *The Shepherd of the Hills*. Trade the solitude for the bright lights and the big shows of contemporary Branson, and you see how things have progressed. This town of about 6,000 has nearly three dozen theaters or performance venues, which must be a record for a town that size. The entertainment emporiums are augmented by the Dixie Stampede, Dolly Parton's dinner and Wild West Show. And there's Celebration City, an amusement park to keep the kids happy while the parents imbibe the country music. The Shepherd of the Hills outdoor theater dramatizes the Harold Bell Wright novel that brought many folks to this town a century ago.

Due north of there, **Camdentown** is in the Lake of the Ozarks region, one of the prettiest parts of Missouri. Bridal Cave is here, a series of large onyx formations and natural colors. Back down south to

Carthage, known for its marble and destroyed during the Civil War but rebuilt thereafter. It is a town known for antiques and for angels. At the Precious Moments Chapel, there are thirty stained-glass windows and hosts of murals using so-called teardrop children to depict events in the Bible. There's also a water and music show called the Fountain of Angels.

Columbia is a college town, home of the University of Missouri, Columbia College, and Stephens College. If you need a break from all that college rah-rah, visit the Shelter Insurance Gardens, a five-acre respite of trees and shrubs and thousands of flowers. **Florida** in north-eastern Missouri was the birthplace of Samuel Langhorne Clemens, later known worldwide as the writer Mark Twain.

Fulton is the site of Westminster College, where Britain's Winston Churchill made his famous Iron Curtain speech in 1946, and now home to a museum in his honor. The college bought London's Church of St. Mary the Virgin, which was about to be struck by the wrecking ball, tore it down, and reassembled it in Fulton. Anglophiles will love the place. Near Joplin the **George Washington Carver National Monument** recognizes the scientist who found some 300 by-products of the peanut and more than 100 from the sweet potato. The monument site includes Carver's birthplace.

Hannibal was the second home of Mark Twain, after his family moved from Florida, Missouri. Samuel Clemens lived here from the age of seven to eighteen, and this Mississippi River town has the feel of Tom Sawyer and Huck Finn, two of Twain's most celebrated creations.

Independence is a town of special importance to me because it's the place where President Harry Truman's Museum and Library are located, along with a memorial to the postwar chief executive. I've been there because I so admire Truman, a man with little formal education, self-taught by reading some of the great writers of the world, who was thrust into power upon the death of Franklin D. Roosevelt and who, historians now say, made many tough decisions in a short period of time and generally made the right ones.

Kansas City is a leading agricultural town—but it is no rural back-water. It's a gleaming city on the Missouri River and the hometown of Hallmark Cards, which every one of us has sent to loved ones for special occasions. This city has some fine museums, including its art museum;

the toy and miniature dollhouse museum is a winner. I'm a big fan of the Plaza, the first planned shopping center in the United States.

The **Ozarks** are a special place in the Show-Me State, one of the oldest mountain ranges in this nation, inhabited by Indians, Scottish settlers, and homesteaders from the eastern states. Visitors come for fishing, boating, picnicking, and camping.

St. Joseph is a town of history, the start of the famous Pony Express mail service in 1860 that took the post clear across the country to Sacramento, California. There's a national memorial recalling the mail milestone. This is also where Jesse James, outlaw to the rest of America, lived quietly among the locals under an assumed name.

St. Louis is a likable, albeit small, city on the mighty Mississippi River. I like this town a lot, from the Gateway Arch to the beautiful Forest Park, from the revitalized Union Station to the Missouri Botanical Garden, from the art museum to the zoo. Oh, and did I mention that it's the world headquarters of Anheuser-Busch, the world's best-selling brewer? It has a big-city feel, but on a small scale. St. Louis is easy to navigate, easier to enjoy. Northwest of town, **Defiance** is the town where the great frontiersman Daniel Boone spent his final days. His home is about 5 miles west.

Springfield is in southwestern Missouri and the site of one of its bigger attractions. Fantastic Caverns is one of the state's largest caves and worth a visit on a cold winter day: The temperature down below is a constant sixty degrees. The oddly named Wonders of Wildlife Zooquarium is also found in Springfield, a museum devoted to conserving the nation's natural resources, even though it also promotes hunting and fishing, which are not things I like to do. I've not been to this place, but it's said to be quite something.

For more information: www.missouritourism.org or (800) 810–5500.

SPECIAL SPOT IN MISSOURI

St. Genevieve, on the Big Muddy. It was the first permanent settlement in Missouri, and it maintains its French heritage and traditions, especially in the beauty of its architecture and in its festivals. There are marvelous old homes and churches to explore in this town that was once as large and important as a Mississippi River counterpart, St. Louis.

MONTANA

On to beautiful, bountiful Big Sky Country, a profusion of gentle plains and rugged plateaus, with some impressive glaciers thrown in. It is a state of natural wonder and natural resources. Witness the town of **Anaconda,** encircled by one of the world's largest deposits of copper ore, which became a leading copper smelter and is today a major tourist attraction in southwestern Montana. To the east is **Bozeman,** home to Montana State University and the Museum of the Rockies. It traces the history of this region, from the age of the dinosaurs, through the early Indian and Caucasian settlers, to more contemporary times. It also houses a planetarium.

Copper made **Butte** famous as well; the town was once said to be the "richest hill on earth," yielding billions of pounds of the precious metal. Copper made many men wealthy. You can still see the remnants of that today.

Great Falls lives up to its name. First seen and mapped by Lewis and Clark in 1805, it is an area still favored by walkers and bikers, especially along the River's Edge Trail. A Lewis and Clark National Historic Trail Interpretive Center is also located in Great Falls.

Some have called **Helena,** the Montana capital, a heavenly place. One reason is the Cathedral of St. Helena, a neo-Gothic edifice pattered after a church in Vienna, Austria. The Montana Historical Society has an impressive museum in town, and its Last Chance Tour Train makes the rounds through the city's historical sites.

On the southeastern Montana border with Wyoming, there is history of another sort. Near the town of **Hardin** is the Little Bighorn Battlefield National Monument, site of Lieutenant Colonel George Custer's Last Stand and the Custer National Cemetery. Custer and his 210 soldiers from the U.S. Seventh Cavalry stood no chance in their battle with hundreds of warriors from the Lakota, Arapaho, and Northern Cheyenne tribes.

Fisher-folk will want to visit **Livingston,** in south-central Montana, and its International Fly Fishing Center. I consider fly fishing a form of art, not just of sport.

In the west of this large state lies **Missoula**—just a lovely town and a pleasant place to visit. The people in **Red Lodge** are proud of their scenic roadway, called the Beartooth. This highway begins its journey at

5,600 feet above sea level and keeps on rising, to nearly 11,000 feet (the summit is actually in Wyoming), providing spectacular views of Absoroka and Beartooth Range. The Indians called the thoroughfare "the trail above the eagles," and you'll know why if you go along for a ride.

Virginia City was one of the most noteworthy and nefarious gold-mining towns in early America. Its reputation for murder and other crimes continues today. You can still pan for precious minerals after visiting several restored buildings from the gold-rush days.

West Yellowstone is a main entrance of America's first national park, still held in high regard by the millions of folks who visit each year. But before you rush to Yellowstone Park, take time to stop at the Grizzly Discovery Center. It's an education center that allows you to watch grizzlies and a gray wolf pack in lifelike surroundings. You could spend days in Yellowstone and never see either species in the wild.

SPECIAL SPOT IN MONTANA

Hands down, it's Glacier National Park, on the border with Canada. Geological processes have left behind some four dozen glaciers and 200 lakes, soaring peaks and deep gorges. Glacier is said to be a refuge for virtually all the large mammal species known to live in the United States. It is a breathtaking place to see—but you may need to hurry. Scientists say the glaciers are disappearing or melting. It may be a result of global warming. See this wonder of our world while it is still majestic.

For more information: www.visitmt.com or (800) 847–4868.

NEBRASKA

The Cornhusker State is bathed in oceans of prairie land and expansive fields. It is long and lean and has some special places to visit.

Way out in the remote northwest corner of this state, the **Agate Fossil Beds National Monument** is worth a visit if you're in the area. Fossils formed some twenty million years ago are embedded in mounds of sedimentary rock. Yet the monument has nothing to do with the mineral agate. The fossil bed is named for James Cook's Agate Springs Ranch. One hundred years ago excavations uncovered a rhinoceros never before seen by scientists at the time. Other species were also found. I have been once to Agate and found it fascinating.

Nebraska was a significant stop along the Oregon and California Trails, as you'll discover when you visit **Chimney Rock National Historic Site** in extreme southwestern Nebraska. The 500-foot-tall rock monolith was a stark symbol for westward trekkers. It announced the end of the prairies and the start of the Intermountain West. As you trek through the state, it's worth pausing for a look.

The town of **Gothenburg,** named for the southern Swedish town, is considered the centerpiece of one of the leading grain-producing areas of the United States. Thousands of people traversing the Oregon and Mormon Trails decided to stop here and become grain farmers. **Kearney,** in south-central Nebraska, is home to two famous flyovers. The first involves the real thing: a massive migratory bird flyway through the center of America. The second involves a way to fly over Interstate 80 in style and comfort. The Great Platte River Road Archway Monument spans the superhighway and has become a leading travel attraction in the middle of this mid-American state.

Lincoln is the Cornhusker State's capital city, with several sites of interest, among them the Museum of Nebraska History, which spans the period from prehistory to the present day. On a lighter note, the National Museum of Roller Skating is located south of downtown.

Go to the other end of this vast state, **Merriman** in the north, to see the Arthur Bowring Sandhills Ranch State Historic Park. It's actually a working cattle ranch that contains a history museum, profiling pioneer life here more than a hundred years ago. Bowring was considered a leading rancher in Nebraska. His second wife, Eve, was a U.S. senator.

Nebraska City is at the eastern edge of the state, on the Missouri River, and is the town where the Arbor Day tradition began. Each year Americans are meant to plant a tree to make the country better. The 260-acre Arbor Day Farm is located here. **North Platte** is the hometown of

---

SPECIAL SPOT IN NEBRASKA

Grand Island, the large island in the Platte River, was a landmark for early traders and remains one for present-day fliers. For six weeks each year (beginning in February), most of the world's sandhill cranes and 250 other species of fowl pack a stretch of the island, resting and revitalizing themselves before heading north for the warmer weather. I have never witnessed this magnificent event, but those who have say it is one of the most exhilarating examples of nature in action.

Colonel William "Buffalo Bill" Cody. There are remembrances of him all over town. **Ogallala** in west-central Nebraska has become a place I will always remember. It was here in 2003 that my family's first rental recreation vehicle developed a flat tire. The puncture occurred right in town, and the rental company acted very quickly to help me deal with the matter. Still, it took some three hours for a local contractor to repair the flat, and it taught me a lesson about how hard it is to fix problems in such a big bus.

Omaha played an important role in the movement west and has continued to play a role in the development of young American males. Boys Town is here, a many-acre facility dedicated to helping troubled children grow up to be responsible citizens. Omaha's Joslyn Art Museum is also worth a look.

Scotts Bluff National Monument is another of those prominent landmarks for early travelers on their way west. Located northwest of Chimney Rock, it also guided those on the Oregon and California Trails. Today it boasts a museum and a scenic overlook some 800 feet above the North Platte River.

For more information: www.visitnebraska.org or (877) NEBRASKA.

NEVADA

Nevada is one of the fastest-growing states in the nation, yet it has vast expanses of uninhabited desert and mountain terrain. You'll find both growing cities and stretches of grass- and farmland. And, of course, it's known for grand hotels, crammed casinos, and flamboyant shows in towns that never shut down.

Boulder City is a charming place that began its existence as a company town. When Uncle Sam began to build the massive Hoover Dam in 1931, named for the sitting president at the time, the government needed a place to house the workers. Bingo! Boulder City. The feds handed the city over to the locals some three decades later. Boulder City is the only Nevada community that prohibits gambling. Hoover Dam itself is located on the Nevada–Arizona border and is a feat of engineering that really must be seen. The dam has created two lakes and a wide swathe of the Colorado River along the Nevada–Arizona–California lines. Lake Mead and Lake Mohave exist primarily because of the dam. Both lakes were affected by the recent half-decade drought in the Southwest.

At the other end of the state, **Elko** is cattle country but it has also become a tourist stop. One attraction is the Cowboy Poetry Gathering, from late January until mid-February. This first-of-its-kind event is intended to preserve the life and culture of the cowpoke.

East-central Nevada is mineral country, and **Ely** was a leader in ore extraction. Two major pits produced $500 million in copper, gold, and other minerals. Marvelous mountains surround the town, and the groups of ghost towns nearby are popular with visitors.

In the south lies the pleasure palace that is **Las Vegas.** It is now a glittering gulch that has made good. Among the sites are the Guggenheim Hermitage Museum, which contains collections from three major art institutions: New York's Guggenheim, St. Petersburg's Hermitage, and the Kunsthistoriches (art history) Museum in Vienna. Pianist Liberace was popular in his day in Las Vegas, and the Liberace Museum continues to pack them in. There are several new and opulent hotels, endless gambling tables, and plenty of fun.

Laughlin is a small but growing gambling town in the middle of nowhere, near the border of Nevada with Arizona and California. Many of my older friends in southern Arizona used to take weekend coach trips to Laughlin to try to win big. No one ever did.

Reno says it is the "biggest little city in the world," and it rakes in the money of gamblers. You can also visit the National Automobile Museum here, in which four street scenes show off special cars from different eras.

Winnemucca has a funny-sounding name but an interesting history. The northwestern Nevada town is home to the largest population of Basques in North America, and the town cherishes their heritage. The Basque Festival takes place every June.

For more information: www.travelnevada.com or (800) NEVADA–8.

NEW HAMPSHIRE

Ah, now we're talking. This has been one of my dozen home states, small but marvelous, underrated but utterly enchanting, site of the nation's first presidential primary and a state of mind. After all, this is the state whose motto is "Live Free or Die."

We begin in the northern White Mountains and **Bretton Woods,** where the highest peak in the Northeast is located. Mount Washington is just 6,000 feet high, yet it endures some of the harshest wind gusts ever recorded. You can visit the mountain by taking the Mount Washington Cog Railway, you can drive up the big hill, or you can actually run or walk up if you are extremely fit. The old steam train is a lot of fun; you'll get covered in soot and smell like a steam engine, but it's a part of history. Speaking of history, the famous Bretton Woods monetary agreement was signed at the Mount Washington Hotel, a grand old palace that still welcomes guests today.

To the south, near the state capital, look for **Canterbury Center.** It's the site of one of the most important Shaker colonies in the United States, and it is huge. You can visit twenty-five buildings in the restored community, first established in 1792. When members of the Shaker sect lived here, they engaged in farming, made wool, and created the elegant furniture for which the now defunct religious group is known.

Concord, the capital, is a charming little city that gets very busy in an election year prior to the New Hampshire primary. Let me call your attention to one local attraction that has national significance: the Christa McAuliffe Planetarium, named for the Concord schoolteacher who was to become the first civilian in space but was killed when the space shuttle Challenger exploded after liftoff in 1986.

On the western edge of the Granite State, the town of **Cornish** is known for one of the longest covered bridges in the nation (across the Connecticut River between New Hampshire and Vermont) and for the Saint-Gaudens National Historic Site. This was the home of sculptor Augustus Saint-Gaudens, and it is a wonderful place to visit, especially on a summer afternoon. Saint-Gaudens was one of several artists drawn to this New England arts colony in the early part of the twentieth century.

New Hampshire is famous for **notches,** cuts in the mountains of the northern part of the state. Crawford, Dixville, Franconia, Kinsman, and

Pinkham Notches are among the best known and the most pictur-esque—all special features of this tiny state.

Derry is one of the most populous communities in the state, but I find it perhaps most appealing as one of the homes of poet Robert Frost. The Frost farm is open to the public on the south side of town. The land provided inspiration for some of his most famous works.

In western New Hampshire, **Enfield** is home to another Shaker village, this one dating to 1854. **Fitzwilliam** is in extreme south-western New Hampshire and is a lovely little place. But it is also renowned for its Rhododendron State Park, famous for some twenty acres of these bushes, which explode in brilliant color each July.

Speaking of Robert Frost, he also lived in **Franconia** in the far north of the state. He left Derry in 1911 and went to England. Upon his return in 1915, he bought a house in the mountains, called the Frost Place. **Hanover,** on the Connecticut River, is the site of Dartmouth College and a typical university town. But I always enjoyed visiting.

SPECIAL SPOT IN NEW HAMPSHIRE

Moultonborough in the center of the Granite State, north of Lake Winnipesaukee, has two places you'd enjoy. The Loon Center has trails that cross an area where loons have lived. You can learn more about these special birds as well as other waterfowl. Up high, in the Ossipee Mountains, is the Castle in the Clouds, a marvelous mansion nearly a hundred years old that offers breathtaking views of the valley below. You can also visit the Castle Springs, which provides water for public sale.

The White Mountains have so much to offer, people tend to spend a lot of time there. In the town of **Jackson,** Nestlenook Farm is a sixty-five-acre estate that offers activities year-round, from snowshoeing and horse-drawn sleighs to hiking and fishing in summer.

Keene is a great place to visit, in southwestern New Hampshire. Its signature event each year is the Pumpkin Festival in October, featuring towers and towers of carved jack-o'-lanterns.

Manchester is the biggest city in this small state and is noteworthy for the Currier Gallery of Art, featuring works by Monet, Picasso, Homer, O'Keeffe, and Andrew Wyeth.

Portsmouth is a great city, well preserved from its days as an important shipbuilding and fishing port. It is an excellent city in which to

browse, full of shops, breweries, bakeries, and restaurants. You'll find many distinguished old homes in the city as well as Strawbery Banke, the preserved waterfront district of the town. The name is derived from a historical event: Famished English travelers who finally reached land here in 1630 found the west bank of the Piscataqua River covered with strawberries. The grateful settlers named the place for the fruit. Off the coast are the **Isles of Shoals,** worth a boat ride out into the Atlantic. You can visit an old hotel, take a picnic, and hike the island. The isles are part of both New Hampshire and Maine.

Lake Winnipesaukee is one of the largest lake in the eastern United States, with some pretty towns on its edges. My favorite is **Wolfeboro** on the eastern tip, known as one of the oldest summer resorts in the country. Good hotels, fine shops, and plenty of water and other activities make this a pleasant place to pass the time. You might enjoy a ride on the lake courtesy of the *Winnipesaukee Belle,* which provides hour-and-a-half cruises of this celebrated body of water.

For more information: www.visitnh.gov or (800) 386–4664.

NEW JERSEY

It's always struck me as odd that New Jersey should follow New Hampshire in alphabetical listings: When my family left New Hampshire, we moved to Jersey. I came to know the beauty of the Garden State, so much more than the ugly petroleum plants along the New Jersey Turnpike. This much-maligned state deserves your attention, especially away from the turnpike.

When I was growing up, my parents took me to **Atlantic City,** the aging and decrepit beach town on the Jersey shore with a proud boardwalk and an embarrassing persona. When the state legislature approved gambling and I returned some years later, I found a Las Vegas East, with a dozen dazzling hotel-casinos but an inner city in appalling condition. You either love the city or hate it, but millions of older folks drop by every year to try their luck.

Farther up the Jersey shore, **Asbury Park** was founded in 1871 as a summer retreat for temperance adherents that would complement the town of Ocean Grove (see below). All that ended in the 1960s when Asbury Park became the new center of rock and roll, making stars of such local boys as Bruce Springsteen, Jon Bon Jovi, and others.

Barnagat Light, the northern community on Long Beach Island, boasts a magnificent lighthouse on the tip of the island. There are actually several beguiling beach towns on the islands offshore. You should plan to visit Seaside Heights, Seaside Park, and Beach Haven. Moving south, the shore communities of **Ocean City, Stone Harbor,** and **the Wildwoods** offer beautiful beaches and balmy breezes. The Jersey shore is an amazing resource, miles and miles of beach and surf. The biggest problem with it is that very little, if any, of this magnificent land is available to the public for free. It always bothered me that I had to pay for beach privileges I could enjoy for free in other states.

At the southern tip of the state, **Cape May** is a beauty, studded with Victorian architecture and some fine sandy beaches. Historic **Cold Spring** village, portraying life here in the nineteenth century, is also worth a gander. The wooded site holds some twenty-five period buildings.

Hoboken is my kind of town, even though native son Frank Sinatra seemed to prefer Chicago, at least in song. Hoboken is directly across the Hudson River from Manhattan, and the view from its main city park is stunning. Shopping in Hoboken is first-class, and you must try the restaurants, including the Sinatra hangouts before he moved west. Nearby

Jersey City is technically home to Liberty Island State Park, the Statue of Liberty, and Ellis Island—the first port of call for so many of the immigrants who flooded our shores.

Lambertville is a lovely little place on the Delaware River in western New Jersey; it prides itself as an antiques center. It also has some fine cafes and eateries. Once you visit a town like this in a rich rural setting, you'll know New Jersey is more appealing than critics say.

> ### SPECIAL SPOT IN NEW JERSEY
>
> I'm very partial to Princeton, site of the elite and architecturally appealing university but also a very inviting small town with fine shops and restaurants. Just being in the town makes you feel smarter. I have spent many rewarding days within Princeton's boundaries.

Because it was close to New York, **Long Branch** became one of the leading resort towns from the late 1890s into the early twentieth century. Its beach location was a draw; indeed, it rivaled Saratoga, New York, as a place to get away from it all. Seven U.S. presidents took their summer vacations here, long before Camp David was created as a presidential retreat.

Morristown is a famous Revolutionary War site: General George Washington chose it as his winter military headquarters on two occasions. It's now a National Historical Park. **Ocean Grove** is an interesting place. It, too, is on the shore and started as a family resort, under the aegis of the Camp Meeting Association. Cultural events and religious programs are held in the Great Auditorium near the beach. When you leave the auditorium area, you'll be impressed with some of the Victorian architecture around town.

Now for something completely different: the New Jersey **Pine Barrens.** This area consists of one million acres of land in the southern part of the Garden State, pine and swamp and river and bog. There were towns and villages here housing foundries and glassworks during the nation's early days. Cranberry and blueberry crops are abundant here, as are recreational activities. One of my favorite places here in the woods is the old town of **Batsto,** an abandoned-then-restored town deep in the Pine Barrens. It's worth a special trip.

West Orange is famous as the laboratory site of Thomas Alva Edison, perhaps America's most prolific inventor. Many of his inventions are displayed at the Edison Laboratories. Visitors can also see Glenmont, Edison's twenty-nine-room mansion.

For more information: www.visitnj.org or (800) VISIT–NJ.

NEW MEXICO

The Land of Enchantment is a place of landscapes and long distances, the fifth-largest state in the nation. It's a land of space studies and special locations; I have always enjoyed my visits.

Alamogordo, in south-central New Mexico, is known for two of its attractions. The New Mexico Museum of Space History traces the space programs in many nations. It features an Astronaut Memorial Garden for those who have died and an International Space Hall of Fame. For train lovers, there's also the Toy Train Depot, with scores of trains and related displays.

Albuquerque is a city interested in arts and culture. The Indian Pueblo Cultural Center and the National Hispanic Cultural Center are both found here, as are the Museum of Natural History and Science and the Museum of Art and History. You'll want to spend some time in Old Town, where Albuquerque began. And if you're not terrified by them, the American International Rattlesnake Museum focuses on some thirty species of the serpent and other relevant information.

In the northwest of this state are remnants of some of the earliest settlers this nation has known. **Aztec Ruins National Monument** is one of the largest and best-preserved pueblo ruins in the southwestern United States. Similar ruins can be found in **Bandelier National Monument,** while **Chaco Culture National Historical Park** is a virtual gold mine, preserving the remains from about a dozen great houses inhabited by the earliest of the Natives. The people of Chaco likely lived here 1,000 years ago, yet they developed public structures and irrigation systems that have awed contemporary scientists and engineers.

At the opposite end of this state, **Carlsbad Caverns National Park**

SPECIAL SPOT IN NEW MEXICO

Taos. I am partial to Santa Fe, but this is a remarkable place—or actually three places. What we call Taos is actually Don Fernando de Taos, the original town and the center of tourism and the arts. The Taos Indians occupy another community, living as they did long before the Spanish conquered this land. The last community, Rancho de Taos, is an agricultural area. I'm told the mission church, made of adobe, could be the most photographed building in the state. Hippies added their culture to the region beginning in the 1960s. And those who love recreation come, too, hiking and rafting in the summer, snow skiing in winter.

shows off an underground spectacle of nature. Some 30 miles of caves and chambers have been discovered in this underground system, which was nearly four million years in the making. This is one of those jaw-dropping places. I found the Bat Cave particularly impressive.

At **Chama,** on the border with Colorado, you can hop the train for a trip through the rugged San Juan and Sangre de Cristo Mountains. The Cumbres and Toltec Scenic Railroad runs narrow-gauge, coal-fired trains into Colorado.

Los Alamos has been famous since 1942, when the federal government converted a local school into an ultrasecret facility to conduct research and testing of the atomic bomb. Some sixty years ago the first A-bomb exploded at the White Sands Missile Range, and the world was changed forever. Los Alamos National Laboratory continues its scientific work on matters of national and economic security.

Down below Las Cruces, **Mesilla** is a charming town where Mexican roots run deep. When southern New Mexico became part of the United States after the 1848 Treaty of Guadalupe Hidalgo, many people moved to Mesilla to retain Mexican citizenship. The 1854 Gadsden Purchase brought the town into the American orbit, but Mesilla retained then, and retains today, its bond with Mexico. I like this little town a lot.

The small but enchanting state capital, **Santa Fe,** shows that great things really do come in tiny packages. This is a city of charm, culture, and community. It retains the look and feel of Spanish and Indian cultures. Its central Plaza, the Palace of Governors, and its arts and culture museums are reminiscent of another country and another time. Its churches and the Santa Fe Opera are legendary in their own right. The capital remains a strong lure to artists and those who appreciate their work, either on canvas or on stage. If there's one town in America I think everyone should see, this is it.

At the northwestern tip of the state is **Shiprock,** which is sacred to the Indian people. The massive geological formation is some 1,700 feet tall, and the shimmering effect on the rock when the sun is setting is magical to most who see it. In south-central New Mexico lies a different phenomenon: the beautiful **White Sands National Monument.** The 145,000 acres of gypsum sand produce snow-white sand that has formed into dunes. On a sunny day, the sand can be almost too brilliant to see clearly. This vast wasteland is quite beguiling.

For more information: www.newmexico.org or (800) 733–6396.

NEW YORK

This is where it all began, for me. This is my native state, and at the time I was born, it was the most populous of all the states. The migration to the Sun Belt has changed that. I have always marveled at the diversity of my native place, from rugged peaks to stunning lakes to dazzling beaches to the biggest city in America. Here are some of the best of these places.

Alexandria Bay is located in the Thousand Islands region of the St. Lawrence River. Among the marvelous homes here is Boldt Castle, on Heart Island. George Boldt, who made a fortune in the hotel business (New York's Waldorf-Astoria and Philadelphia's Bellevue-Stratford), started construction of a summer mansion patterned after a castle along the Rhine River, a gift for his wife. He ordered the project halted when Mrs. Boldt died in 1904. The place sat empty for seventy years. Restoration began and continues.

Adjacent to the Thousand Islands are the majestic **Adirondack Mountains.** They extend from Saratoga Springs and Lake George in the south to Saranac Lake and the Canadian border in the north. The Adirondack Museum is at Blue Mountain Lake. Whiteface Mountain is near Wilmington, one stop on a 6-mile highway with spectacular views of mountains and lakes. **Saratoga Springs** was a snitzy place to take the waters for medicinal purposes, and it became a high-class summer resort. Equestrian events are popular; the summer racing season brings the rich and famous from far and wide. The renowned Lake George Opera Festival takes place every June and July. The town has eight historical districts, brimming with fine examples of Victorian architecture.

Two other regions worth noticing are the **Finger Lakes** in western New York and the **Catskills,** just northwest of New York City. Near the lakes, the exquisite Sonnenberg Gardens and house in Canandaigua should be a summer stop, as well as Chautauqua, home of the famous arts and education institute that brings people in droves to experience a summer of learning on Lake Chautauqua. The Catskill Mountains recall a time of fine hotels just a few hours from the big city. Their halcyon days are over, but the scenery is still impressive.

On to **Cooperstown,** home of the Baseball Hall of Fame, the farmers' museum, and the Fenimore Art Museum. It includes memorabilia of author James Fenimore Cooper, who grew up in Cooperstown. In

Corning, the Museum of Glass traces the history of glass making in a city that made glass famous.

If you are near Lake Champlain, which separates New York from Vermont, visit **Fort Ticonderoga,** which played such a vital role in the early history of the United States.

When I was growing up, my parents took me to the Hudson River town of **Garrison** to visit the Boscobel Mansion, a restored neo-classical home with a spectacular view out over the river.

Hammondsport in western New York is one of the two leading wine-producing regions of the Empire State. The other is the **North Fork of Long Island,** which is more rural and more appealing than the hustle-bustle of the South Fork and the Hamptons. Try some of these wines when you visit New York, because many are first-rate.

Hyde Park is not only my home-town but also that of President Franklin D. Roosevelt. His home and library are here, the first presidential library in the United States. The town is also the site of one of the many Vanderbilt family mansions and the headquarters of the Culinary Institute of America, the leading cooking school in America.

Ithaca is a lovely town and home to Cornell University, one of the Ivy League schools, not to mention Taughannock Falls State Park; this cascade plummets up to 215 feet between some rocky cliffs.

Long Island is the Empire State's beach, stretching from Brooklyn to Montauk Point. Jones Beach, Sunken Meadow Beach, Fire Island, Quogue, the Hamptons, Amagansett, and Orient Point are just a few of the dazzling sandy stretches you can enjoy on the island.

In **Lockport,** on the western frontier, you can tour the Erie Canal, one of the first waterways of commerce in the earliest days of the country. Not far away, no trip to this state is complete without a visit to **Niagara**

SPECIAL SPOT IN NEW YORK

Rhinebeck, not far from my Hyde Park hometown, is famous for two distinctive sites. The Beekman Arms Inn, one of the oldest hotels in America, is still going strong. Also going strong is the Old Rhinebeck Aerodrome, which has old airplanes from the period of 1908 to 1937. If you're not content just looking at these antique beauties, you can go on barnstorming rides in a 1929 open-cockpit plane. But you need to contact the aerodrome for the exact dates when this is available.

Falls, on both the U.S. and the Canadian sides. The *Maid of the Mist,* which comes close to the falls, still packs 'em in.

Then, of course, there is **New York City** and its magic. It is one of our most popular tourist attractions so, as in the case of Los Angeles, I need say little about it. But I would mention one lesser-known museum, the Cloisters. This branch of the Metropolitan Museum of Art is famous for medieval works in five French cloisters. It is located in Fort Tryon Park, at the extreme northern edge of Manhattan Island.

Near the very top of the state in **Ogdensburg,** the Frederic Remington art museum combines the artworks and bronze statues of one of the greatest artists focusing on the American West.

Oyster Bay on Long Island is home to Sagamore Hill National Historic Site, the home of the other Roosevelt president, Teddy. It's a great home, and you'll enjoy your visit. On Long Island's southern side, Old Bethpage Village Restoration is a working Long Island farm from before the War Between the States. Buildings were brought from across the island and placed together in a 209-acre farm site.

In the Finger Lakes region, **Watkins Glen State Park** is crammed with gorges, waterfalls, and a bridge over the chasm. The town is also known for the Watkins Glen International road race each summer.

In the Hudson Valley, the U.S. Military Academy and Museum at **West Point** will tell you about the men and women who were trained here on a beautiful campus overlooking the Hudson.

For more information: www.iloveny.com or (800) 225–5697.

NORTH CAROLINA

The Tar Heel State is a destination of diversity, from bountiful beaches on its eastern edge to mighty mountains at the other end, and some impressive cities in between.

Asheville is one of them, a resort town at the edge of the mountains. It has been a draw for nearly two centuries because doctors sent their patients here to benefit from the fresh mountain air and sulfur springs. One of those visitors happened to be George Vanderbilt, who eventually built a 250-room French Renaissance mansion, which he called Biltmore. Set on 8,000 acres of land, this bucolic estate now draws hordes of visitors annually. The Candlelight Christmas evenings are especially impressive, given your surroundings.

While you are out in the west, hop on the **Blue Ridge Parkway,** a scenic ribbon of road extending more than 450 miles to the Shenandoah National Park in Virginia. It is a wonderful drive; take your time and enjoy every mile of it. Western North Carolina is a highly desirable and highly beautiful area. Many people have cabins, condos, or time-shares in the many mountain communities. My brother and sister-in-law were among them. When it's hot and humid in Atlanta, the Carolina peaks are the place to be.

Boone is named for Daniel Boone, who lived in these rugged mountains in the eighteenth century. The community stages an outdoor musical drama, *Horn in the West,* which traces Boone's efforts to establish freedom and justice in this region. The play is performed from June to August.

Chapel Hill is part of the Research Triangle Park, which also includes **Durham** and the state capital—**Raleigh.** The University of North Carolina and Duke University are in this high-tech hub. All three cities are worth seeing. Then there's **Charlotte,** which is a charming and captivating city. It has become a banking center for the nation, and it has managed to make its downtown look attractive. Charlotte has an impressive array of museums for a city its size and has a healthy commitment to arts and culture in general, but the city also plays an important part in the NASCAR season. The South End is a great place to enjoy good restaurants and enjoyable entertainment.

On the western edge of the state, along the border with Tennessee, is **Cherokee** and a painful chapter of American history. Eleven thousand Cherokees live in their reservation here. But it is the relocation of the Indians from the south to the west that is highlighted here in many ways: at the Museum of the Cherokee Indian, at the Oconaluftee Indian Village, and at the Mountainside Theatre, where an outdoor drama depicts the history of the tribe from the arrival of Spanish explorers in 1540 until the Trail of Tears in 1839.

Fayetteville is the home of Fort Bragg, of the army's Airborne and Special Operations Museum, and of the Cape Fear Botanical Garden. **Great Smoky Mountains National Park,** so called because of the blue haze that fills the park, straddles the border between North Carolina and Tennessee.

At the other end of North Carolina, the **Outer Banks** is a charming place along the Atlantic. From Kitty Hawk, site of the Wright Brothers' first flights, to the beach towns of Nags Head and Ocracoke, it's a very special place. Just ask the thousands of people who come here summer after summer. To the south, there are some lovely beach and near-beach towns that make this state so special. **Beaufort** is a fine example, a charming place with a long fishing history, an appealing old town with some wonderful old homes. **Emerald Isle** is more upscale, a perfect place to retire.

SPECIAL SPOT IN NORTH CAROLINA

Blowing Rock in the mountains, a year-round resort with summer activities galore and snow skiing in winter. You can also visit some unique attractions, like Blowing Rock itself, 4,000 feet high and subject to strong wind currents that make snow fall upward and objects hurled off the rock return to the thrower. Then there's Mystery Hill and its strange gravitational pull, which makes objects actually roll uphill instead of down. And in the nearby resort town of Linville, Grandfather Mountain is another oddity. The rugged rock formation resembles a bearded man looking skyward. There's also a section for hikers and walkers, including the famous Mile High Swinging Bridge.

Wilmington is the site of the Tar Heel State's deepwater port and home of the battleship *North Carolina,* as well as museums, a plantation, and lovely old homes.

Winston-Salem is a center of Moravian culture. You can learn more about the group at Old Salem, a living-history re-creation of the church community, founded in 1766. There are a hundred buildings in the village. The community is also noted for tobacco production, and R. J. Reynolds played a strong role in that. His cigarette wealth was put in part to good causes, among them the Reynolds House Museum of American Art, a sixty-four-room country house that houses indigenous art and furniture from about 1750 until now. It's an impressive collection on an impressive plot of land, some 1,000 acres in all. Reynolds's brother William was no slouch, either. He's responsible for Tanglewood, a former estate and horse farm that has since been turned into a park.

For more information: www.visitnc.com or (800) 847–4862.

NORTH DAKOTA

At the very top of the nation, North Dakota seems to get little respect. But the AAA reminds me that Meriwether Lewis and William Clark spent more time exploring what is now this state than any other. If it was good enough for them, it's got to be good enough for the rest of us.

Beulah, in west-central North Dakota, is the site of America's first synthetic fuels plant. Material from coal is used as a substitute for gasoline or natural gas. **Bismarck** has been state capital since about day one in the Peace Garden State. Its (former) riverboat port and railroad terminal have been as important to the city as is the business of state government. In the land of large inanimate animals, **Bottineau** is home of a statue of Tommy the Turtle riding a snowmobile. The 30-foot statue is the official welcomer to town.

Fort Yates is along the border with South Dakota and is significant as the burial site of the Indian leader Sitting Bull. And take a look at Standing Rock, a stone that looks a lot like a woman in a shawl. There is a legend attached to the stone about love's lost labor, but you'll have to visit to understand. The **International Peace Garden** straddles the border between North Dakota and Manitoba. The park and garden remind us all of the long-term friendship between the United States and Canada.

I didn't know much about **Jamestown** until recently. This east-central town offers many activities, including an arts center, a frontier village, and the National Buffalo Museum and Visitor Center. But get this: The Frontier Village features the World's Largest Buffalo, actually a three-story statue of an American bison. This baby beats the turtle and the cow (see New Salem, below).

Near Bismarck, the Fort Abraham Lincoln State Park at **Mandan** has seen some remarkable moments of history. It was a Mandan Indian village, the site of a fur-trading post, an area explored by Lewis and Clark, and the fort that Lieutenant Colonel George Custer left with his band of troops as they headed for Little Bighorn.

Minot is in the north of North Dakota and offers a Pioneer Village and Museum; its Scandinavian Heritage Park recalls contributions from residents of all the Scandinavian nations to this state and our nation.

New Salem is on Interstate 94, and as you drive through town you can't help but notice Salem Sue, a fiberglas Holstein cow 38 feet high and 50 feet long. She's the symbol of the dairy industry in North Dakota. **Strasburg** is a tiny south-central town made famous by a famous band leader: Lawrence Welk was born and reared here before he headed off to warmer climes.

For more information: www.ndtourism.com or (800) 435–5663.

SPECIAL SPOT IN NORTH DAKOTA

Theodore Roosevelt National Park on the state's western border pays homage to the president's efforts to conserve natural resources. It has its own Badlands (not to be confused with the South Dakota Badlands), and a huge herd of American bison roam the park's 70,000 acres. One last tidbit: It is the only national park named for a person.

OHIO

The Buckeye State has been one of my many home states. I had never set foot on Ohio turf until I moved there for a new job opportunity, but once settled I was sorry I hadn't visited sooner. Ohio can surprise you, as it did me, with some marvelous travel destinations.

Akron, the tire capital, has seen fortunes come and go, including its own. The city has struggled to maintain its image, and it does offer visitors a wide selection of sites. The National Inventors Hall of Fame allows people to try their hands at creating something new and exciting. Quaker Square, site of the former oatmeal factory, has become an in-town entertainment, shopping, and dining destination. And Stan Hywet Hall and Gardens, built by Goodyear co-founder Frank Seiberling, is a sixty-five-room Tudor mansion with art from around the world. My favorite room is the great hall. You may find one you like better, though; there's a lot to choose from.

In the northwestern corner of the state in **Archbold,** Historic Sauder Village is a hit with travelers. It's an early-twentieth-century village with costumed staffers to help you understand life at that time. South of Cleveland, in the town of **Bath,** there's another restored village. Artists and craftspeople re-create life in small-town Ohio in the nineteenth century.

Berlin, in eastern Ohio, is the center of the Amish community, still thriving in the twenty-first century. You can still see people driving the black buggies through the region, shunning electricity and other modern conveniences. **Canton,** the hometown of President William McKinley, is better known for the Pro Football Hall of Fame. **Chillicothe** is south of Columbus and a former capital of the old Northwest Territory. I recommend the outdoor drama *Tecumsah,* which describes the difficulties the Shawnee leader had in preserving his homeland.

Cincinnati is the Queen City, on the banks of the Ohio River, with much to offer visitors. It is chock-full of museums (you'll find an art museum, fire museum, history museum, children's museum, and natural history and science museum), along with a Contemporary Arts Center. Speaking of history, the President William Howard Taft National Historic Site is the boyhood home of America's twenty-seventh chief executive.

At the state's other extreme, **Cleveland** is the ultimate Comeback Kid. After nearly decaying itself into oblivion, it fought its way back to life. The prestigious University Circle area, home of Case Western Reserve University, is also where you'll find the city's performance stage, Severance Hall. It's near the Botanical Garden and the Museums of Art and Natural History. Downtown Cleveland offers the Rock and Roll Hall of Fame and Museum, an absolute boon to the city center. Jacobs Field, where the Indians play, and Gund Arena, home of the Cavaliers, have also helped the downtown district come alive again.

The Ohio capital city, **Columbus,** is a large and diverse city, home to state government, corporations, Ohio State University, and some vibrant neighborhoods. The Franklin Park Conservatory, Columbus Zoo, and Ohio Historical Center are well worth a trip. To the south of town, let me mention **Circleville.** Each autumn this town springs to life for the annual Pumpkin Festival, one of the most interesting of all the festivals in the state.

In **Coshocton** there's more history at Roscoe Village. It introduces guests to an Ohio & Erie Canal town of the 1830s. **Dayton** is a very nice little city in western Ohio once home to two young men who would make the city something special. The Wright Cycle Company building, where Orville and Wilbur Wright initiated their dreams of flight, is on the west side of town, as is Carillon Historical Park recalling some of the history of the region. Carillon concerts are held on weekends during summer months. Outside town, the U.S. Air Force Museum is reputed to be the biggest and oldest military museum on the face of the globe. The Presidential Aircraft Hangar is my personal favorite.

Fremont, a small town in northern Ohio, is where you'll find the Rutherford B. Hayes Presidential Center. It's an impressive house. Note the iron gates around the property: They used to be at the White House in Washington.

If you have a boat or access to one, take a ride to **Kelleys Island** in Lake Erie. It's a summer resort worth seeing and one center of Ohio's wine grape industry. There's a state park on the island as well. If you don't have a boat, there is ferry service to the island. Also in the lake, Put-in-Bay on **South Bass Island** is a place known for wineries, caves, and the water's edge.

East of Cleveland is the town of **Kirtland,** significant as an early headquarters of the Mormon Church in America. The Lake Farmpark is a place where you can see dozens of breeds of farm animals, some rare and some endangered. In **Locust Grove** you should see the Serpent Mound, considered the biggest serpent effigy in the whole of the United States. **Logan** is a place my family and I enjoyed immensely, especially Hocking Hills State Park. There's a trail system which takes visitors through caves to Cantwell Cliffs, a rock house, and some beautiful waterfalls.

Mansfield is midway between Cleveland and Columbus and has two sites I'd point out to seasoned travelers: Kingwood Center is a forty-seven-acre park blooming with beautiful and aromatic plants, while the Bible Walk consists of three religious museums as well as life-size dioramas depicting events from the Old and New Testaments. In **Marion** you can visit the home of President Warren G. Harding, the man who campaigned for high office from the front porch of his Ohio home.

Milan, between Toledo and Cleveland, was the birthplace of Thomas Alva Edison, the brilliant inventor. Edison spent the initial seven years of his life in the home on what is now Edison Drive. **New Philadelphia** is the site of Schoenbrunn Village, a restored 1777 Moravian mission to the Delaware Indians and the first settlement in the state of Ohio. There are some seventeen log buildings and a cemetery on the site.

SPECIAL SPOT IN OHIO

Zoar, not far from New Philadelphia. As one who is part German, I rather liked Zoar Village, founded by German immigrants in 1817. They tried to set up a practical self-sustaining community, which did well until it was dissolved in 1898 because its industries could not keep pace with the Industrial Revolution outside its boundaries. It's a fascinating showcase of an industrious people who tried hard to practice their principles.

Toledo was once a robust northwestern Ohio city, but it has fallen on hard times. Still, the Toledo Museum of Art is a real gem. It has an excellent collection of American artists, as well as works by El Greco, Rembrandt, Rubens, and van Gogh. Remarkably enough, there's no admission charge. **Wapakoneta** is the hometown of Neil Armstrong, first man on the moon, and the site of Armstrong's Air and Space Museum. Here you, too, can fly to the moon in the astrotheater.

For more information: www.ohiotourism.com or (800) 282–5393.

OKLAHOMA

I have been to Oklahoma only a few times, I confess, and I haven't seen all there is to see. Still, let me point out **Altus,** on the southwestern edge of the state, noteworthy for the Museum of the Western Prairie. It describes the history of this country's vast prairie lands, from the time of the Indians to more current conditions. Along that line, the town of **Andarko,** southwest of Oklahoma City, was a key area of settlement by Native Americans. Three tribes lived there. The town now has several sites devoted to its history: Indian City U.S.A., the National Hall of Fame for Famous American Indians, and the Southern Plains Indian Museum. There's also a Pioneer Museum.

SPECIAL SPOT IN OKLAHOMA

Chickasaw National Recreation Area. More than 9,000 acres in southern Oklahoma provide a break from the routine. Forests, streams, waterfalls, and springs are all an enticing part of this package.

Bartlesville is the site of the first commercial oil well drilled in the Sooner State, in 1897. There's a replica of it in Johnstone Park. Outside of town more tributes to the American West can be found at the Woolaroc Ranch Museum and Wildlife Preserve, bulging with art and artifacts and some 700 animals in the preserve.

There are some special sites in **Claremore,** north of Tulsa. It's Will Rogers country and home to the Will Rogers Memorial Museum. It's also the home of Lynn Riggs, who wrote the play *Green Grow the Lilacs,* which inspired the barnburner musical *Oklahoma!* And Claremore is the home of the J. M. Davis Arms and Historical Museum, full of guns and swords and knives and plenty of historical documents and other items. There are 20,000 weapons in the firearms collection.

In northeastern Oklahoma, **Grove** is on the Grand Lake O' the Cherokees; its Har-Ber village recalls life on these plains in the nineteenth century. There are some one hundred log structures representing different aspects of the community. **Guthrie,** near the state's capital, was ground zero for the 1889 rush for land. Nearly all of Guthrie's original commercial buildings are still standing and on the National Register of Historic Places. This is one town worth touring slowly.

Lawton was created by a land auction in 1901 that saw its population grow to 10,000 in less than twenty-four hours. Nearby is Fort Sill, set up in 1869 to control the Indians who lived here. **Norman** is the location of the University of Oklahoma—for college football fans, the equivalent of Green Bay.

The state capital, **Oklahoma City,** is huge in size and has several attractions: the Myriad Botanical Gardens and Crystal Bridge, and the National Cowboy and Western Heritage Museum, to name just two. But it will always be a place of pain after the April 19, 1995, bombing of the Alfred P. Murrah Federal Building. The Oklahoma City National Memorial pays tribute to the victims, survivors, and those who rescued them.

To the northeast, **Tahlequah** in the foothills of the Ozarks has been the capital of the Cherokee Nation since 1839, after the Trail of Tears brought them here. By the way, **Durant** is the capital of the Choctaw

Nation, and **Tishomingo** was the historical capital of the Chickasaw Nation. All three towns contain important structures relating to the tribes.

Tulsa, too, has Indian roots, settled by Creeks who were also victims of the Trail of Tears. Tulsa later became a black-gold bonanza when drillers discovered oil. Today you can visit two fine museums, the Philbrook Museum of Art and the Gilcrease Museum for art of the American West. Oral Roberts University is also here.

For more information: www.travelok.com or (800) 652–6552.

OREGON

What's not to like about Oregon: a stretch of rock-rimmed Pacific coastline, mountains and valleys, deep gorges, great cities, some of the best berries grown in the land, and a burgeoning wine industry?

Astoria is at the very northwestern tip of the state. It's near here that Lewis and Clark built Fort Clatsop in 1805 after arriving at the Pacific to end the first half of their monumental journey. In the city itself, drive up to the Astoria Column, which recounts the Voyage of Discovery and provides marvelous views of the ocean, the Columbia River, and the surrounding countryside. At the southwestern corner of the state, **Ashland**

is known for its remarkable Shakespeare Festival and other stage productions, which run from February until November.

Baker City stands today at the point where pioneers heading west first saw the Oregon Territory. What you can see today is the National Historic Oregon Trail Interpretive Center, which recounts the hardships and heartaches of those who made the trek.

In central Oregon, **Bend** is near the Deschutes National Forest; the Cascade Lakes Highway starts here, a beautiful 40-mile journey through the woods. This is also desert country, and the High Desert Museum explores the past and the present of the Great Basin, proving there's more desert than just Arizona.

SPECIAL SPOT IN OREGON

Crater Lake National Park and some of the bluest water you'll ever see. While the lake is only about 6 miles long, its depth (1,932 feet) and its shoreline both inspire awe. The cliffs surrounding Crater Lake reach as high as 2,000 feet. The 33-mile drive around the crater rim is a must-see in Oregon.

Bonneville is known for a dam as much as for a town. The Lock and Dam on the Columbia River generates hydroelectric power and provides navigable waterways. To get there you'll have to drive through the breathtaking Columbia River Gorge of sheer cliffs and impressive waterfalls. Drive slowly and enjoy it.

The major university towns here are **Corvallis,** home of Oregon State University, and **Eugene,** site of the University of Oregon.

Newport is the center of the illustrious Oregon coast and site of the Oregon Coast Aquarium. In this part of the state, you'll want to see Cannon Beach and the famous Haystack Rock, Tillamook and its famous cheese factories, Lincoln City, the Sea Lions Cave near Florence (don't miss it!), and Coos Bay on the southern coast.

Portland is one of my favorite cities in the country. It's clean, it's well run, and it has a dazzling downtown full of stores, hotels, theaters, museums, and a light rail system that runs efficiently for miles. It's also a city that takes advantage of two rivers. Amid all this, I have two favorite places. Washington Park rises above the downtown, providing views of the city and of Mount Hood. It is considered the crown jewel of Portland's impressive park system. The International Rose Test Gardens, meanwhile, exude the fragrances of 9,000 rosebushes of some 500 varieties. They don't call Portland the City of Roses for nothing. I'm also partial to

Powell's City of Books, which I mentioned in chapter 10, Shopping Sprees. Considered the largest bookseller in the world, this is a monstrous place; it's hard to come out without buying something.

After you view Mount Hood from Portland, drive over to see it up close and hop aboard the historic Mount Hood Railroad at the base of the hill. To the south, on the border with California, **Oregon Caves National Monument** has some absolutely impressive formations and an underground room some 250 feet long. There's a cave tour, but it's long and arduous with a lot of stairs. If you're healthy enough, though, you'll be glad you descended into these caves.

For more information: www.traveloregon.com or (800) 547–7842.

PENNSYLVANIA

I've always thought of the commonwealth of Pennsylvania as big and brawny. My father was from Pittsburgh in the days when it was a big, brawny, gritty steel town. But obviously there's equally dramatic history at the eastern end of the state as well, and a wealth of fascinating tales in between.

In **Ambridge** and **Harmony,** both near Pittsburgh, there are remnants of a societal experiment. George Rapp inaugurated his communal settlement in western Pennsylvania in 1804. The Old Economy Village in Ambridge was one community built by the Harmony Society. **Centre Hall** is located right in the center of the Keystone State, known for Penn's Cave, said to be America's only all-water cavern and wildlife park.

It's a long way from Atlanta, Georgia, to **Clark** in northwestern Pennsylvania, but the Tara looks a lot like a scene from *Gone with the Wind*. It's an inn, with lush lawns, a veranda, and all the southern charm you'd expect. Each room is named for a character from the famous book and film.

Fort Necessity National Battlefield in the southwestern corner marks the start of many important things. The fort was built by George Washington and is where he led Virginia militiamen against a force of French and Indian fighters in 1754. It was Washington's first military campaign as well as the first encounter in the French and Indian Wars. Still, perhaps the most famous battleground in Pennsylvania is at **Gettysburg,** site of a crucial Civil War battle and of Abraham Lincoln's address. Another president lived here, too: Dwight Eisenhower owned a farm in Gettysburg that's now a National Historic Site.

Harrisburg is the capital of this large expanse of land and head-quarters of the National Civil War Museum. Not far away, a sweeter subject. **Hershey** is where the chocolate empire got started by Milton Hershey. The town that made the chocolate kiss a household term features a museum, Hershey's Chocolate World, along with the HersheyPark Amusement area.

Tragedy has struck **Johnstown** not once, but four times. This south-western city has been swamped by floods, the worst coming in 1889, when a 40-foot wall of water leveled the town. It was one of the most destructive natural catastrophes in our history. The city's Flood Museum recalls the tragedy.

Kennett Square is home to the wonderful Longwood Gardens, an arboretum started in 1798 but not finished until the 1930s when industrialist Pierre du Pont had the awesome gardens built. Look for Longwood just over the border from Delaware. **Lancaster** claims President James Buchanan—this country's only bachelor chief executive. He lived at a mansion here called Wheatland for twenty years. The town is also the heart of Amish country and a great place to visit.

My personal favorite town is **Lititz,** home of the Wilbur Chocolate Company and the Sturgis Pretzel House. You may also want to visit Ephrata, Bird-in-Hand, Paradise, Intercourse, and Strasburg.

For a city much maligned, I'm a fan of **Philadelphia.** Its historical district is inspiring, from Independence Hall to the Liberty Bell. Philly has some great neighborhoods and fine restaurants, and its Museum of Art will always be famous as a temple of fine work—albeit more so as a pivotal point in cinematic pop culture.

The **Pocono Mountains** in the northeastern corner of this state remain a resort and getaway area. This used to be a honeymoon destina-

SPECIAL SPOT IN PENNSYLVANIA

Bucks County. North of Philadelphia, this is an area of large homes on big estates, horse farms, gentle rolling hills, the Delaware River, and good taste. It is a wonderful place to get away from the bustle of the big city. Be sure to visit New Hope, a picturesque place where writers and artists congregate, where antiques hunters head, and where the rest of us can find some eclectic little shops to enjoy.

tion when times were simpler; there are still hotels there today. Get out of town and enjoy the countryside.

Pittsburgh has come a long way, baby, from the days when I visited my grandparents' home and would come inside at sunset covered in dirt and soot. This former steel mill town has become a Renaissance community on the banks of the three rivers (the Allegheny, Monongahela, and Ohio). The historic downtown Golden Triangle has been reincarnated, and the riverfronts boast new, environmentally friendly developments.

For history buffs, there are two more military sites you'll need to see, both of which played pivotal parts in the War for Independence: **Valley Forge National Historic Park** and **Washington Crossing Historic Park.** Because of the men who fought in these places, we can celebrate our strengths today.

For more information: www.experiencepa.com or (800) 237–4363.

RHODE ISLAND

The smallest state has a big list of attractions. I lived in New England for many years and was always surprised to come to the Ocean State and discover something new.

Bristol is a delightful old town on the eastern shore of Narragansett Bay. The Audubon Society of Rhode Island has an environmental education center here. A terrific park, Colt State Park, is right on the water and perfect for a day out or a picnic. The Blithewold Mansion, Gardens, and Arboretum—a forty-five-room English-style country manor on the bay— is worth a visit. **Jamestown** is an old town with plenty of charm and a great location. It's an island in the bay between Newport and Wickford, and a great place for a walk, some lunch, or a drive, surrounded by the waters of the Narragansett. The University of Rhode Island is in **Kingston,** and the town reflects it.

For most travelers, Rhode Island *is* **Newport,** and vice versa. This is a fine and fashionable city at the southern tip of another island in the bay. There are many stores and restaurants, but most folks come to see the mansions, sporting such classy names as Beechwood, Belcourt, the Breakers, Chateau-Sur-Mer, the Elms, and more. If you want to see how the rich and powerful played each summer, spend some time gawking your way across Newport. There are two other sites of note here: the International Tennis Hall of Fame and Museum, and the Museum of

SPECIAL SPOT IN RHODE ISLAND

Block Island, an 11-square-mile chunk of paradise several miles off the coast of Point Judith. It is generally quiet (except during the height of summer), less developed than most resort communities, and a magnet for artists with its commanding views of the water. It offers a feel for what life was like in New England decades ago. You must see this spot.

Yachting. After all, this is the place of the America's Cup races. In **Portsmouth,** two towns north of Newport, visit the Green Animals Topiary Garden. Here you'll find some eighty topiary creatures—a lion and a giraffe, among others—all hewn from privet and yew bushes.

Providence, on the western shore of Narragansett Bay, is the state capital. The downtown has been undergoing a rejuvenation in recent years. The 1828 Greek Revival Arcade is worth a look, and do plan to visit the Museum of Art at the Rhode Island School of Design, with some 80,000 works inside. College Hill is where Brown University students and faculty spend their time. It's a lively district of stores, eateries, and entertainment. Speaking of eating, the Culinary Archives and Museum is located at the Harborside campus of Johnson and Wales University, renowned for its cooking and hospitality programs. You might find an interesting menu idea.

The easternmost area of Rhode Island is quiet and rural. I enjoy the towns of **Tiverton** and **Little Compton,** and you might, too. And look for the local winery in Little Compton. The product is surprisingly good.

The neatest town in the Ocean State, at least to my way of thinking, is **Wickford** on the west side of Narragansett Bay. It's an old produce-shipping port that has now distinguished itself as a town of distinctive historic homes and several interesting stores. You can also drop by Smith's Castle, a restored plantation house built way back in 1678. **Narragansett** has some beautiful beaches, as do the towns along the south shore, on Block Island Sound. Surf's up from Charlestown Beach to Watch Hill.

For more information: www.visitrhodeisland.com or (800) 556–2484.

SOUTH CAROLINA

The Palmetto State is not quite so small as Rhode Island. It's the fortieth-largest state in area but still has charm in abundance. Here are some of my favorite places.

Beaufort is a beautiful old port city (pronounced *BEW-fort* here, as opposed to the town in North Carolina). It exudes southern grace in its Revolutionary War and antebellum homes. It has a compact downtown and some fine restaurants. It's also a movie set of sorts: Several motion pictures have been filmed here.

In north-central South Carolina, **Camden** is one of the oldest inland communities. The settlers reached the coast first, then started drifting inward. What Aiken is to polo (see below), Camden is to steeplechases, with races each spring and autumn. The National Steeplechase Museum is ever-so-appropriately located here.

Charleston is one of the truly sumptuous cities in America and in the South; indeed, folks debate whether it or Savannah is the most genteel of the gracious urban ladies. Savannah has its squares, but Charleston has its splendid architecture. The homes range from magnificent to sublime. The best way to see the city is simply to tread lightly from street to street and marvel. When you've had your fill of art and architecture, take in a little history at **Fort Sumter National Monument** in Charleston Harbor. It was here that in 1861, Confederate troops fired the opening salvos of the Civil War, one of the most important events in our nation's past.

Charleston is midway along the Atlantic coast. Nearby are some wonderful towns along with terrific parks and beaches. **Hilton Head Island** is a booming vacation and retirement area, as are **Parris, St. Helena,** and **Edisto Islands.** North of Charleston, the **Grand Strand** struts its stuff, a resort and vacation magnet. Georgetown, Murrels Inlet, Surfside Beach, and Myrtle Beach

SPECIAL SPOT IN SOUTH CAROLINA
Aiken—in west-central South Carolina not far from the Savannah River—is a resort town with an equine embellishment. Wealthy folks from Charleston and up north used to vacation here for extended periods. The Charleston people came in summer when their city was too humid, while the Yankees came in winter. They introduced polo to the region, and now Aiken is horse country—Lexington South, or perhaps Ocala North. The Hopelands Gardens and the Thoroughbred Racing Hall of Fame are just south of town.

are very popular and very crowded in peak periods. But the beaches are special, which is why so many other folks are sharing the sand on a summer day. There's also plenty of entertainment. The Dixie Stampede dinner show, the Carolina Opry, the Medieval Times dinner and show, and Brookgreen Gardens on Murrells Inlet are just a few of the diversions that will keep you occupied away from the beach—and don't forget the NASCAR Speedpark in Myrtle, a seven-track racing amusement park. You can feel young again.

Way up north in **Greenville,** the mountains provide the picturesque views, in this case the Blue Ridge Mountains. Home of Bob Jones University, this is also a classy city with some five dozen parks. Not far away is the town of **Roebuck** with its impressive Walnut Grove Plantation, an eighteenth-century estate full of antiques as well as plantation buildings from the period.

For more information: www.discoversouthcarolina.com or (888) 727–6453.

SOUTH DAKOTA

When people say there's nothing much to see in the Dakotas, I want to wring their necks (or tell them to buy this book). South Dakota is teeming with tourist attractions, as thousands of travelers discover every year. Let's roam across this rich stretch of stark, windswept land.

Most adventurers know of the Black Hills on the western frontier. After all, Mount Rushmore is here and always worth a visit. But don't just stand at the visitor center: Walk the loop and see the presidents above you. Aside from the hills, there are caves studded through this vast wilderness. At the northern fringe of this region are two celebrated old gold-mining towns, **Lead** (*Leed*) and **Deadwood.** The latter has come back strong by opening casinos and luring small-time cardsharps and one-armed-bandit beaters.

SPECIAL SPOT IN SOUTH DAKOTA

Badlands National Park. I find this massive so-called wasteland utterly gorgeous and beguiling. This swathe of rugged stone cliffs, some with remarkably bright coloring, provides an out-of-this-world feeling. Beneath the Badlands one of the great fossil beds of all time remains untouched. You can drive through the national park and be wowed, then realize that the vast bulk of the Badlands are reachable only by long hikes through the peaks.

Jewel Cave National Monument is thought to be the second-longest cavern in this nation, at least 121 miles long. How's that for a hike? But perhaps the most appealing place to me is the vast **Custer State Park,** where the bison do really roam. When my family visited this area a few summers ago, we took along one of our pets, a Siamese cat called Tyler. We drove up close to a mother bison and her baby (a baby that probably weighed 300 pounds). Tyler nearly jumped out of his fur at first, but then he became quite fascinated with the cuddly critters only a few feet away. At the bottom of Custer Park, **Wind Cave National Park** is one of the more noteworthy caverns around here.

Not far away is **Hot Springs,** which was known to the Lakota Sioux as the vale of hot water. Others discovered the waters as well, and many flocked here to soothe their troubles or repair their bodies. There's something else special in Hot Springs, too: the Black Hills Wild Horse Sanctuary, where herds of horses run free. You can take a bus tour through the sanctuary.

The town of **Custer** is dwarfed by another mountain carving. The Crazy Horse Memorial is one of the dominant wonders of South Dakota. Lakota chiefs asked sculptor Korczak Ziolkowski to create a memorial to their revered leader, as well as to all American Indians. Crazy Horse will eventually rise 560 feet and extend 640 feet across. Folks here say it will be the largest statue in the world when completed.

In the eastern part of this state, literature lovers will head to **De Smet,** one of the towns made famous by Laura Ingalls Wilder in her *Little House on the Prairie* books. The Ingalls Homestead is a reproduction of the family property. The Ingallses lived here from 1879 until 1928. **Mitchell,** meantime, is famous for its Corn Palace, a strange building with minarets and flourishes. What's really unusual about the place is that several murals inside and outside the building are made from ears of corn, some colored and some natural. Each year, the pictures change. I found it fascinating. **Pine Ridge** is the headquarters of the Pine Ridge Reservation; its Heritage Center explains the history and culture of the Lakota people. North of here is Wounded Knee, site of a massacre of Indians by the U.S. Army in 1890.

Rapid City is the gateway to the Black Hills and a bit of a tourist trap. I did, however, like the Chapel in the Hills, a replica of a twelfth-century stave church in Norway.

Sioux Falls is the largest city in the state, home of the Great Plains Zoo and a memorial commemorating the USS *South Dakota,* among the most decorated battleships during World War II.

For more information: www.travelsd.com or (800) 732–5682.

TENNESSEE

Residents call it the Volunteer State, but I like to refer to Tennessee as the Slender State. It's long and lean from east to west, with a lot in between.

Starting on the Tennessee River at the eastern end of the state, **Chattanooga** is a trading port that got bigger and better. I enjoy the Riverbend Music Festival each June, and more Americans are coming to enjoy the Tennessee Aquarium, which claims to be the largest freshwater aquarium in the world. I don't know if that's true, but the place is big. It holds some 9,000 animals populating several habitats. Two other places command attention: First, look for Ruby Falls, Lookout Mountain Caverns, and the nearby Rock City Gardens on Lookout Mountain, actually a city of rock formations. Also, the Hunter Museum of American Art in town has an exceptional collection of American works.

Toward the center of the state, **Crossville** is known for Wilson's Wildlife Adventures, a huge collection of mounted animals from across the globe. **Gatlinburg,** a very popular and prosperous mountain resort area near the Great Smoky Mountains National Park, has something for everyone. The Christus Gardens has dioramas depicting the life of Jesus Christ, Ober Gatlinburg is a winter ski area and summer fun park, and Ripley's has a "Believe It or Not" Museum and the Aquarium of the Smokies. It's a family area, so either bring your little ones or avoid the crowds of families in summer.

> ### SPECIAL SPOT IN TENNESSEE
>
> The Hermitage, near Nashville. Andrew Jackson purchased the 1,100-acre property in 1804 and built the mansion we know today. It was finally finished in 1836, and it's a wonderful place. Many of the furnishings are original. I love Thomas Jefferson's Monticello, but the Hermitage is very special.

Dog lovers will head to **Grand Junction** in southwestern Tennessee for the National Bird Dog Museum, whose mission is to recognize the talents of forty breeds of sporting dogs. Tributes are paid to many of the world's most memorable bird dogs. The Everly Brothers would be proud.

Knoxville is volunteer central, home of the University of Tennessee, which has a fine women's basketball team. So it should come as no surprise that the Women's Basketball Hall of Fame is here, complete with a 30-foot-wide basketball at the entrance.

If there's one thing I like about the South, it's a good bourbon. And one of the leading names in the business is in **Lynchburg.** Jasper Newton Daniel (his friends called him Jack) bought his first distillery at a young age from a Lutheran minister. Since the 1860s Jack Daniel's has been served at home and abroad. You can still visit the distillery, seeing and smelling how Tennessee whiskey is made.

Memphis is a Mississippi River gem and the home of the blues. Music is an integral part of the community. A colleague of mine from northern Mississippi also says Memphis is the place where rural Mississippians go when they grow up—because there's not much for them back home. The Elvis Presley crowd comes to Graceland in droves; perhaps you've been one of them. The mansion, museum, and automobile attraction are big hits for fans of the King of Rock and Roll. Memphis is also the site of the National Civil Rights Museum, recalling key events in the fight for equality in America. You must also participate in the

Memphis music scene, either at local clubs or during the many music festivals, especially in May during the Blues Festival. There's an Elvis Presley Birthday Bash in January; the Carnival Memphis comes along late May or early June, and includes a Music Fest.

Then, of course, there's Music City itself, **Nashville.** I'll confess I'm not a big fan of country music, but I love Nashville, as much for the history of the genre as for the music itself. The Ryman Auditorium downtown is where it all began in 1925 with the WSM Barn Dance that later became the Grand Ole Opry. I can remember my wife standing on the stage during our first visit to Nashville, in front of the microphone, pretending to belt out the blues. It's fun to see the music companies where people like Hank Williams, Johnny Cash, Waylon Jennings, Patsy Cline, and many more began their illustrious careers. And that's why a visit to the Country Music Hall of Fame and Museum is essential for fans.

Drop by **Norris,** north of Knoxville, for a different kind of history. The Museum of Appalachia is a re-created pioneer village showing how folks coped in the hills and hollers of this region. I'm told the main museum building holds a quarter of a million artifacts. Nearby is **Oak Ridge,** which played a role in making America a nuclear nation. The American Museum of Science and Energy is a huge place, focusing on the history of energy and especially on the Manhattan Project, which produced the bombs that ended World War II in Japan.

Pigeon Forge in the Smokies is another good-time place, especially now that Dolly Parton is all over it, at her Dixie Stampede dinner show and at the popular Dollywood amusement park.

For more information: www.tnvacation.com or (800) 462–8366.

TEXAS

The land of the Lone Star is about as big as they get, and with all that open range and sagebrush, you know there's a lot to see and do. Wagons, ho.

Let's start at the top in **Amarillo,** where the Cadillac Ranch welcomes folks on Interstate 40 with ten cars inverted nose-first in a field. And in this horsey country, there's the American Quarter Horse Heritage Center. Can you believe it, a museum to the history of the Quarter Horse from colonial Virginia to contemporary Texas? Indeed, it's true.

Austin is a wonderful city, the seat of state government, a high-technology center, a university town, and a music capital. Not bad for a town of 650,000 souls. Among the many arts attractions and state government buildings, there is a remembrance of a national figure at the Lyndon Baines Johnson Library.

North of Corpus Christi, there's an animal kingdom with a difference. **Aransas National Wildlife Refuge** extends for some 70,000 acres, chock-full of armadillos and alligators, whooping cranes and javelinas. And along the Texas–Mexico border, **Big Bend National Park** is a remote expanse of rugged cliffs, deep canyons, and vast wilderness at the big bend in the Rio Grande (large river). I've never been to this remote park, but those who have say it's quiet and majestic.

SPECIAL SPOT IN TEXAS

Fort Stockton. This is a special place for my family even though it's virtually unknown to travelers. The community is midway between San Antonio and El Paso in the middle of nowhere. We stopped here for a rest on a long drive from south Texas to Arizona. We found a hotel and then we found it: the town landmark, Paisano Pete. At 20 feet long and 11 feet high, this is the world's largest statue of a roadrunner. My baby daughter fell in love with Paisano Pete, and I must admit, so did I. Fort Stockton stands out amid all the great places in the Lone Star State.

College Station is the home of Texas A&M University and the George Bush Presidential Library and Museum, bulging with artifacts from our forty-first president. **Corpus Christi** is a beautiful Gulf community and an important international port. Among the attractions are the Texas State Aquarium and several museums.

And so we've made it to the Big-D: **Dallas.** This major commercial and business center is one of the ten biggest cities in the nation. Among its museums, the Biblical Arts Center features religious art from around the world. Fair Park is a national landmark, site of the 1936 Texas Centennial Exhibition. And many who come here still want to visit Dealey Plaza, the spot where President John F. Kennedy was assassinated on November 22, 1963.

Big-D's nearest neighbor is **Fort Worth,** where you can visit the National Cowgirl Hall of Fame, which I'm sure every mature male in America would love to do. This place honors some 160 of the most famous cowpok-ettes in the nation. When you finish there, see the Stockyards National Historic District. What used to be a killing field is now 125 acres of shops, galleries, restaurants, saloons, hotels, and more. Just shows you what good urban renewal can do for you.

Galveston is the urban phoenix rising from the ashes—or in this case, the waves. The town that was wiped away in a cataclysmic 1900 hurricane, which killed 6,000 people, has come back. Victorian-like buildings and horse-drawn carriages along the coast re-create its charm before the storm. This is a city you just explore and appreciate. After that, drop by Moody Gardens. You'll know you're there by the three pyramids made of glass that are the focal point of this mammoth entertainment complex.

Dallas may be big but **Houston** is bigger, a major seaport and oil center. And it is huge. NASA's Johnson Space Center is here, telling the story of space flight from Mercury through Apollo to the space shuttle. For something a bit different, try the Bayou Bend Collection and Gardens, where decorative arts are displayed in twenty-eight room settings tracing their American evolution from the colonies to contemporary times.

If I had to pick my favorite city in the Lone Star State, **San Antonio** would win hands down. Here it's all about the Riverwalk, coupled with the Mexican and Spanish influence and the fact that San Anton is walkable whereas Dallas and Houston really aren't. Then, too, there's the Alamo right downtown; its distinctive design came about because it was a mission before it became a military garrison. This is also a place brimming with museums and galleries, along with the unparalleled activity near the Riverwalk. It's just great.

South Padre Island has become a major beach resort for folks who live inland. It has also become a hot spot for college students seeking sun, surf, and other students during spring break.

For more information: www.traveltex.com or (800) 888–8839.

UTAH

Land of grandeur is the most appropriate way to describe this state that the Mormons took one look at and knew they had arrived. This place is more about natural wonders than wonderful cities. We spent time here for one program in the first year of *The Seasoned Traveler* on TV.

In a state full of arches lies **Arches National Park,** near Moab in the east of the state, close to Colorado. The 2,000 sandstone arches here share the spotlight with lopsided rocks that seem to balance on one another despite the odds. And be sure to take note of the beautiful red rocks and canyons.

In the north of the state, **Bingham Canyon** was made by humans, not your Maker. The Kennecott Copper Company dug it, unearthing fifteen million tons of ore. The hole is so large, we are told astronauts can see it clearly from 300 miles above the planet.

Bryce Canyon National Park is another Utah wonder, this one in the south. It's home to a unique item (with an interesting name): the *hoodoo*. Bryce Canyon contains what many call the most colorful natural rock collection on earth, and over time nature and erosion have formed rock pillars called hoodoos. Who knew? Given its grandeur, you understand why this park is so popular with hikers and mountain climbers. Not far away is **Zion National Park,** named by Mormon pioneers. It, too, has gigantic rock formations, deep canyons, and another of those magnificent arches. Meantime, Congress could meet at the **Capitol Reef National Park** in south-central Utah. White sandstone formations here look strikingly similar to the U.S. Capitol building. There's a lot more to see here as well.

SPECIAL SPOT IN UTAH

Rainbow Bridge National Monument, on the border with Arizona. This is the largest natural bridge anyone's ever found. It is 275 feet wide and rises 290 feet above a stream below it. Its perfect shape reminds viewers of a rainbow. Some deem the bridge one of the Seven Natural Wonders of the World. Many Indian tribes deem it a sacred place.

Cedar Breaks National Monument is something completely different. Drop by and you'll see a natural limestone amphitheater that is 3 miles across and 2,500 feet deep, completely surrounded by soaring cliffs. They don't make 'em like this anymore. In northeastern Utah, **Dinosaur National Monument** contains bones from the Jurassic period; these fossils actually are part of the building at the park's visitor center.

Monument Valley is so grand, it stretches from Arizona into this state. Not far away, **Natural Bridges National Monument** boasts three massive arches formed by watery erosion over eons.

Utah's main city is **Salt Lake,** near one of the largest saline bodies of water in the world. I remember swimming in it years ago, trying desperately to stay underwater without success. The city is the center of the Mormon Church, the site of a recent Winter Olympiad, and location of the Tabernacle—home of one of the world's largest domed roofs without center support. Talk about faith for the 6,500 people who sit below that dome! This city is a charming place to see and stroll in summer and the heart of a major skiing area in winter, at Park City, Alta, Brighton, and elsewhere. If you go there, visit Olympic Park in Park City to relive the glories of the games in 2002. Utah can be a state of mind rather than just a state of the Union. For me, it is clear and clean and natural.

For more information: www.utah.com or (800) 200–1160.

VERMONT

The Green Mountain State is very fortunate. Oh, sure, it's a bucolic beauty, but neighboring New Hampshire has taller mountains, the largest lake in the Northeast, and nearly 20 miles of Atlantic seacoast. Still, people often consider Vermont the best place in the region. I'm not so sure, but I'll admit that it's wonderful. Here are some gorgeous Green Mountain State locales.

Barre is often called the world's granite center. Drive through this town, near Montpelier, and you'll see the huge granite-producing centers at work. All those monuments and headstones have to come from somewhere, and this is the leading place.

Bennington is in the southern part of this small state. It's one of those chic college towns, but at least it has some history, too. The 1777 Battle of Bennington provided an early American victory over British forces; each August the town remembers the conflict. The Bennington Battle Monument and the Bennington Museum are two of the town's draws, as are covered bridges and dazzling autumn leaves in October. Just east lies **Brattleboro,** in a time warp. In typical Vermont fashion, this town looks like a chilly version of Greenwich Village in the 1960s or '70s. Esoteric shops, galleries, and aging hippies are the rage. It'll make you recall the time when you wore beads. Brattleboro is the site of the first permanent settlement in what is now Vermont; author Rudyard Kipling lived in town and wrote *Captains Courageous* here.

Vermont is maple syrup country and a skiers' mecca. You can watch folks make syrup in late winter after you've tamed one of the scores of ski slopes. Those same forests and hills are just as pretty for summer hikes, and roads in Vermont are choked in autumn as leaf-peepers head here to witness the autumn magic and majesty. One of the best thoroughfares for the colorful display is Vermont Route 100—but prepare to be joined by many others.

Burlington is a fine small city on the shore of the crisp, clear Lake Champlain. The Church Street Marketplace is a good venue for shopping and entertainment. You'll also find the homestead of Ethan Allen, head of the Green Mountain Boys. The *Spirit of Ethan Allen* lives on as a cruise ship, which can take you on a trip around the lake from May until October.

Manchester, in southwestern Vermont, is a year-round resort, extremely charming and upscale, and home to some excellent shopping and some great hotels. You should also drop by Hildene, the twenty-four-room summer home of Robert Todd Lincoln, the president's only son to grow old. In west-central Vermont, **Middlebury** is a quaint little burg with another famous small college, which goes by the same name as the town.

Plymouth is home to another former president. The Calvin Coolidge State Historic Site includes the birthplace, boyhood home, and grave site of our thirtieth president. I'm told nearly all of the original furnishings remain.

Shelburne is south of Burlington and home of the Vermont Teddy Bear Company. It's an amazing place to visit, just to watch talented people crafting the cuddly critters. Even more impressive is the Shelburne Museum. From all across New England, artwork and historical items have been brought to the forty-five-acre site and its forty galleries. This museum tells the story of New England, complete with train station, locomotive, and even the steamboat *Ticonderoga*. Don't miss it.

The **Northeast Kingdom** is the rugged land at the top of this state. Heavy woods, hills and trails, maple sugaring, and rural solitude make it a unique place.

For more information: www.travelvermont.com or (800) 837–6668.

VIRGINIA

I've lived in Virginia and loved it. The unofficial motto tells us "Virginia Is for Lovers"—and that's true when it comes to the Blue Ridge Mountains, the Potomac River, Colonial Williamsburg, America's earliest settlements, and the rest of this remarkable state.

Alexandria is the river city across from Washington, DC, but it was here long before the nation's capital. This was the closest town to George Washington's homestead, Mount Vernon, and today its Old Town is where contemporary Washington comes for food, drink, fine shops, and fantastic architecture. On the edge of town is the George Washington Masonic National Memorial, a 300-foot-high structure. Many American presidents, from the Father of His Country onward, were Masons.

To the other end of the state now and the place where the Civil War ended. The **Appomattox Court House National Historical Park** is a re-created village that looks as it did in 1865, when Confederate General Robert E. Lee surrendered to General Ulysses S. Grant in the McLean House. It was the nation's costliest war, claiming more than 600,000 lives on both sides of the political divide.

Heroes of all wars are interred at **Arlington National Cemetery,** including Presidents William Howard Taft and John F. Kennedy, Chief Justice Earl Warren, fighter Joe Louis, and hundreds of military personnel. The land was confiscated from Robert E. Lee, whose Arlington House remains intact, adjacent to the cemetery.

In the southern hills **Charlottesville** is home to two more presidents. Thomas Jefferson's magnificent Monticello sits atop a mountain overlooking another of Jefferson's creations, the University of Virginia. Not far away is Ash Lawn–Highland, the 500-acre estate of the country's fifth president, James Monroe.

I'm a big fan of **Chincoteague,** off Virginia's Eastern Shore. Legends tell of wild horses that swam ashore after a Spanish galleon was shipwrecked here hundreds of years ago. The ponies made it to Assateague Island, Maryland. Each year the horses are herded across the water to Chincoteague and sold as a way of preventing horse overpopulation. Beyond that, this area is beautiful, with fine sandy beaches and warm water for swimming.

Fredericksburg is midway between Arlington and Richmond and also rich in history. After all, it was George Washington's boyhood home and later a victim of Civil War conflict, which left the town in tatters. There are several places recalling the Washington family, including the president's mother's house, and another home used by James Monroe.

Back up north, near Washington, **Great Falls** is a place where politicians and bureaucrats get a rush, although this one is natural. The Potomac River surges through here and plummets nearly 80 feet in a mixture of rapids and falls. It's a wonderful stop, especially just after a heavy rain when the water runs even faster.

Jamestown is where morning really began in America, as the first English settlers came ashore in 1607. The Jamestown Settlement you visit today commemorates that singularly important event. This living-history museum features an Indian village as well.

Virginia is a land of caverns, and cave lovers will want to experience **Luray** and **Front Royal,** both near the Skyline Drive, part of the Blue Ridge Parkway from Virginia into North Carolina and Tennessee. **Norfolk, Newport News,** and **Virginia Beach** make up the Hampton Roads region, with a major military presence at the Norfolk Naval Shipyard and elsewhere. It's an area of outstanding military and maritime museums, the Virginia Living Museum (as in living animals), and the famous Chrysler Museum of Art with its 30,000 works. Virginia Beach adds the fun-in-the-sun-and-surf element to create what many call the perfect place, especially for retirement.

SPECIAL SPOT IN VIRGINIA

The Shenandoah Valley. Two hours from the buzz of the nation's biz in Washington, there is peace and tranquility here along the Shenandoah River. When I lived in DC, I often had the desire to get away. I found the perfect respite here and loved it so much, I bought five acres of land near the river. Roaming the forests and fields, I often felt as earlier settlers may have felt: All's right with the world here. You don't have to own land in the valley, but you can enjoy this area along the 100-mile Skyline Drive. Virginia is really for lovers of beauty.

The state capital of today retains many connections to its past. **Richmond** is home to White House and Museum of the Confederacy, as it was a onetime capital of the secessionist states. There are also exquisite old mansions here, among them Agecroft Hall (built in fifteenth-century England, later dismantled and brought to Virginia) and Maymount, a 110-year-old Victorian estate.

I love the Blue Ridge Mountains, Virginia's backbone on its western frontier. Lovely little towns dot the hills, as do enchanting stretches of farmland. Right in the middle of it all is **Roanoke,** a pleasant city with an impressive cultural center smack-dab in the middle of town. In **Stratford** you can visit Stratford Hall Plantation, the birthplace of Robert E. Lee, who may have been this nation's greatest military leader.

Colonial Williamsburg is a must-see attraction for Americans, whether history buffs or not. This precious city, also the home of William and Mary College, is a vital restoration of Virginia's capital city of the eighteenth century. It is truly remarkable. **Yorktown** is nearby, where a victory by colonial forces sealed London's fate and made the United States an independent land. You can visit the battle site today.

For more information: www.virginia.org or (800) 847–4882.

WASHINGTON

It's called the Evergreen State—though that hasn't been entirely accurate over the past several years of drought. But there's no doubt that Washington is an ever-beautiful state, one I like to visit as often as possible. Mountains, rain forests, coastlines, and coffees: not a bad place to be.

Anacortes is a great little town on the northwest coast. It has a wonderful downtown district, Amtrak stops at the local station, and it is an artists' colony on the water. Aside from ferries to the out-islands, you can hop whale-watching boats out into deeper water. **Bainbridge Island,** west of Seattle in the Puget Sound, offers stunning views of the big city. It's also a great place to walk, so try the Walkabout—a footpath along the waterfront. **Bellevue** is in the other direction, across Lake Washington from Seattle. For those who love dolls, the Rosalie Whyel Museum of Doll Art may be the object of your affections. Two thousand dolls in one place. The museum has some rare specimens on display along with dollhouses, teddy bears, and other works of art.

Even farther east, **Chelan** is a heart stopper. The town sits on a lake and is surrounded by peaks of the Cascade Range. But this isn't just any lake. Lake Chelan is some 1,500 feet deep, clear, and very blue. Some folks say it's one of the prettiest places in the northwestern United States. East of Chelan lies another major attraction, this one human-made: **Grand Coulee Dam** is a huge pile of concrete, something like 12 million cubic yards of it, rising 500 feet and harnessing the Columbia River. It has created Roosevelt Lake, which runs some 150 miles.

Maryhill is on the Columbia River, in south-central Washington, and has become a major wine-producing region. There are nearly half a dozen such areas across the state, and after tasting several Washington vintages, I can attest to the improving quality. Maryhill also has a replica of Stonehenge, in western England. The real thing is located on a flat piece of land, so you might prefer this one's setting: on a cliff overlooking the Columbia. While you are in the neighborhood, also pay a visit to the Maryhill Museum of Art.

Mount Rainier is something special, a perpetually snow-and-ice-clad volcano that Seattle can see closely on a clear day. What always amazes me about it is that there are two dozen glaciers on Rainier. That other active volcano is farther south, near Oregon. **Mount St. Helens** blew her top in 1980 with deadly and devastating results. She sputtered again in 2004 and in early 2005, exciting the tourists, but her bark was more ferocious than her bite. By the way, it's a long drive to the mountain from Interstate 5. Don't think you can drop in for a quickie visit.

Olympic National Park is a true gem, resplendent with snow-topped mountains, glaciers, ocean shorelines, and incredible rain forests. I last visited in the summer of 2004 when the area was hot and dry, but even then the Hoh seemed green and mossy. The trio of such forests are among the very last in this part of the world.

One of the aspects of Washington that is so utterly charming is the **San Juan Islands**—all 172 of them, dotting the northwestern corner of the Evergreen State. It takes a bit of doing to get to these charming places, by ferry from Anacortes or Bellingham.

What gasoline is to Detroit, coffee is to **Seattle.** And there does seem to be a coffee bar on nearly every corner, but that's preferable to a fast-food eatery every few feet. The city is also about water and is similar to an island, with Puget Sound on the left and Lakes Union and Washington on the right. And Seattle's about hills, too, leading down to the docks or up into some of the city's finer neighborhoods. The Pike Place Market and Pioneer Square Historic District are lively and interesting places, Seattle's museums are first-rate (most notably the Art Museum and the Asian Art Museum), and, of course, there's the 500-foot-tall white needle poking the Seattle sky that is so popular with tourists. There's a revolving restaurant up top that gives diners the panoramic view in just under an hour; when my wife and I stopped by for lunch, we were pleasantly surprised with the quality of its food. But Seattle is also about cute and fashionable neighborhoods, and you might want to take some time to stroll through a few. I recommend Queen Ann Hill, University, Capitol Hill, First Hill, and Beacon Hill. Plan enough time to enjoy this town; it's worth it.

Spokane, way out east, is sometimes forgotten but worth a visit. There's the classy Riverfront Park, site of Expo '74, with a waterfall, convention center, Opera House, and other entertainment. And fans of Bing Crosby will enjoy a trip to Gonzaga University and the Bing Crosby

Collection. It's conveniently located in the Bing Crosby Student Center. If you haven't guessed already, the crooner came here to school. He also received an honorary doctorate from Gonzaga in 1937. **Yakima** is a fecund agricultural region and one of the leading wine-producing areas of the state.

For more information: www .experiencewashington.com or (800) 544–1800.

WEST VIRGINIA

Singers have dubbed it "almost heaven," and the locals don't dispute that for a West Virginia minute. It's a combination of mountain highs and good old times. Here are some places to explore.

Beckley is near the bottom of this state and known for its coal production. Visitors may find enjoyment in a local musical: The famous feud of the Hatfields and McCoys is played out at the impressive Cliffside Amphitheater on the New River Gorge National River. Other productions are featured each summer, including Broadway shows. The theater operates from June to late August.

In extreme northeastern West Virginia, history was made. **Berkeley Springs** is said to be this nation's first-ever spa. The springwaters were said to have therapeutic powers. In 1776 George Washington helped establish the town as a health resort, called Bath. That's the town's official name, even though it's more commonly known as Berkeley Springs. No wonder Washington is the Father of His Country. He had a hand in almost everything.

In the east of the state, **Cass** is popular with rail buffs. The Scenic Railroad runs several steam locomotive trains up the slopes of Cheat Mountain. It's quite a ride. And in this former lumber town, the Cass Country Store exists where the West Virginia Pulp and Paper General Stores used to live. What's interesting about it is that it was said to be the largest company store in the wide, wide world.

SPECIAL SPOT IN WASHINGTON

I just love Port Townsend, on a peninsula in the northwest not far from Olympic National Park. It was once a major harbor town and became famously wealthy. The city's charm comes from its sizable collection of Victorian-era homes and storefronts. In fact, the entire town looks like a slice of the early 1900s. There are good shops and better restaurants, along with some grand hotels. I've spent only two days here but look forward to returning to spend many more.

Harpers Ferry and its national historical park recall the ill-fated 1859 raid by John Brown and his followers on the federal armory in the town. Brown wanted to instigate a rebellion by slaves in the area and needed government weapons to arm them. U.S. troops, under General Robert E. Lee, captured Brown and his band and reclaimed the arsenal. John Brown was convicted of treason and hanged. His body lies moldering in the grave.

In **Lewisburg** you'll find the Lost World, or at least the Lost World Caverns. These caves have several big rooms down deep; one geological formation is 40 feet high. When you finish there, explore another cave, Smoke Hole Caverns in **Petersburg,** which contains one of the longest ribbon stalactites on earth. And if you're still not through, then drop down in Seneca Caverns at **Riverton,** which can take you some 165 feet below ground.

SPECIAL SPOT IN WEST VIRGINIA

Try Blackwater Falls State Park. I'm a sucker for waterfalls, and this one cascades 65 feet to a waiting gorge that's 525 feet deep. You can walk down a stairway to the base of the falls, if you're fit enough. There's no admission charge.

In **Wheeling** the Oglebay Resort is a great stop: 1,600 acres of gardens, trails, stables, a zoo, and museums. There's a cascading water show nightly during the summer on Schenk Lake, while in November and December the resort strings one million Christmas lights to get visitors into the holiday spirit at the Festival of Lights. Enjoy.

For more information: www.wvtourism.com or (800) 225–5982.

WISCONSIN

It's almost sad that when most of us think of Wisconsin, we think of tacky Cheeseheads. Yet America's Dairy Land has so much to offer: two of the Great Lakes, the Green Bay, and one major lake. Oh, yes, there's milk and dairy products, and plenty of beer, too. There's something very calming and restoring about Wisconsin. When I lived in Chicago, this state was the perfect place when urban escape was required.

Let's start at the top, at **Apostle Islands National Lakeshore**—and what a place to start. There are nearly two dozen of these isles out in Lake Superior, ranging from tiny to expansive. They've been used for fishing,

lumbering, and sandstone mining; for a while they became a summer retreat for the well heeled. Now they're available to everyone. This is a great hiking area, but not swimming—the water is chilly even in summer.

In south-central Wisconsin there lies a town with a name I love to pronounce. **Baraboo** is actually a bastardized version of the name of the area's French discoverer, Baribault. This was the winter home of the Ringling Brothers circus, which is now the Circus World Museum; you can still see performances under the Big Top during summer months. Just north of town is the International Crane Foundation, which is working extra hard to preserve this special species, as well as the bird's habitat. You can see the real thing here, cranes used for breeding, which are later introduced into the wild.

I've told you about many places across the nation with caves, so let me mention the Cave of the Mounds in **Blue Mounds.** It's a national landmark at the southern end of the state. What's most impressive here is the lighting used to enhance the brilliance of all those stalactites and stalagmites. Nearby is **Little Norway,** which explains the history of Norwegian settlers to this region.

Fresh water from **Chippewa Falls** in northwestern Wisconsin has benefited consumers for years. Springwater has been bottled here for a century and a quarter; other local water goes into making beer. A local brewery will show you its skill.

In the northeastern neck of the woods, there's a peninsula that reaches 75 miles out into Lake Michigan. The **Door Peninsula** features craggy coastlines on both the lake and Green Bay. It is a ruggedly awesome landscape, dotted with enchanting small towns. At least a few people have said it reminds them more of Maine than Wisconsin.

If you travel to modern-day **Eagle,** near Milwaukee, you'll get a sense of the deep history of the state. Old World Wisconsin has some five dozen preserved structures built by the many immigrants who came to this area. They were white Europeans and black Africans, slaves who were later freed.

Green Bay is all about civic pride and a certain football team. This town is gonzo over the Green Bay Packers, whether they win or lose. After all, it was the first team in professional football, and it has an illustrious record of victories and titles. There's a Packer Hall of Fame here, but other museums as well: You'll also find a wildlife sanctuary, a museum dedicated to the Oneida Indian tribe, and the National Railroad Museum with some seventy engines and cars, from steam trains to diesel. One of the trains is called "Big Boy," the biggest steam locomotive in all the world.

Madison is a truly lovely city, a slender spit of land virtually surrounded by Lakes Mendota, Monona, and Wingra. This city has an abundance of green space along the lakes. One of the best places to visit is the Olbrich Botanical Gardens on Lake Monona. There are several gardens, including the only Thai garden in the United States. The gardens are open all year.

On to **Milwaukee,** settled by Germans, joined by the Polish, later the Irish, and then by others. It's Wisconsin's largest city, a main port, and it exudes Old World élan. It is also America's beer capital, although Milwaukee is not what it used to be. There are many wonderful museums; the Mitchell Park Horticultural Conservatory is laid out in three glass domes some 70 feet high. And no reflection on residents is the International Clown Hall of Fame, dedicated to clown art. Now, there's a niche. The best way to see Milwaukee is to take a hike, especially through its older, ethnic neighborhoods. The city can help you find your way.

Down near Blue Mounds, the town of **New Glarus** celebrates its heritage at the Swiss Historical Village. More than one hundred immigrants left Glarus canton, Switzerland, to seek a better life. They found it here in a place the locals call Little Switzerland. The Swiss Village describes the past even though the town itself is reminiscent of the Old Country. You'd expect Swiss migrants to be dairy folk, and you'd be right. This is a big dairy and cheese area.

Northwest of there in **Spring Green,** look for the House on the Rock, a 200-acre empire of gardens, streets, and a remarkable fourteen-room house with pools, fireplaces, and windows looking out on the valley below. Enjoy the Infinity Room and see whether it gives you the shivers.

SPECIAL SPOT IN WISCONSIN

Peshtigo in the northeastern tip of the state has an important historical story to tell. You may remember October 8, 1871, as the date of the Great Chicago Fire. But on that very same day, a much bigger fire, brought about by dry conditions and high winds, devastated a wide area near this small lumber town. Eight hundred residents of Peshtigo died; 400 more perished in surrounding fires. It was the worst tragedy of its kind in American history. There are reminders of the fire and its destruction at the Peshtigo Fire Museum and elsewhere around town. It's amazed me how many Americans have never heard of the town or the conflagration. Here's your chance to learn more about both.

The **Wisconsin Dells,** in the south, is considered Wisconsin's premier natural attraction. The Wisconsin River has chiseled a deep channel through the land, and the surrounding beauty brings travelers here winter and summer alike. There are boat and "duck" tours, Lost Canyon, a Riverview park, children's attractions, and plenty of other entertainment. Opt for the quieter side of the beautiful place.

For more information: www.travelwisconsin.com or (800) 432–8747.

WYOMING

Some would say we've saved the best until last. The alphabet dictates Wyoming's placement, but this wide-open state offers seasoned travelers a warm and welcoming visit. Given the small population in the ninth-largest state of the Union, you'll find plenty of room to get lost in.

We begin our journey in **Casper,** in the east-central region. It started out in 1847 as a ferry site for folks heading west on the Oregon Trail. A decade later a toll bridge was constructed across the North Platte River. And a few decades after that, oil was discovered here. Casper knows how to take advantage of its resources. Today it boasts that it has two lakes, one fish-filled river, two mountains, eleven museums, and the National Historic Trails Interpretive Center. Many people stop by to take advantage of it.

In extreme southeastern Wyoming, **Cheyenne** was a rip-roarin' town of cowboys and speculators, gamblers and storekeepers. It got to be known as "Hell on Wheels." The railroad later rolled in and changed Cheyenne for good. It became the territorial and later the state capital of Wyoming. The Cheyenne Frontier Days Old West Museum recalls the Hell on Wheels era, and the city's Frontier Days celebration each July keeps the memories fresh as well. There are plenty of museums and other sites to explore, and if you want to see the home where the buffalo roam, drive out of town to Terry Bison Ranch, where you can view 3,000 of these beautiful creatures.

SPECIAL SPOT IN WYOMING

Devils Tower National Monument is the most noticeable natural wonder in northeastern Wyoming, and there's something magical about it. In fact, some Indian tribes consider it sacred. The ribbed, rock monolith juts 1,200 feet up from the Belle Fourche River below. If you're fit enough, you are allowed to climb the fluted boulder, but it's quite a hike. And be sure to enjoy the prairie dog colony that co-exists with the tower.

At the other end of the state, **Cody** keeps the Old West image alive. The northwestern town was founded by William "Buffalo Bill" Cody in 1896. But this is also one of the most beautiful parts of this big state, near Yellowstone and Grand Teton National Parks. Buffalo Bill may be gone in the flesh, but he's everywhere today in spirit: There's the Buffalo Bill Historical Center, the Buffalo Bill Museum, the Buffalo Bill Dam, the Cody Firearms Museum—rather like all the George Washington attractions I mentioned in Fredericksburg, Virginia. Hey, if you've got a good thing, run with it.

For every famous cowboy in the West, there are hundreds of unknown pioneers who trekked across this vast land in search of a new life. Their story is exalted at the Wyoming Pioneer Memorial Museum in **Douglas,** on the eastern frontier of the state. It's one of the biggest historical repositories in Wyoming. There's also a natural bridge west of

Douglas in Ayres Park. Not far away in the other direction is **Fort Laramie National Historic Site.** It began as Fort William in 1834 but was renamed Laramie in 1849, with the express mission of helping travelers heading to Oregon and California. By 1890 it had served this purpose and was closed off. The federal government has since rehabilitated Fort Laramie.

Grand Teton National Park is one of the pair of places occupying much of the northwestern corner of Wyoming. The Tetons are some of the youngest mountains in North America, yet they boast a wide variety of glaciated canyons. Park facilities are generally closed in winter, which brings utter solitude to much of this mountainous region. One thing you might want to try in summer is a float trip down the Snake River. There are several float trip providers; some offer meals as part of the trip. Shop around for the best trip at the best price.

Not far away there's an interesting phenomenon called the Gros Ventre Slide. During a 1925 landslide here, some of the land dropped 9,000 feet in a few minutes. That dammed the Gros Ventre River. Within two years, the wall broke and the rushing water inundated the town of **Kelly.** You can hike the affected area.

Just down the road are **Jackson** and **Jackson Hole,** year-round playgrounds for the filthy rich and the rest of us. Along with the National Elk Refuge, you have a Wild West Show, sleigh and float rides (depending on the season), and an alpine slide ride for summer (it becomes a ski trail in winter). Since Jackson is at the southern entrance to the Tetons, you can continue your Old West odyssey through the natural splendor of the region.

Laramie is near Cheyenne, but its history is somewhat less storied than the capital's. Today the rather pleasant town is the University of Wyoming's home, and features a group of museums. Away from campus, Wyoming Territorial Park is a living-history museum of the good old, bad old days before statehood. Among the sites is the Territorial Prison, which housed some of the true miscreants of the West.

Up north, **Sheridan** is another town evoking the rich tradition of cowboy lore. Along with its famous rodeo (and there are many cities that hold many rodeos each year), there's a place you might enjoy that honors the cowboy mystique: the Bradford Brinton Memorial—Historic Ranch and Western Art Collection. This twenty-room ranch house holds dear the life of a properous cattle rancher. As a bonus, there's a mother lode of western art, including works by some of the most famous practitioners of the genre.

Remember that old expression about the last being first and the first being last? It's true here, at least. The last place on this Wyoming list is the world's very first national park, **Yellowstone.** This monstrous landmass, with forests and wildlife, canyons and geysers, is one of the most popular destinations in the nation's incredible collection of parks and monuments. On my first visit to Yellowstone, I came to realize just how massive and diverse it really is. I learned it's best to see Old Faithful and then move on to the more pristine places in the park, even though that can be a tough assignment in summer when Yellowstone is awash in visitors. Do justice to this first national green space. Don't rush through it. See as much as you can. It's worth your investment.

For more information: www.wyomingtourism.org or (800) 225–5996.

My Top Ten Places in Canada

In no particular order, these are among my favorites:

Nova Scotia
Quebec City
Old Town Montreal
Ottawa
Toronto
Calgary
Jasper National Park
Whistler, British Columbia
Vancouver
Vancouver Island

My Top Ten Places in Mexico

Baja California
Puerto Peñasco
Copper Canyon
Guadalajara
Oaxaca
Mérida
Mazatlan

Yucatán Peninsula
Chichen Itza/Uxmal
Mexico City

My Top Ten Places in Europe
Norwegian fjords
Cote d'Azur
Yorkshire Dales
Tuscany
Swiss Alps
Bavaria
Prague
Athens
Scottish Isles
Paris

THE SEASONED TRAVELER ON TV

CHAPTER 13

When I wasn't working on this book, my team and I were traveling and taping episodes of *The Seasoned Traveler* television series on public television. We have created a TV program that does what many mature Americans love to do: travel. We are visiting destinations and taking the kinds of trips seasoned travelers appear to enjoy most. We are going across America, to the rest of North America, and beyond.

The premiere season, fall 2005, had a theme: North America and a Taste of Europe. In these thirteen episodes we spent most of our time close to home. All but four trips were in North America. Of the four shows from Europe, two were destination-oriented, while two focused on types of travel. One profiled river cruises, which have become extremely popular with older wanderers. We compared that experience with longer ocean voyages. The other profiled Christmas Markets, an annual tradition all across Europe, and an idea that is attracting more American travelers to the cold of Europe late in the year. On both these excursions we met people who'd never been on a river cruise or never visited a Christmas Market. We also met folks who are repeat river cruisers or Christmas Market aficionados.

As the years go by and as this series visits new places or focuses on new travel issues, we'll add more and more adventures to upcoming editions of this book.

PROGRAM 101: BERMUDA FOR A BARGAIN

The pink-beach paradise of Bermuda has been known as a playground for the prosperous. That is still true today, but Bermuda is "on sale" each February. The island-nation, 600 miles east of North Carolina, now offers a special new program to lure visitors after the high season each summer. Called Fall into Spring, it encompasses an existing program that benefits seasoned travelers. February has been known as Golden Rendezvous Month, when hotels and attractions offer discounts and other benefits to mature visitors.

On this program we took viewers across these islands in the Mid-Atlantic. In 1505 the sailor Juan de Bermudez first dropped anchor here, but he didn't last long. The British came next, by accident. They were shipwrecked in 1609 near what is now St. George's Island. The group called the place the Somers Islands, after their leader, Sir George Somers. The sailors stayed for a year until they could build new boats, then sailed on to the Virginia colony. But others from Britain followed. London formed the Bermuda Company in 1612 to settle the group of 180 islands. Bermuda has been a British possession ever since. The Victorian upper crust from damp and dreary England discovered Bermuda as a holiday haven; by the start of the twentieth century, others were coming for vacations as well. That changed Bermuda forever.

Today people flock to the islands from the United States, Canada, Britain, Germany, and Caribbean nations. They stay in large hotels, smaller ones, cottage colonies, housekeeping cottages, and guest houses. Many of the most prestigious places are directly on the beach. The South Shore is the home of most hotels, with its surging waves and sandy beaches. The North Shore is quieter. Swimmers there are less bothered by the tides. If you come in February to save some money, you may have to forgo the water altogether. Air temperatures average seventy degrees, compared with eighty-four in July. The ocean reading in February is sixty-seven degrees; in July it's eighty-one.

On the east end, the town of St. George is the original settlement. Given its age and charm, it's now been deemed a World Heritage Site. It's a town of narrow alleyways where the commerce of the community was once carried out. St. Peter's Church in St. George is the oldest on the islands—parts of it date to 1620—as well as the oldest continuously operating Anglican church in the western hemisphere. Fort St. Catherine is north of the town, now a historical museum. You can snorkel at Tobacco Bay nearby; the reefs are just about 40 feet offshore.

The capital is Hamilton, in the center of the main island. Aside from being the governmental center, Hamilton is the place for quality shopping along Front Street and for arts and culture. Cruise ships dock downtown, as well as in St. George and at the Royal Dockyard on the west end. But the government mandates that ships leave port by the weekend. Hamilton is also a place for fine dining and fun clubs. The Art Museum is in city hall, and the historical museum is in the main library near Front Street.

Bermuda has a zoo and aquarium in the small village of Flatts. The two facilities are adjacent. The aquarium is quite appealing; the zoo is not.

Several old homes in Bermuda show off the good times of the past. My own favorite is called Verdmont, in the center of the islands. The Botanical Gardens is a sight to see when things are in bloom (and, alas, they may not be if you venture here in February). It's not far from Verdmont and is next to the prime minister's ceremonial residence. The Royal Dockyard is the former British naval base, long abandoned by Her Majesty's Navy and converted into a shopping and entertainment complex.

February is a perfect time for golf, and Bermuda is just the right place for it. Bermuda has more courses per capita than anyplace on earth: over a dozen in a country of 61,000 people that is just 21 miles long and 1 mile wide. You can come for a week or ten days and play a different course every day.

Because it's an island chain, you'll want to sample the seafood: fish chowder, mussel stew, shark hash, and the locally caught wahoo. The most popular drink here is something called a Dark and Stormy, made with jet-black Bermuda rum and stone-ground ginger beer. You should also try the Rum Swizzle, which can contain three or five different rums.

Bermuda has some magnificent beaches on both shores, perfect for tanning and cooling off in the aquamarine water. There's snorkeling, diving, boating, fishing, parasailing, horseback riding, and much more on these islands in the Mid-Atlantic.

PROGRAM 102: RV—RIGHT FOR YOU?

It seems almost inevitable. When some men and women pass the age of forty, a question begins to gnaw at them: *Should we buy a recreation vehicle?* In fact, nearly eight million American families already have. One in every twelve vehicle-owning households has an RV. And many more folks are joining the ranks, even though the cost of gasoline has risen.

On this program we showed viewers these high-priced toys and the pros and cons of owning one. There are many kinds of recreation vehicles, some motorized and some towable. The latter include travel trailers and fifth-wheel trailers, pop-up camping trailers, and pickup truck campers. The self-contained giants come in three sizes. Class A are the monsters of the interstate (40 feet long and lengthening); Class C are the midsize units (20-plus feet); and Class B are the babies. A simple camping trailer can cost $6,500, while the biggest of the behemoths can set you back $400,000, depending on options.

Before even contemplating a purchase of such magnitude, prospective buyers should do extensive homework. Read up on these big boats, look around, talk to those who own these vehicles, and only then go shopping. Recreation vehicles can come with many options. Be careful of dealers trying to sell you everything in sight. Remember that motor homes are generally financed for ten to fifteen years, which can inflate your monthly payments. An RV depreciates faster than a car or your sport utility vehicle. Maintenance and repairs are more difficult than for the family car.

The good news is that if you purchase an RV as a second home, and spend enough time in it, you may be able to deduct the mortgage interest on your income taxes. Inquire about the rules from the dealer, your banker, and your tax accountant.

Before you buy, do as I did and rent one to see if the RV experience is suitable for you. There are 450 rental outlets nationwide; there should be one near you. I drove to Florida from my home in Atlanta and spent a week living the RV life. I stopped at four of the nation's 16,000 campsites. Put the RV through its paces. Recreation vehicle sales are expected to increase 15 percent by the year 2010. As I've talked to RV folks, they profess their love for the lifestyle and wouldn't have it any other way. They all agree that those who drive these big buses are among the nicest people the world has ever known.

While you may find the prospect of driving a 30-foot monster on the superhighway intimidating, I met one woman who told me that when her husband died, she decided to pick up and drive from the Midwest to Texas for a bit of a break. She was seventy at the time, about 5 foot 3, and she didn't give the drive a second thought. "I never felt more comfortable," she said. "After all, I was up high like the eighteen-wheelers so I felt safe enough."

PROGRAM 103: GULF COAST

America is often called a bicoastal nation. We talk about the East and the West Coasts, the beauty of the Atlantic from Maine to Florida, and the Pacific from Alaska to California. But there's a third coast in the United States, often overlooked but every bit as charming as those in the East or West. The Gulf Coast is not only a wonderful vacation destination but, for many folks, a great place to spend the retirement years as well. The Gulf Coast is a huge geographic arc, stretching some 1,500 miles across five states from the southwestern tip of Florida to the city of Brownsville on the Texas–Mexico border.

On this program I traveled to parts of three states along the coast. I began at St. George Island, Florida, a remarkable island connected by causeway to the Florida mainland. No high-rise condominiums here, just beachfront homes and low-rise apartments. Many homeowners rent out their properties to the hordes of summer and winter visitors from places like Atlanta, Birmingham, and Nashville. Farther west lie a trio of inviting towns: Seaside, Destin, and Fort Walton Beach. These are well-run communities, with miles of white, sugar-sand beaches beckoning vacationers (the sugary appearance is from minute particles of quartz). Thousands of people have discovered this area as a place to call home. Seaside is especially appealing, bright and clean; it served as the backdrop for the motion picture *The Truman Show*. It's a walkable town, with everything close together.

Many people move to this part of the country because of the tax and other financial incentives. That's particularly true for the folks of Fairhope, Alabama, on the eastern shore of Mobile Bay. Founded on utopian principles, the community is funded by a single tax system: Residents hold renewable ninety-nine-year leases on their property, and the single tax colony pays the taxes. You can see how well the system works by looking at the downtown shopping area, festooned with flowers year-round, and the lovely marina on the bay with its charming pier.

Mobile is the old-time charmer of Alabama, the state's chief port and the first American city to celebrate Mardi Gras, well before the natives of New Orleans. There are some fine older neighborhoods here to go with Mobile's civic pride. There's pride, too, in the state's contribution to the past, as the USS *Alabama* is docked along the waterfront. The Mississippi coastline is dotted with cities like the shipbuilding center of Pascagoula, the South's new casino center at Biloxi, and the appealing smaller towns of Ocean Springs and Pass Christian.

Of course, no place is perfect, and this region has suffered repeatedly from hurricanes. Four major storms affected the Gulf in 2004 alone, bringing death and devastation to a wide area. Residents here know the risks and prepare themselves each June to November for the storms.

PROGRAM 104: FOUR CORNERS—HIKERS' AND DRIVERS' DREAM

From the Southeast to the Southwest. Because many mature travelers are still fit and active, *The Seasoned Traveler* wanted to lace up its hiking boots and head off into the wilderness. And the Four Corners region (the only place in America where the boundaries of four states actually touch) is an absolute treasure trove of history, heritage, and magnificent vistas. Several national parks and monuments dot this area, tracing the settlements of America's first inhabitants, the Native peoples of the mesas and canyons.

Today the history coincides with challenging hiking trails, matched by scenic desert drives through breathtaking highlands and valleys.

I decided to walk through a few of these remarkable areas: Hovenweep National Monument, which now safeguards five prehistoric, Puebloan-era villages covering a 20-mile stretch along the Utah–Colorado border. This is a quiet place, known for its undeveloped natural character. Only about 30,000 visitors come to Hovenweep each year, so it's likely to be uncrowded and uncluttered if you decide to drop by.

Monument Valley is along another border, between Utah and Arizona. Its soaring sandstone monoliths have become familiar to most of us, splashed across television and movie screens in commercials and feature films. Farther south, Canyon de Chelly is a special place. At the bottom of sheer red cliffs are ruins of Indian villages dating to A.D. 350—the earliest Basket Makers. Today the land remains part of the Navajo Reservation, and tribal members still live and farm here. Be sure to hike down into the canyon to see the White House cliff dwellings. This path is the only one available to visitors.

The Four Corners is a very special place and well worth a visit. And save time for our best-kept secret: Goosenecks State Park in southeastern Utah. It's magnificent, a lot like Arizona's Grand Canyon but without the crowds of gawkers.

PROGRAM 105: COPPER CANYON

From the Southwest, we travel south into Mexico and the Sierra Madre. We're about to embark on a visit to the Copper Canyon, which is actually one of six massive gorges formed by six rivers, the most prominent of which is the Copper. Scientists say if all six were placed end-to-end, they would stretch four times longer than the Grand Canyon.

There is no better way to reach this natural wonder than by the restored Chihuahua al Pacifico Railroad, known to the locals as El Chepe. I boarded the train in the town of El Fuerte and traveled through the high desert to the Cañon del Cobre. Mexicans actually call the canyon the Barrancas del Cobre, "copper cliffs." When you see the sheer walls, you'll understand. The canyon itself offers breathtaking views for tourists, but it is home to a local tribe, the Tarahumara, who have been living in this region for centuries. I walked down into the canyon to visit an Indian farm and home.

Interest in the Copper Canyon has been growing for decades, since the Mexican government restored the train. And on my trip I discovered a wonderful waterfall, some 80 miles north of Creel, which is also in canyon country. Basaseachi Fall is the highest single-drop waterfall in Mexico, plummeting 800 feet. It's part of a national park.

PROGRAM 106: MEXICO'S HERITAGE

From natural wonders to the legacies of the ancient peoples. I wandered through southern and eastern Mexico, experiencing the pre-Columbian, colonial, and internal influences on the nation south of our border. I viewed the ruins of the country's earliest inhabitants, who were instrumental in shaping modern Mexico. *The Seasoned Traveler* trekked lightly to Monte Alban and Mitla, near the southern city of Oaxaca. Then I went north to Palenque, site of celebrated Mayan ruins, with temples, plazas, and pyramids dating back 1,500 years, a UNESCO World Heritage Site. Some consider this ancient site at the edge of a rain forest the most beautiful of all. Finally, I made it to the Yucatán Peninsula, to visit another UNESCO site, the Mayan ruins at Uxmal. And a visit to the region would not be complete without a stop at the famous Chichen Itza, deemed the most important city in the Yucatán from the tenth through the twelfth centuries. This was a commercial, military, and religious center of 35,000 people. For the past eighty years, Chichen Itza has been a project for archaeologists, who have been restoring this magical place to its former glory. It remains a breathtaking site today.

Mexico's history does not all lie in ruins. I spent some time in the city of Mérida, itself a former Mayan site. A conquistador stumbled upon the place in 1542 and named it for a ruined Roman city in his Spanish homeland. Mérida became an important colonial city and achieved fame and fortune in the early twentieth century when profits from a rope-making ingredient, sisal, made many entrepreneurs rich. The city became home to many millionaires and a center of culture and good living. Many called Mérida the Paris of the West. Its Spanish heritage remains alive today.

PROGRAM 107: TORONTO—A CITY THAT SPARKLES

From south of the U.S. border, we next travel north. Each year on *The Seasoned Traveler*, I'll focus on one distinguished city in the region of the world we're visiting. In the premiere season, it's Toronto, one of the most dynamic, most significant, and safest big cities in North America. It is Canada's leading urban center and its main inland port, home to nearly four million residents. Toronto has grown and modernized but has also managed to maintain its Old World charm; it draws millions of tourists each year (a SARS outbreak in 2003 reduced those numbers for several months). My visit takes me to some of the most interesting parts of this Ontario metropolis, from the top of the mighty CN Tower to the underground shopping districts. There's some wild and wacky footwear at the Bata Shoe Museum, often called Toronto's most unique museum. The collection spans the ages, from ancient times to the present. The footwear belonged to the unknown and to the well known.

In the middle of the city lies a majestic castle, Casa Loma. Once the ninety-room mansion of Canadian financier Henry Pellatt, it's now a sight for travelers. It's a house of lavish suites, secret passageways, tall towers, and an underground tunnel to the stables. We also paused at Canada's largest museum of natural history and human cultures. The Royal Ontario Museum has more than five million objects of art, science, and archaeology.

Toronto is brimming with exciting neighborhoods, and I stopped by at the trendy Bloor-Yorkville area. Those who seek nightlife are lured to the Distillery Historic District, the city's newest cultural, entertainment, and dining area in a former distillery. And along the way, I sampled some Canadian delicacies, including a special sandwich called a peameal: Canadian bacon in a special "wrapper." The locals love it. Ask for it if you visit.

PROGRAM 108: THE CANADIAN

All aboard for one of Canada's proudest rail rides, the VIA Toronto-to-Vancouver express service. The Canadian travels from Toronto westward, gliding past the picturesque lakes of Ontario, racing through the prairie lands of middle Canada, and coming face-to-face with the majestic mountains near the town of Jasper, Alberta. The train stops here so passengers can tour this region of the Rockies. Then it's on to the western terminus in British Columbia. The complete journey takes three days and offers three classes of service, two of which include luxury sleeping accommodations and first-class meals. You can also travel west to east on The Canadian. The Canadian lures train buffs and mature travelers who want to see a lot but don't want to expend the energy of driving across the continent. Ride along with me to see why so many people can't wait for their chance to savor The Canadian.

PROGRAM 109: VANCOUVER ISLAND—AWAY FROM IT ALL

When the train pulled into the station, my next journey began. It was on to one of the most cherished of Canadian cities, Vancouver. I did all the sights. First came Chinatown, which grew dramatically after Great Britain returned sovereignty of Hong Kong nearly a decade ago. Then I toured the original Gastown district. It was first called Gassy's in honor of saloon proprietor Gassy Jack Deighton, who stunned the locals by getting his bar up and running in just one day. A fire in 1886 destroyed the wooden structures, and when the village was rebuilt, it was named Gastown.

On the western edge of Vancouver, Stanley Park is a gem—the largest urban green space in Canada. Because the city's growth is restricted by waterways and mountains, the locals are proud their city has resisted the urge to develop its parkland and create new high-rise structures for a growing population. North of the central city are two tourism highlights: First is the Capilano suspension footbridge, which spans some 230 feet above a densely wooded gorge below. Those who brave the bridge can traverse the Tree Tops footbridge through a living forest. Next is Grouse Mountain, which I scaled for a panoramic view of this magnificent region.

Hopping the ferry, I headed to Vancouver Island, still largely undeveloped. It has Canada's mildest weather and attracts growing numbers of visitors. Quaint Victoria, the provincial capital, reminds travelers of how the island might have looked years ago. And, of course, there's Butchart Gardens, in Brentwood Bay, which lures flower lovers back time and time again. One of its most stunning scenes is the sunken garden, created in a former quarry. I also traveled to Tofino on the western shore of Vancouver Island, a popular resort and surfing town. Pacific Rim National Park is found here, as are some excellent whale-watching adventures.

PROGRAM 110: CRUISING EUROPE

River cruises have become one of the hottest tourism adventures for seasoned travelers, so I decided to join them. Landlubbers can cruise down almost any river nowadays. In the United States there are trips on the Hudson, the Ohio, the Mississippi, and the Willamette. Elsewhere you can travel the Thames, the Seine, the Rhine, the Mosel, the Danube, the Elbe, the Po, the Volga, and the Moskova in Europe; the Nile in Africa; the Ganges and the Yangtze in Asia; or the Amazon in South America. Such cruises are popular because they allow visitors to unpack only once, even though they will visit several towns and cities during their water journey. The vessels used are smaller, more intimate than large oceangoing ships, with 140 passengers instead of the 1,400 or more you'd find on a typical sea cruise. There is plenty to see both on and off the river ship.

The Seasoned Traveler took off on a cruise of Europe's Rhine River. In this part of the world, the shores are replete with appealing towns, castles fit for a king, dramatic hills and mountains, and lush vineyards. Riverboats offer three first-class meals each day, a lounge for entertainment and conversation, a small library for quiet endeavors, and a bar (which generally charges passengers for beverages). There are several excursions off the ship and optional tours. The more fit among the crowd will cram in every shore visit and every activity. The more mature and less fit will be content to remain onboard, to read or play cards and games with others.

On my river cruise I met several women who were knitters. They engaged in their craft on days when the vessel was traveling from port to port, or during shore visits when they preferred not to abandon ship. This is a wonderful way to spend a week or two away from home. You really should weigh anchor and set sail.

PROGRAM 111: GERMAN GEMS

River cruises ply the waters throughout Europe, from England and the Netherlands, to France and Germany and Switzerland, on to Austria and Hungary, and even to the Black Sea. Often it is best to get off the boats to see what Europe truly has to offer. Such is the case in Bavaria, southern Germany.

For this program I stopped in several glorious cities and towns. Koblenz is at the confluence of two well-traveled rivers and the city closest to Marksburg Castle, one of the best-preserved castles along the Rhine. It is the only hill castle along the river never destroyed by war, fire, or other natural disaster, and it is the repository of the world's largest literary collection on medieval castles. Rudesheim is a romantic little river town, but often overrun by tourists. Most make a beeline to the well-traveled Drosselgasse, an alley of shops, bars, and eateries.

Mainz is a large city, but its claim to fame centers on businessman Johannes Gutenberg. He invented the printing press in Mainz; from 1452 to 1455 he printed 180 copies of the Bible. Of the forty originals that remain, one sits proudly at the Gutenberg Museum. The university town of Heidelburg was a favorite of American author Mark Twain and remains a cherished city today. Its high-on-a-hill castle is the most overwhelming site in the city. I also checked in at the Student Prison, where scofflaws were sent to do their time after being arrested for petty crimes.

The fairy-tale town of Wertheim is relatively undiscovered. A quaint reminder of ages ago, it's also now the glass-making center of Germany. Wurzburg has a special winery, the Juliusspital. In 1576 the prince-bishop of the region developed a hospital for the needy. To pay for its upkeep, a winery was created. The relationship remains intact today.

Rothenburg is one of the most beautiful and best-preserved towns in Germany; its Old Town is surrounded by walls some 800 years old. It's a charming blend of towers and turrets, Tudor buildings and cobblestone streets. It is one of the most visited communities in Germany.

Our final stop is Bamberg, which dates to A.D. 902. One of its charms is the city hall and its dramatic exterior mural. Another is the eleventh-century cathedral, where the first Roman Catholic pope from Germany, Clement II, is buried. (He would not have a German counterpart, of course, until the twenty-first century.) And when you visit Bamberg, try the famous, or infamous, smoky beer. It's a dark brew with a distinctive taste; most people liken it to drinking smoked bacon. The story goes that Bamberg's brewery was damaged heavily by fire, but the owner couldn't bear the thought of destroying the liquid product, so he decided to market it as smoky beer. The tradition stuck. Try it and let me know if you like it . . . or hate it.

PROGRAM 112: LIECHTENSTEIN AND THE OTHER LITTLE LANDS

There are five tiny independent nations within Europe, and on this episode, I highlight the little lands. I visited Liechtenstein, just 160 square miles—about the size of Washington, DC—and nestled in the Alps. It is connected to Austria on one side and separated from Switzerland on the other side by the Rhine, which is much narrower by the time it reaches this area. Above the small capital city of Vaduz is the princely palace, home of the ruler of the principality. The regal family spends much of its time here but also has extensive holdings in and near Vienna. People come to play here at the very top of the principality, skiing near the town of Malbun on a dozen trails almost a mile above sea level. Others visit, and walk, the miles of hiking trails that snake through the mountains and low-lying areas. Businesses come here for the favorable financial climate. You'll also find a handful of wineries, including one owned by the prince himself. Given its ties to Switzerland, Liechtenstein accepts Swiss francs, but merchants also take euros.

Another little land is Andorra, a principality in the Pyrenees, on the border between France and Spain. It is larger than Liechtenstein and another place pursuing tourists and their money. This is a land of duty-free shopping and superb ski slopes, mostly in the western part of the nation. The currency of choice is euros.

Along the Mediterranean coast lies the principality of Monaco, on the eastern edge of France. It is the second-smallest land in Europe but rolling in money. One of its two towns, Monte Carlo, is home to the world-famous casino. The current facility is actually the second casino here. The original was constructed in 1862; it brought visitors from around the world, who luxuriated in Monte Carlo's spectacular climate, berthed their behemoths at the marina, and stayed at fashionable hotels and resorts. This first casino still exists, but today it is a tourist attraction where you can play slot machines only. Spend euros here.

The smallest of the five is Vatican City, headquarters of the Roman Catholic Church. It is home to the pope and 900 or so other religious men and women. St. Peter's Basilica is one of the most venerable and remarkable churches in the world. And this enclave within the city of Rome has no trouble attracting visitors. Millions pour into St. Peter's Square each year to visit the Basilica and the renowned Sistine Chapel, to await a papal blessing on certain holy days, or to attend services canonizing new saints of the Catholic Church. Spend euros here, too.

The lesser-known small nation of Italy is north of the Vatican. San Marino is the third-smallest state in Europe and claims to be the oldest republic in the world. The mountainous land was founded in A.D. 301 by a stonemason called Marinus. Three million people cross the Italian line to visit San Marino each year—indeed, tourism is responsible for 50 percent of the country's revenue. San Marino's appeal: rugged mountains, fantastic local cuisine, and centuries-old structures in the center of San Marino City, the capital. And by all means, spend euros here as well.

The five little lands of Europe are worth a visit, especially if you have been to most places on the Continent but have somehow missed these tiny ones.

PROGRAM 113: CHRISTMAS MARKETS

In a European tradition dating back 500 years, shopkeepers converge on the town square or the center of an urban neighborhood each Advent and set up shop. The locals come around in search of Christmas foods and gifts. The tradition continues, and now Americans are flocking to the many Christmas Markets, from Sweden to Spain and from Paris to Prague. On *The Seasoned Traveler* I take it upon myself to visit markets in Austria and Germany, where this festive holiday tradition began. It's a tough task, but someone has to do it.

Vienna has a marvelous market at the Rathaus, or city hall, but each of the city's twenty-three districts has its own market. Altogether Vienna has a citywide total of forty markets. I drop by city hall, as well as a small neighborhood market in the Spittleburg district, and to the magnificent Schloss Schoenbrunn (the Schoenbrunn Palace) on Vienna's western edge. This former summer residence of Austrian emperors is open to the public but makes an especially charming destination around Christmas. The palace has 1,441 rooms, 45 of which are available for sightseers.

Seven million people visit each year, many to see the Christmas Market. In western Austria, Salzburg has a wonderful market in the Domplatz, the square adjacent to the Salzburg Cathedral. Mozart's hometown is alive for the holidays, especially along the famous Getreidegasse, the city's most famous shopping alley.

In Germany these celebrations of commerce, community, and Christmas are called Christkindlmarkt, or "Christ child market." This is where the tradition started, most likely in Nuremberg, which still has one of the largest markets in Europe, so large there is also room for a special children's market. These festivals can be swarming with visitors, especially on the opening weekend in late November. Germans, Europeans, and hordes of foreigners on package tours stream through these marketplaces. The Christkindlmarkt is open until Christmas Eve. I also decided to visit some smaller markets in the towns of Passau and Regensburg, the latter town noteworthy not only for its main market, but also for a crafters' market near City Hall.

Christmas Markets are great holiday traditions, unlike almost anything you might see at home—except, of course, in Chicago. That city has created a Christmas Market at Daley Plaza in the Loop area, fashioned after the very famous market in Nuremberg.

I invite you to watch *The Seasoned Traveler* on TV. In our second season we'll be traveling to some U.S. states, a Canadian province, the island of Puerto Rico, Eastern and Western Europe, and South America. I hope you'll enjoy the ride.

INDEX

ABOUT THE AUTHOR

George Bauer is an award-winning journalist and broadcaster who has traveled extensively across the United States and overseas. He's always been a tourist, even when working as an anchor, reporter, and producer for both public and commercial radio and television, at local and network levels, in the United States and Great Britain. He is also creator and host of the companion American Public Television series, *The Seasoned Traveler.*